"I loved *Tough Titties* and didn't want it to end! Through her insightful wit and sarcasm, Laura Belgray speaks to the late bloomers and slow starters in us all."

—**Kelly Ripa**, *New York Times* **best-selling author of** *Live Wire*

"Nobody makes me laugh like Laura Belgray. She's got a one of a kind knack for taking the shame out of life's most humiliating moments. *Tough Titties* is a hilarious, must-read permission slip to be 100% you."

—**Marie Forleo, #1 New York Times best-selling author of** *Everything is Figureoutable*

"Where has Laura Belgray been all my life? Hilarious, eloquent, wise, she writes with delicious honesty about coming of age, falling in love, and finding meaning in these weird and chaotic times. I loved *Tough Titties* so much, I want to press it in the hands of everyone I pass on the street!"

—**Joanna Rakoff, international best-selling author of** *My Salinger Year* **and** *A Fortunate Age*

"I've been a fan of Laura Belgray's hilarious, tell-it-like-it-is writing for years. She was an early influence on my own craft, and I count her among my teachers. Laura is for anyone who keeps waking up disappointed to find they didn't become a different, more pulled-together person in their sleep."

—**Holly Whitaker,** *New York Times* **best-selling author of** *Quit Like a Woman*

Tough Titties

Tough Titties

On Living Your Best Life
When You're the F-ing Worst

Laura Belgray

hachette
BOOKS

New York

Hachette Books
Hachette Book Group
1290 Avenue of the Americas
New York, NY 10104
HachetteBooks.com
Twitter.com/HachetteBooks
Instagram.com/HachetteBooks

First Trade Paperback Edition: June 2024

Published by Hachette Books, an imprint of Perseus Books, LLC, a subsidiary of Hachette Book Group, Inc. The Hachette Books name and logo is a trademark of the Hachette Book Group.

The Hachette Speakers Bureau provides a wide range of authors for speaking events. To find out more, go to hachettespeakersbureau.com or email HachetteSpeakers@hbgusa.com.

Books by Hachette Books may be purchased in bulk for business, educational, or promotional use. For information, please contact your local bookseller or Hachette Book Group Special Markets Department at: special.markets@hbgusa.com.

The publisher is not responsible for websites (or their content) that are not owned by the publisher.

Print book interior design by Amy Quinn

Library of Congress Cataloging-in-Publication Data

Name: Belgray, Laura, author.
Title: Tough titties: on living your best life when you're the f-ing worst /
    Laura Belgray.
Description: New York, NY: Hachette Books, [2023]
Identifiers: LCCN 2022037460 | ISBN 9780306826047 (hardcover) | ISBN
    9780306826054 (paperback) | ISBN 9780306826061 (ebook)
Subjects: LCSH: Self-actualization (Psychology) | Courage.
Classification: LCC BF637.S4 B4258 2023 | DDC 158.1—dc23/eng/20230209
LC record available at https://lccn.loc.gov/2022037460

ISBNs: 9780306826047 (hardcover); 9780306826054 (trade paperback);
    9780306826061 (ebook)

Printed in the United States of America

LSC-C

Printing 1, 2024

For Alice and David Belgray
Mom, maybe skip Chapter 9? Dad, if you're up there, you, too.

Contents

Part III

Introduction

Up and Up and Up

When I was rounding forty, my husband and I had dinner with our friend and his new girlfriend, a dewy-faced, twenty-nine-year-old Condé Nast worker who'd come straight from her spin class. Twisting her shower-fresh hair into a perfect knot, she sighed.

"All I do in my career is move up and up and up. It's like every time I walk into the office, I get promoted."

Shaking her head no to the server's offer of bread and smearing a fingerful of Vaseline on her plump lips—at that age, a complete beauty routine—she added, "I'll probably be publisher in the next couple of years."

I remember thinking (as I buttered a second sourdough roll, thank you), *I'm ten years older than this glowing go-getter and have never in my life moved "up and up and up."*

If you don't know me, and however you found yourself with this book in your hands, I know I'm supposed to inspire you with how far I've come from my disadvantaged or troubled beginnings. How I've turned lemons into lemonade, or some boozy, sassy version: skinny margaritas, limoncello, Patrón Silver lemon drops. I know this from sampling influencer books and their intros. Not that I consider myself an influencer. I'm too old for that now, I've graduated to "thought leader." (You're never allowed to call your-self either of those things, by the way. But other people can.) Just like in acting, where the stages for a woman are *ingenue, mom, district attorney*, the online phases are *influencer, thought leader, sea hag*. I'm hoping to stay comfortably in the thought leader cat-egory for as long as possible before sprouting a tuft of hair from my giant face mole, living in an underwater lair, and eating chil-dren who frolic in the waves.

But anyway, I have to tell you what my existing audience knows: I've carved out a pretty great career, allowing for a #NoHomeworkLife that makes people say, "I want to be you when I grow up." Because somehow, they got the impression I'm a grown-up. Supposedly, you're one of those when you can drive. When you're a parent. When you review your monthly cash flow on a spreadsheet. When you can open a bottle of wine. I check none of those boxes. Despite having waitressed and bartended, I'm even scared to pull out a cork. I fear the leverage will fling me across the room and I'll break everything *and* spill the wine. I picture my husband sighing, "This is why we can't have nice things." I do have a grown-up marriage, unless you ask our build-ing staff, who have seen us on the elevator camera punching each other's crotches. We imagine them editing our antics into one extended "sizzle reel."

In addition to hitting basic milestones of adulthood like cre-ating new life and knowing how to roast a chicken, you're now expected to: know your "Why," face your fear, be a boss, unlock your purpose, live your passion, live your best life, be your best self, be of service, yet put yourself first—actually, that one, I've got in the bag! I should be more selfless but I'm told I should also stop "shoulding all over myself."

If you don't check the usual boxes either, or you're far from the person you know you could be but are too resistant or just plain lazy to become, this book is for you.

It's for you if . . .

. . . you've ever tanked relationships or sabotaged your career because something in you recoiled from success or being a responsible, fully developed human.

. . . you say "unpopular opinion" at the start of a post you hope will be wildly popular.

. . . you want to be your authentic, unselfconscious, live-out-loud self but catch yourself kissing the ass of someone you don't like, or fake-laughing too loud, then thinking about it all day—whether everyone noticed, is now discussing it, and is taking turns reenacting it at a secret party you're not invited to.

It's for you if . . .

. . . you hate-follow old nemeses online, hoping they get enormously jealous of you.

. . . you've ever measured your worth by how many bartenders found you sexually attractive enough to let you blow them. (Just me?)

. . . you've ever joined a cringey self-help thing where you felt very much not yourself.

. . . or, you wake up with your mind racing about everything you should be doing but know you probably won't do any of it.

I see you. I wrote a book for you.

No, I wrote it for me. Because I always wanted to write a book. But the fact that I actually did, and followed through to completion, should give you hope.

Born five days late, first make-out at fifteen, sprouted big tits at twenty-one, entered "slut phase" also at twenty-one—coincidence? First *job*-job at twenty-three, left the nest at twenty-six, first and last drag on a cigarette at twenty-eight, "rebellion boyfriend" from twenty-nine through thirty-two, married at thirty-seven, had kids at—wait for it—never.

I tried (and dropped) yoga in 2017, found my career groove at around forty-eight, and, at fifty, earned my first million dollars within a year. A mark I know most people never hit, but one I'd always drooled over and had seen many colleagues in the online space sail past by their thirties. Also at fifty, way later than most authors named as "late bloomers," I sold my first book, which you're reading. (Thank you!) In some fugue state of thinking I was a different me, I expected to crank out this puppy in a few months. LOLZ.

I've always felt behind, like I'm scrambling to catch up and can't do life the way you're "supposed to." The signs were there at my preschool interview, where, my mother tells me, I sat on the floor saying, "Oh ship, oh ship" (Baby's first obscenity) while trying—*literally*—to jam a square peg into a round hole.

And that's why it blows my mind that I've "made it"—without hitting the right achievements at the right life intervals; without wearing pantyhose, climbing a ladder, running ideas up a flag-pole, or any of the other corporate rituals I was so unsuited for in my first jobs, working in my shrunken baby tees. (Hey, it was the '90s, it was cool to dress like a seven-year-old with knockers.)

Essentially, I now get paid to be myself.

But I'm still a flaming hot mess of a human.

I miss deadlines. I pretend I missed your text. I'm late. Late to the Zoom call, late to the party—metaphorically and liter-ally. (Unless I thought the party started an hour earlier. In that case, I'm practically on time.) I'm still forever teenager-weird about food and body image and rigid about my workout sched-ule. I still want my sixth-grade bully to see I've made it. I don't clean or take care of things. I have sneeze marks on my laptop screen, sticky fingerprints on my glass desk, and coffee rings on the insurance paperwork I was supposed to do in 2018. I don't get waxed. My nails are shit. And before you say boo about need-ing self-care, NAIL CARE IS NOT SELF-CARE. Neither is getting your pubes ripped out by the root. It's a public service, a courtesy. One I rarely extend. I take a stand in my business about being fully me, like it or don't, but desperately hope you do like it because being disliked, which I have been, leaves scars, the raised keloid kind that make people say, "What happened *there*?" I'm a coward. I still say yes, let's get together, when I want to say no, let's not. And then I try to wiggle out of it. (Ram Dass said, "We're all just walking each other home." I say, "We're all dying for the other person to cancel so we can *stay* home.")

If you're raising your hand (and checking for a pit stain), you're who *Tough Titties* is for.

And why "Tough Titties"?

First, because I say it a lot. Because, basically, I'm twelve.

Second, it evokes late-'70s, early '80s, dirty, scuzzy New York, which I consider my point of origin, the shell out of which I rose in all my nerd glory. It gives top notes of terry-cloth halter top and roller skates, the waka-waka of Pac-Man, fear of getting mugged, vintage comic-book stores, Bloomingdale's with Mom, hot sidewalk with a touch of urine.

Third, tits. I haz them. They're a whole chapter. The *tit*ular one, if you will. (Told you I was twelve.)

Finally, "Tough Titties" is my favorite non-apology, the original "sorry not sorry."

Want me to work nine to five? Tough titties.

Want me to have kids, like you do? Tough titties.

Want me to watch less TV? Tough titties.

Want me to close my eyes, take a deep breath, and then massage the person next to me at this conference? Yeah, hell no. Tough titties. Being touched by strangers who make intimate, piercing eye contact: one of many awful things I don't love but am supposed to.

It turns out my stubborn refusal to be a "supposed to" person has gotten me right where I'm supposed to be, and, if you ask me, the same can go for you. That's right: you *can* get ahead while feeling like you're a giant step behind. And you *can* live your best life . . . even if you're sometimes the fucking worst.

If you're thinking my "it all works out" perspective comes from a place of privilege, you nailed it. White, cis, hetero, able-bodied, now dealing with crepey neck skin and other horrors of aging but still cute enough under good light and filters and, hello, camera angled from above, please. I also need to cite clean water, not living in a war zone, access to feminine hygiene products (though CVS is always out of the pantyliners for your thong). Plus, I had loving parents who put my finger paintings on the fridge and kept me on their insurance 'til the cutoff at age twenty-six. Lotta cushion for making questionable life choices and blowing opportunities, not to mention all those undeserving guys. (Yes, they get a chapter.)

Tough Titties is not an epic triumph of the soul or an instructional book. It's less a how-to than a *how not to*, a permission slip to be your bad self if you don't, can't, or won't follow the rules or timeline of "being your best self" and are tired of pretending to. What a strain.

My only instructions are, go ahead: screw up, take your time, go down that weird and windy path. Treat "supposed to" as a serving suggestion, not a federal law, and be who you are. Even if "who you are" doesn't always fit in, and changes as often as the ports and charger inputs of your Apple products. (Seriously, Apple. What the fuck.)

And to you, the go-getter running laps around us, right on. You go! Get your gold star, check all the boxes, rise up and up and up. Order without me. I'll meet you after.

Tough Titties

Part I

Deb Fishbone Likes This

Like most people who are "my people"—the former dweebs, bookworms, misfits who collected comics and wore sandals with floppy socks—I was bullied in sixth grade. We didn't call it bullying then. But today's definition easily applies to what Deb Fishbone did to me. Whenever I talk about Deb—in therapy, in my emails, on the stage (bullies are keynote gold!)—people ask, "So what happened to this buttmunch?" From her presence on social media, limited mostly to likes of major retailers, I can tell you this much: she grew up to be incredibly basic.

I've determined this, and seen her activity (Lululemon: Deb Fishbone likes this), because we're "friends" on Facebook.

First, I know: Facebook is now less a social platform than an obit section for relatives, aging rockers, and pets. I also know *Facebook friends* doesn't mean *real friends*. Lately, it seems to mean a green light to message me about my "health journey"—not on one, thanks!—so you can pitch me essential oils.

Still, it felt like a dork move to friend Deb Fishbone—who, if you were wondering, likes Zara, Saks, and Bed Bath & Beyond. Why friend someone who made my middle-school life pure hell? Someone whose year of organized cruelty had such lasting effects on my psyche, I credit her for all my shortcomings? I need outside validation because of Deb Fishbone. I get writer's block and miss deadlines because of Deb Fishbone. I leave hair in the sink because of . . . you know it: Deb Fucking Fishbone—who likes The Container Store, and stole my best friend.

That best friend was Deb Yoveda, or Deb Y. In fifth grade, we'd been a unit. Sneaking off to seedy Times Square to play video games. Listening on repeat to Donna Summer's "Love to Love You Baby" and screaming "Ewwww" at the part where she climaxed. When everyone was speaking a version of Pig Latin gibberish called "Idigoo Idigai," we made up our *own* secret language, because fuck fads. We did everything together. And we had a pact: in sixth grade, we'd take Spanish together.

In assembly on the first day, the head of middle school told us, "If you're taking French, sit on the left. If you're taking Spanish, go to the right."

I went to the right, *claro*. And Deb? She went to the left.

I looked around, confused, and saw her already sitting next to Deb Fishbone—or, as I called her, Mean Deb.

They clasped hands and raised them in the air like champions. "Yay, French!"

Looking right at me and cupping her hands around her mouth, Mean Deb called out, "Spanish is for losers!"

Como se dice *what the fuck*?

We'd been Laura and Deb. Now, they were Deb and Deb. Or, as one teacher called them, Deb Squared. (Adorbs!) I was booted from my friend group. No longer invited to Wednesdays at V&T pizza, to play Pac-Man at our hangout, Baronette Card Shoppe, not even to go buy leg warmers. I soon got a fake "secret admirer" letter that said I walked like a duck. In chorus, two older girls pointed to the trash can and informed me, "You sing like that garbage." Thinking it was a compliment, my sweet little sister reported the buzz from her second-grade classmates. "They said you're a spazz!" Every day, kids snatched and tossed around my signature green felt hat—admittedly, a sorry fashion choice. As was the massive, metal-frame backpack I boasted was "for my slight scoliosis." The lowest blow: Deb Squared spoke in Idigoo Idigai. "Didigon't tidigell Lidigauridiga gidibabidigout thidige pidigartidigy." ("Don't tell Laura about the party.")

I faked sick a lot. Hated school. At least once a day, I felt the "about to cry" sting in my nose like I'd walked into a plate glass door (something I've done many times).

Refusing to give up, I returned from our family trip to Mexico with little gifts for all my friends—and for Deb Fishbone. I'd had a vision of this gesture melting everyone's hearts and possibly winning back Deb Y. As they walked away examining their souvenirs, I heard Deb F. say, "This is so stupid."

Nothing, though, scarred thicker than the lunchroom incident. I'd just gotten back a short story I'd written for class called "Liddy and Me," a purely fictional and NOT AT ALL autobiographical piece. It was about a New York sixth grader named "Liddy"—not Laura, because it totally wasn't me—who'd become a social leper at school. Deb Fishbone could sniff out vulnerability like a truffle hog, and grabbed the story from me at lunch.

Over my protests—"Hey, that's *mine!*"—she flipped through, selecting the perfect line to read aloud:

"'I have good friends, but I feel like I'm losing them . . . slowly.'" She looked up, delighted. "Ohmigod, this is you!"

"Uh, no it's not!" I said in a "duh" voice. "It's fiction!" I felt panicked and exposed—like when someone opens the bathroom door on you right when you're wiping. SOMEONE'S IN HERE!

This is why creating art is so risky! You couldn't pick a more literal way to infect someone with the twin beliefs—those gleaming pillars of self-doubt—that "It's not safe to be me" and "It's deadly to be disliked." I'm sure not *all* my insecurity comes from one line of my story being read out loud at lunch. But of all Deb's offenses, this was the crown jewel.

So why, again, would I friend her on Facebook? Because a friend request said, "I'm the bigger person. Sixth grade? Don't remember it." As opposed to what it really meant: "I want you to see that I'm thriving and super cool, someone you should've been nicer to—and, most of all, I'm here to feed my revenge fantasy that your life turned out, if not a total shit-show, at least wildly unexceptional."

There's not much to go on, but I make do. Deb Fishbone rarely posts anything besides pics of her kid, winning at lacrosse. She's tagged in the occasional girls'-night-out photo: angled three-quarters to camera (red-carpet style), one knee bent like everyone else's in bachelorette-party formation; frizzy hair pulled back; workish glasses that make her look every bit the corporate stiff she became. She's in insurance—something with auto accidents and trip-and-falls. She's probably the one who trips you.

Mostly, all I've seen of her in my feed is her name—atop retail ads.

J.Crew: Deb Fishbone likes this.

Macy's: Deb Fishbone likes this.

Shopbop, Revolve Clothing, Nordstrom's: Deb Fishbone likes them all—as well as Eileen Fisher, H&M, Club Monaco, Gap, ASOS, and Sephora.

Deb Fishbone likes Starbucks and anything you can find at a mall. Money says she also likes dish towels that say "wine o'clock."

I bet Deb Fishbone would like to go back in time and click *Like* on the things from when she was large and in charge. Deb Fishbone likes Reggie! Bars. Deb Fishbone likes ice-cream-cone shoelaces, satin jackets, the song "Jessie's Girl," and exclusive roller-skating parties. Deb Fishbone likes ribbon barrettes, aka friendship barrettes, but she's not trading any with you, because Deb Fishbone likes everyone but you. Deb Fishbone likes ruining your life.

I like to picture a split screen: On one side of it, I'm with my husband and friends at an impossible-to-get-into restaurant, being sent a procession of off-menu dishes we didn't order, "compliments of the chef." By day, I'm under a sun umbrella, comfily propped on outdoor throw pillows, sipping a frosty summer drink and typing something that will earn abundant money, fame, and accolades. It's a fantasy, go with it. And, by the way, if this fantasy sounds "girlboss" basic bitch, well, yeah, I'm a little basic, too. But is it basic if you're aware of it?

Back in my vision, I smile at the laptop. A private joke to myself. The joke is about how good it feels to get paid for the exact thing I was bullied for: being me! Splice this imagery with scenes of me on stage in front of thousands, making them cry-pee-laugh with my signature talk. It opens with a story of how I stopped giving a shit about Deb Fishbone. Which, as you can tell, I totally did.

On the other side of the split screen is Deb Fishbone, sitting in a harshly lit office, in a depressing office park. She's neck-deep in reports she was supposed to look at weeks ago, staring into a bleak Dell computer. Botox keeps her brow from furrowing, but it's bad Botox, which makes her face look like a melting candle. (I saw this on a former boss who fired me. The schadenfreude is too delicious not to graft the same cosmetic mishap onto Deb Fishbone.) She abandons a work email to browse for a jewel-toned cardigan that will look good with her nondescript black pants on Casual Friday. A popup tells her, "Like us on Facebook." And so she does.

Liking things on Facebook: Deb Fishbone likes this.

It's not the things she likes that make her basic. (I myself order way too often from Shopbop: easy returns, peel-and-stick label.) It's more the constant, robotic liking. The bland, unoriginal obedience. One day, you're the alpha of sixth grade, deciding everyone's fates. Who's invited to the birthday party, who stays home in loserville watching reruns of *Diff'rent Strokes*. Next, you're clicking a thumbs-up button because a department store told you to.

I know: I'm still not over this shit? My life is great! Deb Fishbone's is irrelevant. So is what she did when we were tweens collecting Hello Kitty erasers.

The key to creativity, business, art, self-expression, any kind of success I value, is to remind yourself that life is *not* sixth grade. In fact, it's the opposite. Standing out is where it's at. Samey and "normal" are the kiss of death, and only the weird survive. And once you're a grown-up, one person disliking you can't destroy you. Unless they sue you. Which is why I'd never use Deb Fishbone's real name. Except, of course, in my private daydreams of her dull, dopey existence . . . which are totally sixth-grade-bitch of me, but *hey*: it's my turn.

And while it's my turn, how fun is it to imagine that, this very moment, someone who once tortured you for so much as wearing the wrong jeans is probably Googling "How to be more unique"? Obviously, the evolved thing is to stop scrolling. Unfollow. Have compassion for the miserable child Deb F. must have been to deliberately cause me pain. I should wish her love and light. Bless and release. Stop giving energy to people who've wronged me. Biiitch, what fun is that? My pettiness gives *me* energy.

Sure, it's helpful to drop our ancient stories of why we're so needy/guarded/people-pleasing/controlling/cheap/unemployable/slovenly, or selfish. Why we're addicted to Häagen-Dazs, bad with money, bad at relationships, or bad at follow-through and social skills, or can't figure out the cable remote. No one wants to be the bore saying, "I wish I had the courage to live my dreams and be my best self, but I'm emotionally hobbled from being picked on in 1980." At the same time, there's joy in privately creeping on someone who once made you feel less-than and now looks to be a big nothing-sandwich of a human. I say, troll away. Hate-follow all the fuckheads: bosses who fired you, posers who trigger you, flings who never called. My hope for you is that their lives look every bit as unremarkable as you dreamed, and that the occasional scroll through their *blah* beach vacation at a timeshare—one they were probably suckered into and now regret—is as satisfying as successfully plucking a barely surfaced chin hair. Especially if it's some dodo who once made your life hell and now likes Jennifer Fucking Convertibles.

Nope, I'm still not over this shit.

And Deb Fishbone likes this.

How to Be Popular

A few weeks into ninth grade, to fit in better, I went out and bought a wood file (as one does). The guy at the hardware store asked if I was going to bake it into a cake and help spring someone out of prison. *Ha ha, no.* I mumbled something about a woodwork thing. A dollhouse for my sister? I didn't want to explain it was for my shoes. I know—file? For shoes? To fit in? I'll get there.

For context, I had just switched schools, from the relaxed, progressive, Upper West Side school I'd been at since preschool to a traditional, more academic all-girls school on the Upper East Side. They were as far apart as you could get, both in city blocks and vibe.

My parents had switched my sister the year before. She cried for days. Lots of slamming doors and wailing about her friends. They wanted to get her into a more focused environment before it was too late. For me, I guess they figured the damage had been done. I was in seventh grade, might as well finish out middle school.

When the time came, I went willingly. Deb Fishbone had lifted the ban on me in seventh grade when she'd discovered that my home, across the street from school, was the perfect place to catch *General Hospital*. Even so, I had no solid friend group to be torn about leaving behind.

I was part of a small exodus of high-school-bound nerds who wanted to go where it was cool to be smart. At my old school, where I had gone upstairs to take advanced algebra with the juniors and seniors, the popular girls only talked to me when they wanted help with their homework. And then they'd go back to demonstrating how to apply eyeshadow that matched a feather earring.

I started touring more academically rigorous schools, most of them on the ritzy, polished Upper East Side. In my first interview, the admissions officer asked me what I liked to do after school. "Besides homework," she winked. I told her I liked art museums. I hated them. They made me tired, and still do. I get a thing I call "museum feet." But when you're trying to get into a fiercely competitive school, you don't tell them your primary extracurricular is "hours and hours of *Donkey Kong*."

"Wonderful," she said, crossing her legs. We sat in opposite-facing stuffed armchairs. "New York has such terrific art museums. Who's your favorite artist?" This was like when you lie to someone that you were in the Marines, and they ask, "What platoon?"

"I like . . . Calder?" My parents had bought a bunch of his lithographs when he died. The walls of our Upper West Side apartment were splashed with red, yellow, blue, and orange blobs. "And, um . . . Rothko and Picasso, I like?" I had a framed Rothko poster in my bedroom, and in the foyer hung a "Picasso," a far-fetched copy my dad had painted for my mom to focus on when she was in labor with me. The interviewer asked what I liked about those artists, and I guessed: The colors? And fun shapes?

I didn't get in. Lesson learned: If you're going to lie, you have to be super specific.

I also spent a day at one of the big, smart schools up in Riverdale, with a campus, and found it intimidating. A girl from my old school, who'd gotten skinny, pretty, and outgoing since switching to this one, was bent over with nothing but a towel around her waist, disingenuously yelling "Look at my fat rolls" when I toured the locker room. In classes, while the boys raised their hands to answer questions, the girls twirled their hair, the way flirty females did on TV.

At the school I ended up going to, I saw blond hair and thin, prim lips on girls studying in the library. At the other all-girls schools I'd visited, the students paired their kilts with tauntingly perfect Ralph Lauren button-downs, sleeves rolled up their hairless arms just so, along with jewelry and makeup. Even in their uniforms, they were too glam for me. At my new school, however, the girls were refreshingly bookish and plain—true to a very-last-century saying I would later hear: "School X and School Y girls grow up to marry doctors and lawyers. School Z girls (that was my new school) grow up to *be* them." These girls raised their hands in class. They bounced with anticipation at the elevator, which I found overly school-eager, if also comforting. At a place like this, even if I was The Jew, I wouldn't be The Nerd. I spent a day and felt at ease. But when I got there, I had some adjusting to do.

My old school had been informal and wacky, a 1970s experiment made of concrete, glass, and leniency. Because it looked like a TV, people called it "The TV School," but officially, it wasn't even called a school. It was a "Learning Center." Homerooms were "clusters," homeroom teachers were "cluster advisers," and classrooms were "areas," as there were no walls to separate them. We called teachers by their first names: Eva, Jim, Suki, George, Jodi, Shelley. As in, *This year, I'm in Shelley's cluster.* Or, *George yelled at me in health ed. He's a dick!*

When our communications teacher announced an assignment, the hot girl, Carney, would let her striped boatneck tee slip to show her bra strap as she raised her hand and protested in a breathy purr. "Um, Larry, I don't think it's fair that you gave us so much homework."

"Uh, okay," Larry would agree. At my old school, education was a *dialogue*.

At my new school (established 1883), you started French in fourth grade and Latin in sixth, wore uniforms through eighth, couldn't talk in the elevator if there were more than six people, and had the same gym teachers who'd taught my mother in the 1950s. Those gym teachers were over seventy, and their names started with "Miss." I'd never even called a parent "Mr." or "Mrs." I was nervous about calling teachers by their last names. Or getting a feminist teacher and forgetting it was "Ms."

At my old school, there had been no cafeteria. Just a lunchroom, where we'd eat sandwiches our parents had packed into our Fonzie, *Charlie's Angels*, or *Muppets* lunchboxes, which later gave way to more mature brown paper bags, which we dispensed with as soon as we hit seventh grade. That's when we were allowed to leave the building to score bagels at H&H. At my new school, the cafeteria offered individual Cornish game hens, a salad bar that included a very good Oriental sesame beef, goose

liver pâté, triple-cream cheeses left over from the Thursday trust-
ees meeting, and a thing called "Joey rolls." These were addictive,
croissant-like rolls made by the assistant chef, Joey. We clustered
around him like pigeons when he put out a fresh bowl.

The mascot of both of my schools: the Beaver. Take that in:
ALL-GIRLS SCHOOL. BEAVER. And they were all about
the beaver. For the centennial year, they handed out pins: "100
Years of Eager Beavers." The school's crest had beavers. The lit-
erary magazine was called *The Beaver*. At an assembly, the magazine's editor in chief famously announced a "big *Beaver* meeting
after school." In the earnest spirit typical of our school, she
added, "All Beavers welcome!"

My old school—to use a term that wasn't yet un-PC or un-
woke because neither had been invented—was what we'd then
call *jappy* (meaning, Jewish American Princess-y). My new
school was preppy. Not that my old school wasn't, also. This was
the age of the flipped-up polo collar. The perfect white tee under a Benetton sweater vest. But my new school embodied prep
in the old-money, drive-a-beat-up-Volvo-in-the-Hamptons-and-
don't-show-how-rich-you-are way.

My old school was children of orthodontists; my new school
was children of the Pilgrims. At my old school we came back
from summer camp; at my new school they returned from Switzerland. On my first day, I heard one classmate say of yogurt, "All
summer in Europe, I ate nothing but."

At the new school you dressed to show how long you'd been
there. Starting in ninth grade, there was no real dress code.
Those who'd attended elementary and middle school had waited
years to ditch their uniforms and wear jeans, cords, any pants.
East End Avenue, right by the East River, could be a cold, windy

place. Still, some girls in my class voluntarily came to school in their old uniforms. Not the recent one, that wasn't cool. Cool was a collector's item you owned if you'd been there forever: a navy, pleated skirt that had been discontinued. You wore it really short, a little frayed and beaten up, dotted with a mix of Adam Ant and Duran Duran pins or just plain safety pins for rebellious flair. A look you might call "legacy punk."

I couldn't do the uniform, but I could work on my shoes. Having learned the perils of not fitting in at my old school, I was determined to sew myself into the social fabric of this one. The most urgent place to start was on my feet. The real mark of status in this prepster motherland was, How scuffed are your boat shoes? Beat-up brown leather boat shoes were *it*. Even better if they were handed down from your older sibling who was now off at Choate. You could wear Docksiders, or you could wear L.L. Bean Bluchers, pronounced BLUE-kers. If you called them "BLUE-chers," you were someone's embarrassing mom. And if you wore them, you had to have the leather laces curled up on the ends in a spiral dongle thingy I had no idea how to make.

I bought Docksiders, and realized as soon as I got them home that they looked wrong. They were too new, just like my Danish Schoolbag. You didn't call it that. You called it a "Chocolate Soup Bag," after the Upper East Side store where most kids bought theirs. Those of us on the West Side, the crosstown bus girls, bought ours at a Columbus Avenue store called Mythology. No one called it a Mythology Bag, though. The scrappy, less-posh Upper West Side wasn't a point of reference. Since these had been "in" for at least a year, everyone else's Chocolate Soup Bag was threadbare and floppy. Mine was factory fresh, to match my glaringly virginal shoes.

Their leather was bright, stiff, unblemished, and a little or-angey? I didn't have a summer to acquire a patina by wearing them around my dad's sailboat on Cape Cod. I didn't have a dad's sailboat, or the kind of dad who sailed, or a family cot-tage on Cape Cod, the Hamptons, or any place with sand dunes. Our country house was a suburban ranch home in Stamford, Connecticut, where my mother's parents had retired and died. The spare rooms were occupied by surgical-store, flesh-colored old-people gear. Crutches, walker, folding cot, a terrifying com-mode. The kids at the swim club were all local and on the diving team. Their hair was bleached not by sun and surf, but by chlo-rine, and anyway, I didn't know them. I can hardly whine about growing up with the wrong weekend home, but I envied my new classmates' access to chumminess and salt-air corrosion.

I coveted the weather-beaten luster of belonging. Of having put in your years, and being comfortable in your skin—or in your leather, leather which was impossibly soft and broken in. It was the look of not trying. You don't have to try when you've had sunny afternoons riding rusted bikes to get ice cream at a wharf, with kids you've known since preschool. The question was, how to fast-track the process.

My efforting was transparent. I was the picture of wanting and pushing. That's the picture you put behind the other pictures, be-cause trying too hard is not pretty. But then, most of us are try-ing too hard. Especially to look like we're not trying at all. Not trying is a multibillion-dollar industry. We have warring best sellers about not giving a fuck. Every morning, we who make a living on the Internet scroll through our camera rolls faced with a riddle: How can I be extra-authentic today? How can I be the poster child for ease? How can I express, in a fun, fresh way, my fucks are all gone, come back tomorrow, we're fresh out of fucks? I believe zero of the people who claim they give zero fucks. Announcing it means you give at least a partial fuck. Me, I've always given more of a fuck than I'd like.

Here are some ways I fucked up at not giving a fuck at my new school, in the form of handy dos and don'ts I'd like to hand thirteen-year-old me for this adventure (they're all don'ts) and to you, too, because, P.S., we're all still thirteen.

DON'T Be a Grind

There were two things you didn't want to be called in our class. The first was a *grind*, someone seen as doing too much homework. Yes, you were supposed to be smart, but effortlessly so.

From day one, I got pigeonholed as a grind, which was unfair. I wasn't used to the volume of homework, so I sat at my desk during free periods—for some reason with my bulky CB ski jacket on, which is the quintessential look of "not at ease"— in a frantic attempt to keep up. What was I supposed to do, not hand in my homework? Do a bad job and get a C? That wasn't cool, either.

Asking for an extension or skipping school to work on your paper, or (god forbid) asking a classmate for help, were all considered cheating. And even worse than being a grind was being a cheat. When word got around that I'd asked a fellow student for help with my biology worksheet, our class prefect, an A+ student named Josie, who only ate carrot and celery sticks at lunch, got on the case. She rounded up a group of classmates, including some I badly wanted as friends, and confronted me in an empty classroom about my cheating. On the wall, the portrait of a former headmistress looked on sternly as if she'd give final say. I ugly-cried and said all those things people say on the show *Intervention*: "This is an ambush, I'm out of here." Which was it? Don't work too hard, or *do* work hard?

The same lose-lose proposition exists now. There's hustle culture, where serial entrepreneurs like Gary Vaynerchuk, aka Gary Vee, appear on every platform to scream at you to prioritize work over all else (but also, be *kind* to yourself). Everywhere I turn, there's Gary, finding time in his jam-packed day to tell me I'm not doing enough. On YouTube, he's telling me to put out sixty-four pieces of content daily. On LinkedIn, he says to skip dinner with the family. Better yet, skip Christmas! But don't skip TikTok! Oh hi, Gary, there you are on Instagram in a repurposed video from 2009, literally telling me to work 'til my eyeballs bleed and to stop watching *Lost*. Guess what: I started watching *Lost* because Gary Vee told me not to. (And then I stopped all on my own because it was too stupid after they got off the island.) I keep expecting Gary Vee to appear behind me in the bathroom mirror. *Boo! Caught you going after a chin hair instead of going after your dreams!*

Then there's anti-hustle culture. Do what brings you joy! Work smarter, not harder. Get in flow and alignment, choose ease. Sure, sign me up. Problem is, sometimes I have to work all day to get the things I want. But that's too hustle-y to broadcast (except here, I guess, in this book). Relaxed: good. Strenuous: bad. You're not supposed to show the pushing. You're supposed to show the hammock. If you're on your laptop all day, it'd better be at the beach. (Caption: "My office for the day!")

It's as confusing now as it was back then. I guess if you're a grind, go be a grind, but don't look like one. Work in a bikini, not your puffy coat.

DON'T Be a Climber

Worse than *grind* was being called a *climber*. I was that, too. As soon as I could, I brutally ditched my nerd group and started sitting with the popular girls. Yasmin, a classmate who wore a full arm of Fiorucci bracelets and overused the phrase "This summer in Monte Carlo" (serving up a throat-clearing French *r* every time), tried to muscle in at the cool table, too.

It hadn't taken me long to figure out Yasmin was a pushy wannabe. On the first day, she told me, in her continental accent—giving each word a clap of the hands—"You must, come, see, my shoe, collection, I'm like Imelda, Marcos. But with even, more, shoes." The way she spoke, you expected all her sentences to end with "darling." She lived in a Park Avenue hotel with her family and two hairless cats who looked like they disapproved of the thread count. She was a modern-day Eloise, if Eloise (a) had a credit card to use freely at Benetton and Bloomie's yet never paid you back after you covered her frozen hot chocolate at Serendipity, and (b) summered on the French Riviera at a beach club favored by French Royals, tax dodgers, and lesser members of Wham! Whenever the song "Forever Young" played on the radio in our homeroom, Yasmin put her hand to her heart and sighed, "Ohhhh, this was my song with my boyfriend in Monte Carrrrlo." We heard from credible sources that said "boyfriend" was an unreciprocated crush Yasmin kept pushing into the pool.

Yasmin's worst offense was her bald social ambition. She was always saving a seat for someone higher-ranking. "You can't sit here," she warned when we entered math class, her hand covering the chair next to her. "This seat's for Mandy." Here was everything I didn't want to be. My humiliating, socially desperate shadow self.

When Yasmin headed with her foie-gras-loaded lunch tray toward our table—at least that's how I thought of it, "ours"—I rolled my eyes and sighed, "Oh boy. Look who's trying to sit with us." One of the popular girls, who wore the coveted, shabby-chic vintage uniform and whose family had a real Renoir in the TV room, said, "No offense, Laura, but who are you to sit here, either?"

And so, I did what any confident, strong, self-respecting young woman would: got up and started my own table, where all were welcome. The nerds, the dorks, the grinds, the climbers, the other new girls. Ha, as if! What I did was let my face turn red, butter a Joey roll, and continue to wedge myself into that same table as if no one had said anything. Baller!

DON'T Openly Compare Grades

At my old school, when the teacher handed back a test or paper, everyone would ask, "Whadju get?" We answered each other freely. "98." "73." "Failed! Got a 51!" When smarts aren't currency, grades aren't personal. It was as if everyone had received a single jelly bean, and then asked each other, "What flavor did you get?"

At my new school, the first thing we were handed back was an algebra test. "Whadju get?" I asked the classmate next to me. She, like everyone else in the class, had carefully folded over the top corner of the test page, covering the grade. She gave me an aghast look as if I'd just asked her, "How much money does your family have?" or "Can I see your vagina?"

"That," she said, sliding her test paper an extra inch away and curving her arm around it as a shield, "is none of your business."

Correct. And I love info that's none of my business. In the online-entrepreneur world, publicly sharing your income is considered vulnerable, transparent, and authentic—the holy troika of trustworthy brand traits—and I guess I've always been suited for that trend. I'm comfortable in a "whadju get" kind of culture. Once I had a million-dollar year, I myself wrote several articles with some version of "I Made a Million Dollars" in the title. It's tacky and gauche, but the sort of headline that gets clicked on and shared—and shows people what's possible for them. So I went with it, even as I imagined my mother cringing and these former classmates circulating my articles with a cluster of eyeroll emojis.

So maybe don't ask for anyone else's grade, but feel free to share your own. Just read the room first, and know that even in the "right" room, some people might give you shit.

DON'T Home-Distress Your Shoes

I thought I had the answer. In the same spirit of hope with which I now bring home any new, expensive face cream promising "rapid cell turnover" and "collagen repair," I pulled that brand-new wood file out of the paper bag, nested one of my spankin'-new Docksiders on my lap, and went to work. I was determined to have preppy, weather-beaten footwear by dinnertime.

I attacked those spotless genuine leather uppers from every angle for several hours in front of the TV.

Result? Drumroll please . . . and . . . Ta-da! They looked psychotic. Like a mama tiger had read them as a threat to her cubs. Or, simply, like they'd been filed. Light crosshatching all over dark brown hide: it was a look. I had begged my mom for the Docksiders, so I had to wear them to school—where they drew the question, "What happened to your shoes?" I said they got scuffed, which was not a lie.

Despite my fumbles, I was at least liked enough to assemble what felt like a respectable "group of friends" for my birthday party in late October. That's fast work for a new girl, the equivalent of a *Top Chef* Quickfire Challenge. You make do with what you've got in the time allotted. I nervously called a list of girls that felt socially aspirational but not a huge reach. No queen bees, no top Beavers. They said yes and showed up with good gifts: stacks of rubber bracelets, 45s of "Safety Dance" and "Puttin' on the Ritz." I felt reasonably popular.

Safe to say, though, no one had been won over by my trying-too-hard shoes. But you know what? Who gives a fuck?

See Ya at Studio

Other ninth graders, especially the ones who looked ten years older with a little eyeliner, went to all the clubs: Peppermint Lounge, Danceteria, Area, the Pyramid Club, and, of course, Studio 54, which—unless you were a dork or the nightly news—you called "Studio."

Studio was a "must." You wanted someone to shout to you at the end of school, "See ya at Studio!"

I was late to the party, literally. By the time I nervously lined up to get in, Studio was already four years past its "Final Party," where stars like Diana Ross and Ryan O'Neal had bumped booties in a cocaine-dusted bon voyage to the owners on the eve of their prison sentence.

"You had to go in the late '70s," my husband, Steven, likes to remind me. "That was the heyday." He's nine years older and talks as if I should revise my sad Studio timeline like you change a restaurant reservation.

At eighteen, he went all the time, alternating between a canary-yellow parachute jumpsuit and leather pants with an argyle sweater. ("Preppy-punk," he describes it. "Very Fiorucci.")

When we hear the speedy bridge of disco hit "Born to Be Alive," Steven always says, "This is the part where everyone at Studio would break open and sniff their amyl nitrite"—adding, as if I haven't read fiendishly about every drug, "That's poppers."

Steven and his friends were nobodies from New Jersey, but they sailed past the legendary throngs of desperados outside the club—even the ones who pulled up in limos. They had juice. The famous doorman, Marc Benecke, sublet an apartment to Steven's suave older brother, Sibby.

Sibby had a 1970s porn mustache, lots of girlfriends, a construction business, and property in Aspen. He was the kind of guy people owed and granted favors.

Steven saw all the people you were supposed to see. "Always Halston. Andy Warhol, Blondie, Liza Minnelli, and Scavullo—" adding, for my benefit, though again, I know, "—the photographer."

In 1984, I didn't know or care that this crowd was gone, that the "heyday" was over. As far as I was concerned, this was The Moment, and I was way behind—just as I'd been the last to get "layers" (feathered hair was now for mall rats) and leg warmers in seventh grade.

Rob Lowe still went to Studio. So did all the cool kids from different schools who knew each other and drank, smoked, and made out. Some even finger fucked. We heard them say so in the school library.

I wasn't in that crowd. I looked too young. I didn't have the right "going out" clothes. I had braces. I didn't know what you did once you got there. That first year at my all-girls school, I went to a co-ed dance and discovered I didn't know how to dance. I kept trying to copy my new friend Sara's side-to-side snaky move and couldn't pull it off, even trickier when fake-mouthing lyrics you don't know to "Melt with You." If I couldn't cut it at a school dance, what business did I have going to Studio?

To go to Studio, you had to be Mallory—the rich, perfect-looking, strawberry-blond goddess in our class whose favorite phrase was "Last night at Studio." Mallory had acknowledged me once. In the school elevator, she looked at my Girbaud Complements khakis, with the trademark label across the fly, and said, "I have those same Complements." It was a big day.

Mallory was bad at school but great at boys. Boys, and fashion. I once saw her cutting class with her sidekick, Lisa. They sat against the lockers with their legs out in front of them, sharing a magazine. "I need this leather jacket," Mallory said, studying an editorial spread as I walked past. "It's *Vogue*, but not so *Vogue* that you couldn't wear it? To like, wherever. Like, Studio."

I didn't have anything that was any type of *Vogue*. Not even *Seventeen*. I was still *Dynamite* magazine. Okay, maybe *Bananas*. (*Dynamite* for teens.)

Through my *Bananas* mind's eye, I could picture what Studio would be like: a tight bunch of friends on velvet sofas, in un-tucked Oxford shirts, girls lying on boys, boys on girls, heads on shoulders and laps. Laughter. A Shangri-la of togetherness.

"My group" was a phrase I always wanted to say.

I didn't have that at my new school. I had a handful of friends, who invited me to their massive Park Avenue apartments to watch TV, do homework, and make cookie dough (which the maids cleaned up). I had the twelve or so who had come to my birthday party. They'd squealed watching *Psycho* and enjoyed the make-your-own-sundae bar my mom set up in the kitchen. They got to mix Oreos into vanilla ice cream. That combo wasn't yet available in pints. It was the best thing you ever ate, and the most daring thing we did.

These were the semi-cool people, and pushing my way in was already a feat. But they weren't the kind of crew who'd say, "See ya at Studio," and know how to get in and what time to meet, in what part of the club, in "our spot."

By the spring of ninth grade, I got tired of saying, "Nope, never been to Studio. I keep meaning to go"—as if it were a movie I hadn't seen and not a daunting venture like signing up for the marathon or deciding to go buy drugs.

I was still connected with two friends from my old school, Jill and Danielle, through Jewish confirmation class, which is like the grad school after your bat mitzvah. The three of us agreed, *enough already*, we'd go to Studio. They hadn't been either, and it was time. We refused to remain losers. We had just a couple of hurdles: getting in—but we'd cross that velvet rope when we got to it—and our parents. Chiefly, Jill's mom.

Jill's mom was a tiny woman with a tiny head, giant eyes, and a heavy New York accent. A Jewish-mother version of E.T. Her hobbies were: driving around in a new Jaguar (leased), picking up prepared foods from Zabar's, stirring up rumors, and looking for Jill. Her name was Janet, and we heard it a lot in my house. "Janet called. She wants to know if you know where Jill is." "Sure, Jill can stay for dinner, but I don't want to have to deal with five phone calls from Janet." "Janet accused me of coming on to her."

This last one from my dad, who was colleagues with Janet in the psychoanalyst community. True, he'd often say old-school, inappropriate things to women without meaning anything, like, "You have quite a figure," but he was unflagging in his fidelity to my mom, and didn't think much of Janet, professionally or otherwise. "She's totally unaware of her feelings," he'd marvel. "I don't know how she has any patients. She's a crazy." Years later, Janet would be in the news for allegedly stabbing her second husband—another shrink who was a parent from the school— with a challah knife.

Other than ice-skate and shop for clothes, Janet didn't want Jill doing anything. Especially not nighttime activities where Janet couldn't call to check up. The one exception was any synagogue youth group event, including sleepovers at our temple. These were called "shul-ins," and Jill was allowed to go.

At one shul-in, Jill gave a hand job to the guy I had a crush on, right in front of me. At least she had the decency to do it inside her North Face sleeping bag. At another, she gave a blow job to an older boy in the sanctuary pews. We called these "pew jobs." Guys always wanted to fool around with Jill. She had a tiny mouth—which I pictured being a liability for pew jobs—but a great body from ice skating.

Senior year of high school, Jill would be spotted by one of my parents' friends in a ground-floor apartment window, fucking her boyfriend—or, as my father reported, "making the scene." This boyfriend was the president of our temple youth group. He and Jill had met at a shul-in. None of this was what Janet pictured at shul-ins, but I'm sure it's the exact scenario she imagined at Studio.

Danielle's parents, on the other hand, were pretty damn disco. Her dad had his own ad agency and a pinball machine in his office. Her mom was tall and thin and always wore the right patent-leather Calvin Klein skinny belt. Their brownstone, and Danielle's dad, had made a big cameo in a box-office hit starring Jack Nicholson. They were friends with George Lucas and got free *Star Wars* tickets. One time after school, Danielle's mom was putting an anthurium flower in a vase and said to us, "It looks like a penis on a heart." Danielle was embarrassed but I thought it was cool—though it would've been cooler if she had said "a dick."

Danielle's parents had gone to Studio themselves. It was that kind of place in that kind of era—you'd see everyone from nine-year-old Drew Barrymore to the eighty-year-old lady known as Disco Sally.

Danielle got permission to go to Studio.

I told my parents I was going. I thought this was the most mature approach. "I don't want to lie to you or sneak around," I said, "so you should know that I'm going to Studio 54 this weekend." My parents applauded my honesty. They probably figured I'd never get in.

Jill would say she was sleeping over at my house. We'd wear our coolest outfits and meet at our old school. Jill still went there; Danielle, like me, had switched. Unlike me, she'd enrolled at a co-ed school and had guy friends. One of them, she told us, "lets me practice blow jobs on him—even though I have braces." *I need some guy friends*, I thought.

We'd kill time by seeing the Parents' Association production of *Once Upon a Mattress* at our old school. And then, we were going clubbing.

I dressed for a wild night, or did my best: black pants I thought were edgy because they had strange round pocket openings, a yellow loose-knit Benetton sweater that showed off my spring vacation tan, flat jelly shoes, and my one Fiorucci metal link bracelet, stacked with a couple of black rubber ones, all in a weak gesture of punk. My hair was in a straight bob because that's all it could do. And, braces.

Danielle's outfit was preppy, but in a summer camp way, not a Studio way. Not "preppy punk."

Jill wore something Madonna-esque. Her ice-skating body was just right for wide, studded hip belts; her curly hair ideal for that shaved-on-one-side bob, made funkier with a touch of Dippity-do. She looked right.

Leading up to our caper, I nursed my Studio fantasy:

Someone lighting a ciggy and passing it my way, me confidently saying, "No thanks," and no one caring. Then: a super-cute boy who looks like Jake Ryan from Sixteen Candles—*but not so frighteningly manly as Jake Ryan—plays with my hair and says into my ear, "I've had a crush on you all year." He's from one of our brother schools, and everyone is watching me, including the girls from my old school who tortured or ignored me until they wanted to watch soaps at my house (a block from school) or cheat off of me in Spanish. I overhear one yelling, over the music, "When did Laura Belgray get popular?" And Deb Fishbone, eyeing my Jake Ryan–esque boyfriend, shrugs, "I know, she's like, cool now." That's the precise moment she trips over someone's foot.*

We got to Studio by cab and joined the long line snaking from under the giant "54" on the famous marquee. My stomach fluttered.

I heard a smoky voice: "Hey." It was Mallory. Skinny, pretty Mallory, saying "Hey" to *me*. She looked like a model. Her outfit was *Vogue*, but not so *Vogue* that you couldn't wear it.

"I didn't know you came to Studio," she said.

"Yeah," I told her, adding the most uncool thing I could possibly say. "First time, let's hope. Cross your fingers!"

Already not listening, she said, "Have fun," and whooped as one of the boarding-school boys lifted her on his shoulders and sailed her through the door.

We'd barely joined the line and I'd already seen Mallory. Iconic! Like going to the Hard Rock Cafe and spotting Matt Dillon and Ally Sheedy, which one girl in our class always claimed she did, but I didn't believe her.

As we got closer, Danielle and Jill and I coached each other: "Remember, smile, but without showing your braces." I knew I didn't look a day over fourteen. In fact, people still guessed I was twelve.

Danielle was a little taller but didn't look any older than I did. Self-conscious bounce, picked-at cuticles, and a smile that screamed puberty. She went to the "cool" orthodontist, who was famous for having video games in the waiting room and giving out colored dental rubber bands. Danielle's were hot pink.

Jill was another story. With her big boobs, her braces looked like adult braces. Jill had a special sexy confidence. Not wanting to confine her gifts to the ice rink, she often jumped and spiraled in the air during school, shrugging after she landed, "Just an axel." She also liked to do backbends. Conveniently for her, someone once started a game of limbo in Hebrew school. As Jill shimmied under the broomstick, head thrust back and chest up, a boy in our class commented, "I call this portrait, 'Mountains Rising to the Sun.'"

"Here goes," one of us said at the ticket booth. I worried. What if my friends got in and I didn't? Would they go in without me? Would Mallory look around for me, not see me, and know I didn't get in?

The guy in the booth didn't ask us anything. Didn't ask for ID. Didn't even glance at my strange, closed-lipped smile. Skin stretched over metal. If he noticed anything, it was probably Jill's chest. Our collective proof of age.

We were in. We were going into Studio 54.

We walked down what I remember as a long hall (but might have been a short lobby), through massive metal doors. People were dancing. People were making out. We smelled pot. We lingered near the entrance and hung around a sofa, taking it all in. We were at Studio. *We were at Studio!* Should we go on the actual dance floor? Buy drinks? Find the bathroom and put on lip gloss? Or should we stand where we were for a bit and just, y'know, "people watch"?

If we wandered around, we might come across Mallory and her crew in their spot, flopping around on each other, smoking and drinking. Would they wave me over? If they did, would I bring Jill and Danielle?

I didn't have to worry.

I once fainted getting out of a ski resort hot tub in Colorado and had an entire dream that seemed to last an hour. When I woke up, with concerned, wet grown-ups around me, I asked how long I'd been lying there. They said only one second. They'd seen me crumple and shaken me awake right away.

My few moments at Studio now feel like that. In my head, we were there for hours, dancing and mingling—amid an eternity of gyrating butts, teenagers sipping drinks, probable D-list celebrities I didn't recognize, sickly sweet marijuana smoke that scared me, and the song "99 Luftballons."

In reality, we were probably there for five minutes, clinging like wallflowers at a school dance to that seating area near the entrance. There wasn't room for us to sit, so we hovered near it. Danielle tapped me, nodded toward the dance floor, and, with her mouth open in an expression of "I'm wild," did that embarrassing mock-disco down-up-down-up finger point. Her braces glittered in the flashing lights.

And that's when it happened.

Those imposing, solid doors we'd fought so hard to get through crashed open with the operatic force of a DEA squad. But this wasn't a drug raid. It was a furious, Jewish E.T. in a massive fur coat, barreling into the club.

It was Jill's mother, Janet.

"JILL?" Janet screeched at a pitch that cut right through the din.

In my TV-influenced memory, this is where the music stopped with a record scratch and everything went into super slow motion. Jill's mother plowed through the crowd like she was acting in a terrorist-plot chase through a Middle Eastern souk. "JILL!! WHERE'S MY JILL? WHO HAS MY JILL?"

As soon as I took in what was happening, Janet was on us. She plucked Her Jill from our midst like a pterodactyl grabbing dinner and dragged her out by the arm. Frozen in place, I could feel the whole stack of Madonna-esque rubber bracelets rolling against Jill's skin—giving her what we then called an "Indian burn"—and Jill screamed the thing you hope never, ever to scream at Studio: "MOMMY, NO!"

Danielle and I made pathetic half-motions to stop it, not unlike when you're going to hold the elevator for someone but miss it. Or when the server takes your dessert plate with a bite still left on it. A weakly mimed, "Wait, no. Come back."

The doors clanged shut after them, silencing Janet's rant that no doubt rang through the lobby to the street and into the shiny, leased Jaguar Jill's father probably had idling outside: "You're lucky I found you before you got drugged and raped and killed and how were you even thinking of being out this late when you have a skating tournament coming up do you know what I pay for that rink and those lessons and from now on it's school, temple, and ice skating and that's IT!"

"Oh my god," Danielle and I both said a moment later. We were stunned stupid. How had Janet found us?

A man dancing his way off the dance floor drunkenly bumped into me. "Jesus!" he spat. I said sorry, though I was standing still. In tight jeans and black leather straps criss-crossed over his white T-shirt, he was the type you see in photos from the club's previous era. A relic. He probably spent his nights waiting for the DJ to play one disco song, even though everyone knew disco sucked.

He danced away. I realized we weren't going to have the kind of night you're supposed to have there, the kind I imagined Mallory had. The kind my husband now tells me he had. He has no photos from those nights, but he took one crappy keepsake: tinnitus. When a neighbor's smoke alarm goes off all night, he'll tell me, "That's what it sounds like in my ear all the time." It's constant, low-grade torture, but he likes the way he got it: from sitting inside the club's giant music speakers. It's his version of a war wound.

People have picked up way worse at that place, and they're lucky if they're around to tell about it.

"You wanna go?" I asked Danielle, who was twanging her hot-pink dental bands.

"If you want to." We each wanted the other to lay claim to giving up.

In our cab back to the Upper West Side, Danielle and I didn't have much to say besides, "I can't believe that happened," and "Janet, like, ruined everything." But I felt free. It was like finally not being a virgin, even if the sex was painful and not much fun. Not that I'd know that for another three years. Disastrous as it was, I could now say, "I've been to Studio."

When I walked into the apartment, my parents looked up from the living room sofa. They were watching Johnny Carson. My night hadn't even lasted 'til Letterman.

"Hi," my mom said, in her not-pleased tone, as if I'd snuck out. "I spent the whole night dealing with Janet."

"You *told* her?" I demanded, shedding my jacket and taking off my jelly shoes as though they were four-inch stilettos. Janet had called and demanded to speak to Jill. My mother, who can't lie and hadn't promised to, told her where we were.

My father shook his head. "That woman is crazier than my patients."

Though seething at my mother's pathetic cover-up skills, I was relieved to put on my sleep clothes and retreat to my bedroom with a bowl of Golden Grahams, to hear my dad's explosive "Ha!" through my shut door. He loved Johnny Carson's guest comedians. I turned on my own TV (a bat mitzvah gift) to catch the rest.

The worry that plagued me was that Mallory might have seen the horror go down. What I didn't know was that there were other witnesses. In a long, nostalgic Facebook message session with a classmate from my old school—she was in the popular group, those people who made fun of me in middle school and the very ones I'd fantasized about awing with my coolness— she brought up "that time Jill's crazy mother dragged her out of

Studio." Turns out she and her friends saw it happen and had been joking about it for over thirty years. However, she didn't remember me being there, which is a retroactive relief to my teenage self. Also an insult.

Forever after that, I fancied myself sealed in the memory glass of Studio 54 history. I must have written my name and address on a clipboard on the way out, because I got promotional postcards from Studio for years. Invitations to magazine-sponsored parties, decked out with sparkly graphics of lips and champagne glasses. For the first couple of months, I tacked them up on my bedroom bulletin board and felt very "on the list" without actually going anywhere. My life's goal to this day.

As for Mallory, she left for boarding school the next year, taking the party to her dorm room. I wouldn't see her until our ten-year high school reunion—where she said several times to the same people, "Me, I'm just looking for my first husband." She'd gone into floral design with her mother and looked more ordinary now, her outfit conservative. It was *Better Homes & Gardens*, but not so *Better Homes & Gardens* that you couldn't wear it.

She wouldn't reappear again until our twenty-fifth reunion, where she looked awfully puffy. "My mother told me I'm fat!" she said, swirling a glass of vodka. "I was like, yeah, Mom, but it's all from alcohol, so it doesn't count."

I thought then of my most cherished dividend from our ruined night. At the end of ninth grade, I'd shyly asked Mallory to sign my yearbook. In the ads in the back, over a drawing of a bear, she wrote: *Cute bear. See ya at Studio.*

Watch the Potato Chips

"Watch the potato chips." That's what my pediatrician used to say when he weighed me. He drew out the words in a hesitant whine, like it pained him. "Waaaaaatch the potato chips." I wish I'd told him to watch my middle finger and then mimed cranking it to full mast. I was eight or nine, tops, and already had a complex about my weight. Normally a late bloomer, I can claim it's one area where I got a head start on my peers. (The other was arm and leg hair. Jealous?) It's also one area where it's become dicey to tread. Size and body image are a cultural can of worms. But worms are low-fat, and treading burns calories, so here's a deep dive on how this issue has shaped my life.

As early as age five, I stared at other kids' stomachs when they sat down. Somehow, theirs stayed flat rather than oozing into mud pies like mine. When I got out of a pool, I quickly wrapped a towel around my middle or covered my abdomen with my forearm, holding it like a low sling. Kind of a revolutionary-soldier-crossing-the-Delaware pose.

Now, looking at pictures, I see I wasn't fat—just pudgy enough for kids to tease. One hid my Hershey's Kiss at lunch and said, "Maybe you could do without it." Another said she wanted to squeeze my chubby cheeks. "They're like Arnold's from *Diff'rent Strokes*." I wanted to look like Kimberly, the slim older sister who looked perfect in her Ralph Lauren polo sweaters and always had a date.

In middle school, I made up a four-week stomachache so I could sit out gymnastics. Gym sucked enough as it was. Like any unathletic kid, I stood wax-museum-still in dodgeball. I wheezed and doubled over when we had to run a mile. Struck out first, got picked last. But gymnastics was a whole other level of *fuck no*. While other girls did triple back-handsprings, I barely managed a somersault. Mine wobbled off to the side. The deal-breaker, though, was the outfit. They let the boys dress in regular gym clothes while making us girls wear a leotard. A LEOTARD. The garment that might as well say, "Ask Me About My Fat Rolls." Hello, doctor's note.

Next, I hated my butt. I thank the designer-jeans boom. Suddenly, everyone at school was wearing skin-tight, midnight-blue denim with bold logos on the pockets. Calvin Klein. Jordache. Sasson. The Jordache ad said, "You've got the look." Not me, in my drab Wranglers, I didn't. I announced at home, "We need to get me some decent jeans."

My father, having read about designer denim in the Business section, wasn't having it. "The jeans are free. What you're paying for is the name and the rent." Also: "Dungarees aren't for style. They're knockaround clothes. It's a rip-off!" He bought his suits from the sidewalk sale racks outside a bargain place on upper Broadway called Fowad. They were short-sleeved, which didn't make them cheaper but is worth mentioning. Short-sleeved suits. "You want me to buy designer clothes," he'd say, opening the jacket to show me the label. "Well what do you say to Pierre Cardin?" He pronounced it "Car-DAH," like the first part of Kardashian.

My mom had mercy on me and my need to fit in and overrode my dad.

Having fought for it made our shopping trip that much worse. From Bloomie's to Macy's to Gimbels, from Juniors and Young Miss to full-blown Women's Casuals, I tried on every designer jeans brand under the sun. Even last-choice Gloria Vanderbilts— which promised on TV to fit "like the skin on a grape," but not, evidently, like the skin on a chubby rump. I couldn't pull them over my butt meat. I came out of the dressing room in tears. "Sorry, my dear," my mom sighed. "You inherited many things from your mama. Some of them good . . . and others, well . . ." At this, she patted her own tush and made a regretful "them's the breaks" teeth click.

My mom had always struggled with weight. Tab in the fridge, fat-free yogurt pops in the freezer, Weight Watchers scale on the counter. Guilty face if you caught her eating peanut butter on the sly. I'm sure she wished I'd inherited my dad's speedy metabolism. My sister had. Not only that, she could make a Blondie or a Ring Ding last for two episodes of *The Brady Bunch*, while I wolfed mine down before the first commercial. "Ha ha," she'd taunt. "I still have half left."

In seventh grade, I started trying to get skinny. I signed up for after-school Jazzercise with two friends. Wearing shiny dark-tan

L'eggs pantyhose under our shorts and terry-cloth sweatbands on our wrists and foreheads, we did crunches and leg lifts to the Go-Go's "Our Lips Are Sealed." I didn't see progress.

That year, I bought a booklet at Woolworths called *Thin Thighs in 30 Days*. The pink cover featured a gorgeous pair of toned, bronzed legs coming out of white, silky shorts. I followed it to the letter. I did wall-sits and donkey kicks. I walked a mile every day, counted out in blocks on Broadway. Papaya King at Seventy-Second Street was my turnaround point. All that, and my thighs still met at the top.

Finally, I worked up the nerve to tell my mom I wanted to go on Weight Watchers. I felt shy talking body stuff with her. She said I was beautiful just the way I was, but had no problem with conscious, healthy eating. My first day on the plan, she counted out twenty red seedless grapes (that equaled one fruit) and added a twenty-first. "You deserve one extra."

I lost weight and liked how I looked in shorts. I got my hair feathered. As they do when you look a little more like them, the pretty girls started being nice to me. "We like your haircut," one reported for the whole group, like the head of a workers union. "You have to flip it more often." She showed me how to turn my head upside down and throw it back, which worked for a few seconds. My fine, slippery hair didn't hold feathered wings for long. But she was satisfied with her work and threw in a bonus compliment. "You look skinny, too."

The infamous Deb Fishbone said, "I realized recently: you were never that fat before, just dumpy."

"Thanks," I said gratefully.

I was twelve. I would never again eat without considering the outcome.

Getting truly cuckoo with food, however, started later. In eleventh grade, I got mono and tonsillitis. I kept my own Ben & Jerry's Heath Bar Crunch in the freezer, off limits to my sister. "It's contaminated," I said, licking my spoon and sticking it back in. Universal law: Calories don't count when they're for a sore throat. I ate a pint a day, a habit that lasted well beyond the mono. Pair that with a year of skipping gym—the school nurse was a pushover—and I was struggling to snap my Girbaud jeans. A friend, leafing through a past yearbook, opened to a photo of me with a thinner face and said, "Ohmigod, look how good you looked last year." I felt a shameful lump in my throat. I started sucking in my cheeks in the mirror.

A few girls at school had gotten super skinny on Jenny Craig. I tried it. It allowed little more than cottage cheese and Wasa bread—which, if you've never tried it, is cardboard sold in the cracker aisle. At school, a friend saw me smearing butter on my Wasa and asked, in her most innocent, inquisitive voice, if butter was allowed on Jenny Craig. "I'm just curious," she said. I angerate the Wasa.

That summer, I spent two weeks with a friend's family in Switzerland. For months, she'd been telling me about the country's dietary wonders: super low-calorie yogurt so thin you could drink it; fat-free gummy candies with a sour-sweet coating. (The miracle of "Sour Patch" had yet to arrive in the United States.) It was everything she promised. We lived on liquidy yogurt and gummy fish. We biked, hiked, and swam. Then, at one family dinner outing, we rewarded ourselves with sundaes, which we tried to throw up when we got home. We took turns in the bathroom.

"Anything come up?"

"Nope. You?"

"Nothing. I think I'm bad at bulimia."

"Same. Oh well."

I'd already devoured every novel, pamphlet, encyclopedia entry, and after-school special about eating disorders—*Best Little Girl in the World* stands out—and knew habitual barfing could make your face puffy and rot your teeth, not to mention stop your heart, so I was half-relieved I couldn't get the hang of it.

Back home, I started having "phases." For a while, I'd eat nothing but grilled vegetables, grilled without oil. When we had dinner out, my parents called ahead to the restaurant to see if my needs could be accommodated, like they were an advance team for the president.

I returned for twelfth grade with my jeans hanging loose. I loved that I could pull them off without unbuttoning them. I loved being told I was skinny. Even better? "Too" skinny. "You're a real *lokshen*," my great uncle said. (Yiddish for "noodle.") My friend's dad congratulated me on turning down peaches and Häagen-Dazs. "Your discipline's working! Turn sideways and you disappear." Someone at school said I looked "even skinnier than yesterday." A friend reported her sister's high compliment: "What's Laura been eating, iceberg lettuce?" Pretty much. Who needed calories? I had verbal reinforcement for fuel. "You're finally, actually skinny," another friend said, as though I had, at last, begun to fulfill my potential as a human. The attention confirmed my lifelong suspicion: being skinny was the key to life. I began weighing myself every bathroom visit, before and after I peed. At parties, I brought my own liter of Diet Coke and swigged from it all night. I wouldn't even look at pizza.

I went to aerobics every day after school, on Seventy-Fourth Street—me, the gym dodger! I became one of those people who get there early to snag a spot in the front. I got in a fight with an older woman (she must have been about thirty) who insisted her spot was her spot, even if she didn't get there first. I felt sorry for her, a grown woman living like that.

Senior spring, I worked at Steve's Ice Cream on Columbus and never had one scoop. Not a lick. I brought fro-yo from Zabar's for my ice-cream break. I lusted for real ice cream, but as a booby prize I got to feel smug serving it to customers and thinking how fat they'd get. Especially when they mixed in fucking Reeses.

I started college with abject fear of the Freshman Fifteen. Instead of joining friends in the cafeteria, I spent lunches in my room, where I assembled a 200-calorie sandwich of fat-free turkey slices and one Fat-Free Kraft Cheese food Single on Pepperidge Farm Light Bread. I know, can't you just feel it sticking to your teeth? But to me, it was heaven. Knowing the calorie count added delicious zip to any meal.

On Snack Nights, when my dorm gathered in the hall for chips, cookies, and pizza, I emerged from my mauve-carpeted single with a bag of carrots, a carrot scraper, and my mauve-plastic wastebasket to catch the peel. They had their snack, I had mine. *Scrape scrape scrape.* I ate so many carrots, I turned orange. Carotene poisoning. I was okay with it, so long as my hip bones stuck out.

I wasn't even the one to worry about. Three doors to the right, Vicky did aerobics in her room for hours while defrosting Birds Eye vegetables on her radiator. No one was allowed in, but when she opened the door a crack to talk, you could smell a mélange of sweat and broccoli.

Another hallmate, Marla, kept a waist-high Binge Basket next to her bed, full of Ho Hos, Ding Dongs, Doritos, Fritos,

Twinkies, Sno Balls, anything you'd buy drunk in a 7-Eleven.
Her feet were always turned the wrong way in the bathroom, fac-
ing the toilet to throw it all up.

At the other end of the hall, a group of roomies weighed themselves together mid-semester and shrieked. "Oh SHIT!" I heard.
"I gained eighteen pounds!" "I gained twenty-two!" It was from
their nightly Domino's. Sure, I thought, they've been having fun,
but was it worth it? I hugged my carrots to my chest.

Sophomore year, I lived with housemates in a unit with sliding
glass doors onto a central courtyard. Through those doors, any
time of day, people could see me in our living room, sweating
my life away on my stationary bike. I was always climbing back
on that creaky seat to pedal off what I ate. A guy at a party said,
"Hey, you're that girl on the bike." *Yup, that's me.* For Hanukkah,
my parents gave me and my sister T-shirts. Hers said, "Go Marian! Co-Pres," because she was student body co-president. Mine
said, "Go Laura! Stationary Bike Team." Because . . . yeah.

Junior year, I started running eleven miles a day. I ran so hard
my toenails fell off. (P.S., they never recovered. Decades later, my
Google history is full of searches for "toenail replacement surgery.") "You're always running, running, running," my psychotherapist dad said over the holidays. "You're running away from
your feelings. But they're still there!" I rolled my eyes. "Dad! It's
not about feelings and it's not by choice!" Try explaining exercise
and weight to a man who drank milkshakes growing up because
he was too skinny and takes down whole bowls of Breakstone's
sour cream as a snack.

My reward for eleven miles was a Weight Watchers ice-milk
sandwich. I was convinced I had a rare, tragically slow metabolism that made real desserts off limits. On group Baskin-Robbins

runs, I purchased nothing, but requested samples of nearly all thirty-one flavors on those pink plastic mini-spoons. Like a panhandler, I'd then ask each housemate for a taste of her Quarterback Crunch. They'd grunt, "Why didn't you get your own?" Then, an embarrassing low: One afternoon, my wire-thin housemate Kelly brought home a half gallon of Hershey's ice cream. I watched her eat a dainty bowlful and put the rest away, her name Sharpied on the side. Later, I crept downstairs in the dark and ate a spoonful right out of the freezer. *Fuck, real ice cream's good.* Next night, same thing. It became a ritual. I couldn't fall asleep until I'd had my secret spoonful. Weeks later, Kelly remembered, "Hey, I have ice cream!" My heart pounded as she opened the freezer and found all that remained of her Fudge Ripple: a sad little mound, clinging to the corner of the carton like it was trying to hide from me. "Talk about consideration," Kelly yelled, slamming the box in the trash. Wondering how soon I could salvage that last bite from the garbage, I said, "Wow. Who *does* that?" She gave me a look like, "Just stop." I switched to sneak-eating Brian's Cookie Crisp.

During break, I got together with three high school friends to make dinner and cried in the supermarket because the jar of sauce they voted on contained cream.

Post-college, I met Victoria. She was instantly my partner in crime, as well as my partner in ordering steamed spinach with a side of mustard. As an entrée. I needed that friend.

In my mid-twenties, I never, ever skipped Aerobox class—not even for a single Saturday to meet my boyfriend's grandmother. I tried therapy, hoping it'd free me from my cycle of stuckness. My therapist said, "What if you gained ten or so pounds but stopped being consumed with food and exercise?" *Ten pounds?* I looked at her like she'd suggested, "What if you tried killing your parents in their sleep?"

At twenty-nine, I discovered salsa dancing. I was extra obsessed because it was a great workout. I became so desperate to master it, I made myself fall in love with a much older, mustachioed, married salsa instructor who taught me for free and promised to make me great, so long as I agreed to be with him. Sweet deal, right? He was fat and gluttonous and gave not one fuck. He described himself as a "sexy, roly-poly dancing motherfucker." We followed dance sessions at Joe Jr.'s diner on my corner, where he ordered banana pancakes, cheese omelets, extra bacon, a waffle "just to taste." Through a mouthful of hash browns, he said, of a woman on the salsa team, "Wow, her ass got fat. I can't have her on stage looking sloppy like that."

And then, in my thirties, I started dating Steven. He worked in the restaurant business. I was a restaurant person's nightmare—requesting tomato sauce instead of cream, pan-fried noodles steamed instead of fried. (That's like asking for cake, but can it be a cucumber?) Meanwhile, Steven ordered the way "chef recommends" and put sugar and half-and-half in his coffee, which—go figure—always tasted better than my skim milk and Equal.

I'm not sure why and when I started to relax my rules. Maybe because Steven liked to sit at the bar and share things, which felt romantic. "Wanna split the gnocchi with butter and the duck?" I balked at first. But the butter was delicious. As butter is. And the thick, fatty duck skin—*fuckin' a.*

When I was little—before I was told to watch the potato chips—I remember begging my parents for the strips of fat they cut from their steak. "That's not fat, it's gristle," they'd warn, moving the plate out of reach. "You'll choke." I'd beg harder, willing to take my chances.

Decades later, much as I'd tried, I'd never lost my taste for a mouthful of pure fat.

Gradually, I stopped asking for substitutions. I got what I wanted instead of picking the menu's best calorie bargain and then eyeballing my friend's Bolognese. I loved the freebies the kitchens sent out to me and Steven. Fried risotto balls, béchamel lasagna, a parade of items I never would have ordered. I ate it all. I was done with my diet-y ways.

And then, I came to accept and love my body unconditionally, no matter what I weigh.

LOLZ. Kidding! Don't I wish.

True, I shifted from the girl who turns orange from carrots and runs her toenails off to someone who fights her boyfriend for the fatty end of the ribeye. But I can't exactly claim I've "totally reset my relationship with weight and food." It's a lifelong relationship, after all. You've heard of COVID long-haulers? I'm a body-issues long-hauler. An "OG," if you will.

These days, while I don't "count calories" or keep a food journal, my mind is still always calculating in the background, like an app I can't quit out of. *Did I get my steps in today? Enough to burn off what I ate?* I check myself in the mirror every time I'm naked. Mostly from the side. *Am I skinny? Am I fat? Is it PMS, or from too much bread and butter when we eat out?*

Other people with "food stuff"—women who've grown up watching the potato chips—can probably spot me just like I spot them. I tunnel through fruit pie, eating only the filling, because, in that primitive, 1980s part of my brain, anything fruit-based is allowed and pastry crust is not. I eat around nuts, even spit them out like they're cherry pits. I practice the Hamburger Haircut, where you rip the bun overhang off a burger and then keep trimming as you go to eat the beef patty without all the bread. My

plate ends up looking like a hurricane-stricken region waiting for
FEMA. Steven shakes his head and says, "What's all that debris?
I can't even look."

He should see inside my head.

It sucks up all your bandwidth, this body-image business.
I've let it hold me back and limit me in a whole Skittles rainbow
of ways. I've turned down or lost jobs because I needed time to
work out in the morning (but not *early* morning). I've freaked out
about trips where there's no gym, no walkable road, too short a
beach, too many activities and meals, or, god forbid, an itinerary spreadsheet—a SPREADSHEET—without enough blank
space for working out. I had a two-year falling out with a friend
because I couldn't make time to see her on her once-a-year visit
to the city. I didn't say why, but I think she knew the conflict was
dance class. I wanted to be extra lean for an upcoming trip.

I'm not supposed to admit all this. Body positivity is the thing
now, and you're not even allowed to fat-shame yourself, especially if no one would consider you fat. Drew Barrymore got in
trouble for saying she had to be careful or she'd be "the size of
a bus." Every day, I see another influencer on Instagram in tiny
boy shorts, sitting on her kitchen counter, laughing, eating something nutritious from a bowl. (As one does.) The caption warns
us, "Don't mistake a ripped body for happiness. The girl in this
picture starved herself for three days before the shoot and was really grumpy!" If you serve up a self-development thirst trap, you
must present the secret downside.

Weight-loss coaches have come to me for help with their copy,
saying, "I don't want to mention losing weight. That shouldn't be
the goal. It's about feeling good and loving yourself." I mean . . .
awesome, if people will go for it. Will they? I think they still

want to lose weight. I probably sound like I'm from the "Living Well Lady" generation—and we've established, yes, I am! I grapevined and ponied in aerobics studios, some of them carpeted. I chowed SnackWell's, because if the box was green and said "Low Fat," you could go buckwild. I'd love to un-drink the Kool-Aid of diet culture, which is, of course, not Kool-Aid but Crystal Light. Which you better believe I carried in my bag when it came out in single packets for dieters on the go.

That's all to say, I don't have the answer—but I'm right there with you when it comes to the question: Will girls and women truly ever stop wanting to be skinny? If yes, hallelujah and count me in. Pass me the cookie dough. I guess if it was once the height of chic to be fleshy and flaunt your bare fat folds on a chaise while dangling grapes in your mouth, we could conceivably go back to that. After all, we went back to bushy eyebrows—and that was once unimaginable. When that daydream seems too unlikely, I've switched to a fantasy of everyone in the world being blind, so how I look in jeans wouldn't matter. In this joyscape, I'd be the one person with sight. Because I still want to see my food. I just don't want to have to watch it.

Boys Don't Like Me

In tenth grade, I got a little sloppy at a cast party for the interschool production of *Anything Goes* and humiliated myself. I was barely in the show, with a bit part I'd had to beg the drama teacher to give me after a sucky audition. My father made me call the man at home on a Sunday evening and use his favorite script for getting hotel upgrades: "If you accommodate me, I'll make it worth your while." Mr. Warble said "Okay" in a "suit yourself" tone and agreed to let me sing in one all-cast number, "Blow, Gabriel, Blow."

At the wrap party, to feel more loose and chummy among people who didn't even know I'd been on stage with them, I chugged down two Budweisers. I was a lightweight, so the night was a blur of cavorting and being social in ways I couldn't later recall. (Except for one moment: a guy with bad breath who was too old to be there ran his finger over my teeth when I said I'd gotten my braces off. I was grossed out, but also flattered.)

The next day at school, a classmate told me, "This drunk girl was talking to Cornelia and Dan"—a beautiful, rail-thin girl from the class above us and her boyfriend from our brother school—"and the girl kept saying, 'You're so lucky! You're so lucky to be a couple!' It was so embarrassing."

"Ewwww!" I shook off the image. "So pathetic! Who was it?" The classmate said she didn't remember. Later, my face heated as I realized she'd been trying to tell me *I* did that. It added up. I had little memory of the party, but "You're so lucky" sounded mortifyingly like me. I thought anyone with a boyfriend, or anyone boys liked, was sooooo lucky.

A boy liking you wasn't just someone to go to the movies with. It was a green light to like yourself. A gold medal, a beauty queen sash, a royal flush, and a winning Powerball ticket. A stamp of authenticity, hotness, excellence, *je ne sais quoi*. Citizenship. A right to walk tall. You could get 98s in geometry—which I did— or be the funniest in your class—which I thought I was—but as far as your worth went, the only unit that mattered was a boy.

Maybe part of it was going to an all-girls school, where boys were rare, exotic creatures who sometimes showed up in the lobby to meet a few lucky girls. *Behold! A young, private-school male.* But more than from lack of access, my fetishizing of that whole gender probably came from them not liking me.

They didn't, I have receipts: At Jill's seventh-grade make-out party, the hot guy yelled "Do-over!" when his bottle spin landed on me. Another classmate had the same luck and had to spend "Seven Minutes in Heaven" with me in Jill's closet. As we closed the door behind us, he said, "Uh, we're not doing this." I was like "Yeahno. I mean. I would never." As a formality, we closed our eyes and mimed frenching, waving around our tongues and making that "mwahmuaaumuaaaah" sound of pretend kissing.

Now, by tenth grade, nothing had changed. Still no takers for touching tongues.

I knew it wasn't just looks or clothes. Girls who were good at being liked were at ease with boys. They could call one on the fly and talk for hours. What do you talk about with a guy? I wondered. Do you make a list of topics? Classmates you hate, teachers who suck, what's the best new Atari cartridge? How do you be your natural self, the way you are with your girl friends? That was the secret. Grown-ups and *Seventeen* said so. Being yourself was how you got his feelings to shift, so he'd realize with a thud: he can no longer bear to be "just friends" . . . because he's falling in love with you. Being yourself would "drive him wild." It also helped to stand close, touch the arm, laugh at the jokes. Some girls were just naturals. It was like watching someone do a cartwheel. How the fuck does she do that?

That spring break, my family went to Club Med, where I met two girls in the pool. They were pretty and wore a lot of aqua-blue eyeliner. One was blond and the other had loose, dark ringlets, the kind that looked good in a mesh bow like Madonna's. My stick-straight hair didn't work with that look. Both girls could sit up in a bikini without any stomach folds. They had an ease about them. *These* were the kind of girls guys liked.

On the final night of our week, the Club Med had a circus show that my sister was in, and then a cascading champagne pyramid. I took part in the champagne. I grabbed two plastic flutes and chugged them in quick succession. My parents saw me going back for more and intercepted. Thankfully, I'd already sucked down enough to be a touch giggly and borderline confident. Like I might know how to flirt.

My two flat-abbed friends had wrangled a guy they thought was cute, which he sort of was. He was vacation cute—the kind when there's not a big selection. The plan was to go hang out on the beach and get high.

"Well, I don't really smoke pot," I warned, as if anyone cared. "But I am *in!*"

We grabbed pool towels and spread them out in the dark on the sand. They passed around a joint, which one of them called a "roach." I shook my head and put up a "no thanks" hand when they tried to pass it to me. Not only was pot a dangerous gateway drug, but I was afraid it would make me vomit. Same gaggy-sweet odor as the burning leaves we passed on family road trips. The smell always made me carsick.

I felt compelled to explain all this while they held in the smoke, coughed, and giggled at each other.

All three lay back on the row of towels, the vacation-cute boy in the middle, and started cuddling. I was on the left side of the left-side girl. The outside side. He stroked both of their heads at the same time. He didn't have the reach or the interest to stroke mine.

As they all three started kissing, I scooched my way down like an inchworm and curled my body mostly off the towels on the cold sand at the boy's feet. Only my shoulders and head got a place on the towel.

Listening to the sloppy tongue and lip sounds, I did my bit in this *ménage à trois* (or *ménage à trois* and a quarter?) by hugging the boy's ankles for a very, very long and boring time.

My champagne buzz had long worn off, but I forced a few giggles into the quiet Caribbean night to seem engaged. I wanted to be in bed.

One day, I thought, I want to be one of the ones all the way on the towel.

Those girls were soooo lucky.

That summer, after tenth grade, *I* finally got lucky. I went to Spain through an exchange program, in a tiny town north of Salamanca where my stock was high because I was American. The boys yelled "Las Americanas!" when they saw the girls from our group. I wasn't the prettiest in our cohort, but I was the best at Spanish. After a week or so there, I could reasonably joke, flirt, and hold center stage with the local boys in their language. I was a whole different, self-assured me. And my tan was *sick*. I wrote in a letter to a friend, "I'm not shy here."

I ended the summer with two boyfriends who fought over me. They literally tussled in the dirt. The second boyfriend was my boyfriend's best friend and my best friend's boyfriend, an ethical pickle that made for lots of lying, sneaking around, and making out 'til four a.m. in the cool, stone alcoves of ancient buildings.

It started with a dare one night in the town plaza. We were two couples. Me and Tomás, Joanna and Mateo. Mateo said, "Let's kiss each other's dates," and it was the first time I ever felt the mythical sparks I'd heard about. So *this* was a kiss. Tomás, my boyfriend, was the best looking of all the guys but his kisses were slobbery, and he never had much to say. Mateo and I could spar. Even with my developing Spanish, we had a back-and-forth like Maddie and David on *Moonlighting*.

"Hey," my boyfriend said in Spanish as Mateo and I pulled apart, "that was a little too long." "Yeah," Joanna said. "Get a room. Kidding." As Tomás and Joanna took their turn, Mateo said in my ear, "Me ha gustado" (I liked that). We made a secret plan to meet up after the other two went home to bed, and we did the same every night after that. I spent the next few weeks goosebumped with excitement and guilt. Joanna did have a boy-friend at home though. And she *had* said, whenever she watched us banter, "You two should be the ones going out." It was practically her idea.

It was my favorite summer. I thought of it as The Summer Boys Liked Me. I didn't trust that my magic translated on US soil. It was like Spain had its own planetary atmosphere that made me sparkle with sex appeal. My value seemed higher there—just like the US dollar.

That fall, I wanted my friend Julie's boyfriend, Ezra. "I want your boyfriend," I said on the phone. I didn't understand that you don't say that. I still didn't get "girl code." Julie was blond and had no body fat and no hair on her arms and got asked out all the time, so of course I couldn't have her boyfriend. What threat was me wanting him? It's like telling someone, "I want your cute jumpsuit." It's not like you're going to rip it off of them.

"Ezra" is not the boyfriend's real name, by the way, but he's a rabbi now. A rabbi doesn't want people to Google him and find out he was a big-time dry-humper.

Yup. Rub a dub dub.

I'd met Ezra at a weekend retreat for temple youth groups. He was loud and outgoing and flirted recklessly. The Charming Ass-hole. My friends and I would mope to each other, "Why do we like assholes?" Life would be so easy if we liked nice boys, but no. Had to be the assholes.

You could tell who Ezra had a crush on because he'd wander over to her table at Shabbat dinner and tear off a piece of her challah bread.

The first of these weekends I went on, during the singalong, the cool rabbi with a guitar strummed a few chords and everyone started singing a song about the Bible's Jonah and the whale. A bunch of kids substituted "Ezra" for "Jonah" so it went, *Who did, who did, who did, who did, who did swallow Ez-Ez-Ez-ra?*

After every "who did," one loudmouthed girl, Cassie, yelled out, "I DID!"

Like so:

Who did,

"I DID!"

Who did,

"I DID!"

Who did, swallow Ez-Ez-Ez-ra . . .

It was great for Ezra's reputation, because it established him as a guy who got BJs.

Amy, the first of my close friends to go out with Ezra (after he ate her challah), revealed the BJ thing to be false. All Ezra wanted to do was dry hump, which we referred to as "DH-ing." Amy told me she and Ezra had DH'd in The Meadow in Central Park, right out in public. DH-ing sounded appealingly easy. You didn't have to know your way around a penis. Amy said it was boring. "I thought about my algebra homework the whole time." Still, I envied her. She got sexual experience without having to touch anything. And she had a boyfriend. So lucky!

After Amy broke up with him, Ezra moved on to blond, perfect Julie. That's when I started having a real crush on him. "Let me know when you guys are hanging out," I told her from my bubble of cluelessness. Weirdly, she never did.

And then, one Shabbat, during a retreat, Ezra came over to my table and ate my challah.

I repeat: HE ATE MY CHALLAH.

I laughed super loud and felt my face grow hot, but I didn't think it meant anything. He was DH-ing Julie.

He was the ultimate surprise at the surprise sixteenth birthday party my two best friends threw me. He showed up in a suit, which inspired my friends to call him "Bar Mitzvah Boy." I was good with it, it showed an effort. All evening, he followed me around and ate birthday cake off my plate.

As the party wound down, Ezra sat next to me on the window seat. I went cold with nerves. "I want to kiss you so badly. But I can't 'til I break up with Julie." I thought I was in a dream.

"I want you to, too," I said. "When do you think you'll break up?" Turned out I *could* have what I wanted. I could take it right off of her.

Ezra went out with me for six weeks.

I missed him all through our family ski trip. I bought him a stuffed penguin in the ski-lodge gift shop because he loved Opus the cartoon penguin.

Soon after I gave him the penguin, he started giving me the brush-off. On one of our last dry-humping sessions, he stopped rubbing his fully clothed body up and down on mine and said, "This isn't working. I can't come. I need to be able to trust the person I'm with, and I don't feel that with you."

Which, let's face it, is something you say when you're over someone and want to eat another person's challah.

He was soon holding hands with my classmate Alexandra— and, I hoped, chafing her through her Levi's.

For several months, I cried if I saw a picture of a penguin or heard the Starship song "Sara"—*Sara, Sara . . . no time is a good time for goodbye*—because a friend of his named Sara had been the first to report Ezra liked me. "He finds you very, very attractive."

Ezra married another of my friends from that youth group before becoming a rabbi. On any given Yom Kippur, she and their five sons—a product of much DH-ing—sit in temple, stomachs growling, while the Rabbi Formerly Known as Bar Mitzvah Boy leads the service.

This Ezra experience revealed an important lesson: if you can steal a guy from his current love interest, someone else can steal him from you. (I didn't say I *learned* the lesson; just that it was revealed.)

The deeper lesson of all this should have been about my value as a person, my worthiness. But the idea of worthiness kept shape shifting, and still does. The same magazine will tell you how to attract the men you deserve (to make you feel worthy) and how to find the inner worthiness you're born with, all in the same issue. Brought to you by L'Oréal. *Because you're worth it.* It's no wonder I didn't learn I was more than who liked me—who wanted me all the way on the towel, who wanted to steal me from his best friend, who wanted to eat off my plate and do some jean-jerking.

Instead, my takeaway—then, and for years to come—was, *Boys still aren't into me. So when they are, I'd better take what I can get, even when that's someone else's crush, boyfriend, or husband.* You can never get enough of what you think you don't have enough of, especially if it's something you think makes you worth taking up space on the planet. Like money. Or, say, attention from boys. This, in the self-helpy online industry, is what they call a "scarcity mindset," or "coming from a place of lack." Basically, a doctor's note to be a thirsty asshole.

Measuring our merit by the sexual attention we get—I know it's about biology and procreation, but it sometimes seems so arbitrary and random. It may as well be about the length of your fingers. Or how many hot dogs you can eat. What if everyone trained in school for the hot dog eating contest, and that was the ultimate culmination of your life? And all the *Seventeen* articles were about how to fit more hot dogs in your mouth without choking? (I guess that's more *Cosmo*.)

Best thing about getting older, unimaginable as it was in my teens (or even my forties), is you stop caring so much about being noticed and attractive to the opposite (or same) sex. Not that I don't desperately buy every neck cream and still want to be considered "hawt." But these days, "You're so lucky" is what I say to a friend who can sleep all night without getting up to pee. And you know what? I'd rather be on my own damn towel.

The Most Driven Person You Know

Driving is a handy and popular metaphor for being an evolved, self-actualized person. Being in the driver's seat means taking charge of your destiny, making your own choices, choosing your path, being an adult. When you're in park, you're stuck in your life. Pedal to the metal means you're taking action. Got your foot on the gas *and* the brake? You're letting fear stop you. "Jesus take the wheel" means you're giving up control. I'm Jewish and don't believe in Jesus—except that he existed at one time and was very charismatic and I probably would've been attracted to him in spite of his long hair and sandals lewk. But I like the idea of surrendering and sitting back. It's my jam.

And while I'm sitting back: Don't ask me to navigate and then ask "Are you sure?" at every turn. I'm only as sure as Waze, which sometimes announces your turn after you've passed it. Not my fault.

You know what else I like? The expression "driven," meaning ambitious.

And the most driven person you know?

It's me.

I get driven everywhere.

Because I. Don't. Drive!

My husband, Steven, loves driving. But when he's tired and has to wait for his glass of wine to wear off before we hit the road, he'll sigh, "I wish you drove." I ask if he really wants me to.

"No," he says, "I mean I wish you were good at it."

I know you're supposed to get out of your comfort zone, crush limiting beliefs, fail your way to success, yadda yadda. Be willing to suck. I'm all for that. If you're a bad dancer, go ahead and do it badly. Your overbite and awkward pointing won't kill anyone. But if you're terrible at something that could kill people, then no. "Comfortable being uncomfortable" doesn't do much when you run over a guy trying to get the Chinese takeout home to his kids. There's a reason the expression isn't "*drive* like no one's watching."

I do have a license. I want to be able to drive in an emergency. Like, if Steven suddenly slumps behind the wheel and I need to get us to the nearest hospital. As if I'd have the presence of mind to find our way to a hospital, much less remember which pedal is which.

The last time I drove was in 2002. Our first road trip together. As I pulled up to the curb where Steven was waiting with his neat, leather weekend bag, I nearly took him out. He motioned for me to roll down the window.

"I'll drive," he said.

And he has ever since.

Fine by me. I know "Driver" is in one of those *Discover Your Work Style* personality tests everyone loves. My boss at a TV network took it and announced she was in the top right of the top right quadrant: a "Driver Driver" or "Double Driver." I never wanted to be a boss. I like being a passenger. If there's a "Drivee," or even "Double Drivee," that's me.

Drive me. Take me. Do it for me. Tell me where to sit (but seat me with someone good). Tell me what I should do with my life, and then shuttle me there. Let me nap in the passenger seat. If that means I have no say about the radio and can never have my '90s hip-hop, so be it.

Unlike most kids, I didn't long to drive. Didn't race for the bumper cars at Rye Playland, didn't beg my parents to let me sit in their laps and try steering the Chevy.

My first friend to drive was Anna. On warm days after school, we'd get in her red convertible, which was parked for free in one of her dad's chain of garages. She drove barefoot and by instinct.

"How do you know when the light changes without even looking?" I marveled.

She shrugged. "I just feel it."

We drove through Harlem, down to SoHo, wherever we felt like, and stopped when we spotted another of Dad's garages. We parked and walked around, got banana FrozFruits, maybe found a Putumayo and tried on skirt-and-top combos. Bought matching hats.

It was the kind of new freedom I'd felt exploring the city unchaperoned in fifth grade with Deb Y. But I was perfectly content with the freedom of being driven. I wasn't *driven* to drive.

Anna never suggested I give it a shot behind the wheel. Probably because she'd let me try driving the family's ATV in the country. I'd hopped on, expecting to zip easily down the road. Instead, I careened slowly into a stone wall, where the force of impact ejected me—also slowly—over that wall. Anna still does an impression of me going over the wall like a giant tree falling languidly. Or like an elderly tree lowering itself onto a beach chair. I walked away unhurt, if not exactly confident.

In twelfth grade, I enrolled in driver's ed like everyone else. You learned to shave your legs. You learned to kiss with tongue. You learned to drive. That's what you did. It was an interschool program, which I took mainly to meet boys. On that front, driver's ed was a bust. As for making the gearshift my bitch and scoring a license? Also a bust.

I failed the road test without even pulling out of the space. Checked the rear view, side mirror, pedals, to remember which pedal was which. Put transmission in D and foot on the gas. The car jerked violently.

The DMV official was gaping at me. She'd just slammed her dual-control brakes. "You gotta look before you pull out!"

"I did," I said. "I checked the mirrors and everything."

"That was ten damn minutes ago." She shook her head.

"Oh. Sorry. Can I try again?"

"Sure you can," she said, scribbling on her clipboard. I sighed with relief, until she finished the thought:

". . . when you make a new road test appointment."

She handed me the sheet, marked with a giant, cartoonish "F."

Shaken and embarrassed, I scheduled a new road test, but blew it off. I was okay not taking the wheel ever again.

But soon, in college, I had to acknowledge life would be way better if I could drive. Frosh year—that's what you had to call freshman year at my school—I was homesick. I had buyer's remorse about my college choice. *90210* didn't exist yet, so I didn't have the term "Peach Pit" to describe the feeling of cozy camaraderie I wanted, but I knew it was missing. I'd gone to visit a friend at Amherst and loved it. It felt more "college-y," and some of her guy friends flirted with me. I decided to be a regular visitor.

To get there, I had to take a Peter Pan bus from downtown Middletown. The first one I took, right under its Peter Pan signage on the side, said "Slightly Soiled." In official lettering. Like "Slightly Soiled" was a brand extension, the way Marriott has Courtyard by Marriott. True to its promise, the bus smelled like dirty diapers. Over the hour-plus journey, the odor intensified like the bus had shit itself afresh.

To get home from school to New York, which I wanted to do often—hauling weeks of laundry with me, of course—I could take the bus or the train. The train was faster and less likely to smell like feces. On the downside, the station was a half-hour drive from campus. I had two choices: impose on a friend to pick me up or take an expensive cab. And for that, I had to call from the station's pay phone and then wait in the cold.

The first and last time I took a cab, the driver asked if I wanted to ride with him up front. I did not. On the road, he griped about his other passengers. "You're real nice," he said. "Not like a lotta them stuck-up types at your school, think they're too good to talk to me. But with you, I feel comfortable, you know? You treat me like an equal. Like you don't look down on me."

"No, never," I stammered. "I mean, we are! We're equals."

"Well, good. You're a nice girl. Also, a lot of the students are Jews, you know? Real snobs."

"Oh. Wow." I decided not to offer that I, too, was a Jew.

"Should we turn off here and get something to eat?"

"Thanks, yeah, I would—but I have to get to school." I looked at my watch and added, "Got people waiting for me."

"We could pull over and hang out or rest. Lie down? Bet you're tired."

"I'm good." I touched the door handle, wondering if I'd have to jump out at a stoplight.

"Well that's too bad. I thought you were different. Seems like you're just another one of them stuck-up Jew bitches."

Miraculously, he took me all the way to school. I guess he wanted to get paid more than he wanted to murder me, an equation I was nauseously unsure of until I got out.

I started thinking how great it would be to heave my dirty laundry into my own car and drive home anytime I wanted. No train schedules, no Slightly Soiled buses, no murder-y, Jew-hating cab drivers.

And no riding with drunk drivers after Dino's pizza. That was another problem. The people with cars drank whole pitchers of beer, and they were my only way home. My weak pleas of "Shouldn't someone be designated driver?" were met with burps. Campus Safety would drive you to Genovese Drugs to pick up meds for your UTI, or around campus when there was a spike in rapes. But no way were they coming to get you from Dino's when you were done eating garlic knots.

My dad said if I got my license, he'd buy me a used car. It was time to become a driver.

I signed up for lessons at Big A Driving School, first one in the Middletown Phone Book. Probably because it was Middletown's only driving school.

Its owner and only teacher: Uncle Mike. He was grandfatherly, or uncle-y. Or pervy, but gently pervy—unlike a friend's driving teacher, who'd eyed the foil-wrapped bagel between my friend's knees and said, "I wish I were where that bagel is."

Uncle Mike spoke about himself in the third person.

"Take this curve niiiice and slow. That's it. Uncle Mike's got you."

Unlike other driving teachers, Uncle Mike didn't use dual controls. Instead, he leaned over from the passenger seat, placing his hands on mine to guide them.

"There we go. Smooth. Like ice cream. Uncle Mike style."

Again and again, Uncle Mike had me practice the route the DMV would take me on for my road test. He assured me it would go better than my first attempt, with that meanie in New York. "Every guy at the DMV knows Uncle Mike," promised Uncle Mike. "Right here's where they'll see if you stop for a stop sign. Kinda hidden, but you know it's there. Easy. 'Cuz Uncle Mike showed ya."

Indeed, this road test went differently. This time, I actually drove . . . and I did it horribly. At the first turn the inspector told me to take, I said, "Oh. Okay. That's not what Uncle Mike said we'd—Okay." My turn was rough and jerky. He looked at me funny the whole time, marking his clipboard and shaking his head. If he was trying to throw me off, it was working. I didn't roll to a stop; I screeched to a stop. And then I missed a stop.

The inspector slammed on his brakes. "Miss Belgray, are you nervous?"

"Uh, a little," I stammered. "This is different from the route Uncle Mike showed me. He said we'd go left after Dunkin' Donuts."

"Miss Belgray, I don't know your uncle, or why you keep talking about him, but I do know you should be prepared for any way I take you. Tell your uncle *that.*"

The photo on my license from that day features a red nose and pink, puffy eyes.

After reviewing all my infractions and making me cry in the car, the guy said, "Miss Belgray, I'm gonna give it to you 'cause of the inclement weather." (It had been beautiful all week, but on this day, it was pissing rain.) "But you'd better practice. Maybe with a different family member next time. No offense to your uncle."

That summer, I read up on the blue books, as my dad showed me, and found the best used car around: an '87 Camry with just a few thousand miles on it. It was a stick. My dad said those saved on gas—and that once I knew how to drive one, I could also drive in Europe. (I have never driven in Europe.) The license plate ended in GCD, which my mom said stood for "Good, Careful Driver." I spent the summer learning stick, and proudly but nervously drove myself back to school, where I was now one of the People Who Have a Car.

I could drive us to New York, to Baskin-Robbins, to the gym. I could drive my running route and measure how many miles I was running every day (eleven) so I could calculate how many calories I was burning (1,100), so I knew how many Weight Watchers ice-cream sandwiches and how many rice cakes I deserved (one and infinity, respectively).

That's not to say I could drive *well*. While I'd mastered shifting gears, I was less handy at the rest. You know—signaling, merging, parking, sensing when a car is too close, spotting my exit sign before it was right over my head . . . that kind of stuff. If there was a choice of cars to get in, mine was last.

Senior year, I drove to Northampton with my boyfriend and picked up my friend Jess and her boyfriend for a comedy show— Judy Tenuta. (We'll leave that there, it was the '80s.) In the dark, I ran up on a curb and blew out a tire. The boys spent the evening changing the flat in the freezing rain. Jess and I shivered under a bus shelter, which wasn't very feminist of us. We missed the whole show. And Emo Philips was opening, too.

Even though I was terrible and he wasn't, my boyfriend refused to drive. He didn't want to be responsible if there was an accident. He preferred the strong possibility of injury or death at my hand over the lesser chance of causing it himself. I get it. I, too, would rather be dead than have something be my fault. Which personality quadrant is that?

On a trip home from school, I had my boyfriend in the car as well as my housemate, who I had a crush on. Wanting to show off, I stayed in the left lane. I drove fast, feeling like hot shit. We heard a police siren behind us, quickly getting louder.

"Oh no! What am I supposed to do?"

My passengers both yelled, "Pull over!"

A cop yelled from the speaker. "PULL OVER!"

"Pull over WHERE?" I wailed. There was no shoulder. The fucking Merritt Parkway. More scenic than I-95, but she's a curvy, dangerous beauty. The answer—as you know if you're one of the many people who drive—was "to the right." But I didn't get that.

"PULL OVER. *PULL OVER!!* YOU NEED TO PULL OVER!!!"

The cop car gave up and swerved around me. If you want to know what the whole highway heard next, cup your hands around your mouth, make a crackling loudspeaker sound, and yell, "UNBELIEVABLE!"

My housemate and boyfriend used this all year as a comedy callback. "KKkkkkchh. UNBELIEVABLE."

And that drive got worse. In standstill traffic at the George Washington Bridge, I let our car drift into the one ahead of us. There was an old man in the back seat. His head wobbled like a bobblehead doll's and his hat fell off, but no one was hurt. I mouthed "I'm sorry" as big as I could.

After enough close calls, I felt I was pressing my luck to keep it up. Sure, I've had many near-death moments as a pedestrian, almost getting flattened by a bus (usually because I was looking at my phone) or almost walking into a tree planter (same), and that hasn't stopped me from walking. But you don't kill someone by walking into them.

I know it would be a smart personal growth move to get comfortable at the wheel. There's a reason it's a metaphor for self-empowerment. *Be the driver in your life!* Nah, I'd rather be the person who can lower the seatback in my life, and nap.

When I've mentioned that I don't drive, people get this knowing look: "Oh, right! You grew up in New York!" I don't explain that even if I'd grown up in Ohio, I'd probably still be the same professional passenger I am today. Let them think my not driving is part of being a cool New Yorker: I was on *Sesame Street*, I rode the subway by myself at age ten, I see the Empire State Building every day, and I don't drive.

I'll keep up my license, just in case—because there's no way I'll ever pass the test again. Not unless I do it in Connecticut and, this time, am lucky enough to get that mythical, easy friend of Uncle Mike.

Part II

Tough Titties

In my twenties, my boobs got huge and kept going. There should have been a Dr. Seuss graduation book just for me: *Oh, the Places You'll Grow.*

Friends thought I'd had a boob job.

"Where did *those* come from?" a guy asked at a post-college bar night. "And can I hug you again?"

You might think this kind of surprise would be like winning the lottery. (In two lump sums! Hee hee.) No, it was more like getting sent a cumbersome wedding gift that wasn't on your registry. Say, a set of plaster garden gnomes. *I'm supposed to put these where? Nope, no gift receipt. Couldn't they have completed our china serving set instead?*

I'd been a happily flat-chested teen. A late bloomer who wasn't keen on blooming at all. Unlike the girls in Judy Blume books, I didn't covet any effects of puberty. Not in fifth, sixth, seventh, or even eighth grade. The main character in *Are You There, God, It's Me, Margaret* thought getting her period last among her friends made her a loser. I thought it made her so fucking lucky and

77

wondered if there were any tricks to keep mine at bay . . . for life. And boobs? No thank you to those. When I read about the chant, "We must, we must, we must increase our bust," I thought, *Really? Must we?* Sure, a couple of times, I tried putting two rolls of socks under my T-shirt to see how it would look, but I didn't think the front humps brought anything to the table. I did not want to look "womanly," or ever, *ever* hear my dad say I'd "developed." I didn't even want him to know I shaved my legs. I sure didn't need another thing for boys to tease me about. They grabbed and threw around my notebook, my jacks ball, or my green felt hat, but at least they didn't call me the nicknames they called my early-blooming friend Vanessa, like "Fat Tits."

And bra shopping with Mom? Ick. Having her stand outside the dressing room while I tried on designer jeans was horrific enough.

"Can't I just see?"

"Mom, stay out, they don't fit, *okay*? I SAID STAY OUUUUUT!!!"

About my life, I'm happy to pull back the curtain. Embarrassing sexcapades, items I've shoplifted, even my income. TMI served here. But when it comes to my body, I'm a hugely private person. I don't know whether it's despite, or partly because of, the hippie naked summer camp I attended in Vermont, where everyone swam in the nude and did gardening chores topless. Flashback to the waterfront director standing above us on the raft, whistle hanging from her neck and tampon string from her hoo-ha; to counselors with bare jugs swinging in the sun as they led us in picking bean pods and singing "Johnny Appleseed"; to the redheaded cabin counselor saying goodnight with her massive, orangey bush at eye level (peril of calling dibs on the bottom bunk). The camp's Quaker philosophy referred to being un-clothed as "the Fifth Freedom," but to me, it felt like a trap. My first summer there, I wore my Speedo swimsuit around the clock. I even slept and showered in it, so no one, at any time, would get an eyeful of my naughty bits.

Even as early as age four, I cried at the doctor's office, saying, "I want my underpants on!" I kicked my parents out of my room when I changed into pajamas. Of all human reflexes, my strongest was yelling, "I'M IN HERE! DON'T COME IN!" during any state of undress. As an adult, I won't go to a day spa and get naked with friends. I can't get dressed fast enough in a locker room. And I still hate bra shopping. No matter where you go, the shopwomen assault you with their dry, cold hands and tape measure. No fitting room is safe.

Before the pandemic closed everything but banks, there was a tiny bra place in my neighborhood, on University, that got famous from being on *Sex and the City*. A photo of Charlotte and Carrie graced the window. When you were in the fitting room, the owner would say, "How we doing in here?" and yank open the curtain without waiting for a reply. Many visits, I panic-yelled "It's not on yet!" and held the curtain shut while she tried to jerk it open, her fingers busting through from the other side. It was like fending off a murderer. If you were lucky enough to have the bra on and not be bare, she'd say, "Look at that bra on you. Your tits look GORGEOUS! Don't they? Come ON, look at those, I told you I'm good at this! You need the matching panties. Got a boyfriend? Husband? Trust me, he'll go nuts for the matching panties." (I reported this to Steven, thinking he'd scoff, but he tilted his head from side to side and agreed, "The nice bra with the old beige thong *is* a little discordant.")

At first, my new tits didn't even need a bra. I still wore a flimsy Gap B-cup number as a gesture, but they were perky enough to stand up on their own, without any scaffolding. I could even wear them bra-free around a mixed-sex group. When I was twenty-three, a bunch of us stayed at my friend Vic's family condo in Florida. I walked into the living room in a white T-shirt and Vic said, "That's such a good bra on you." I proudly and truthfully said, "Oh! I'm not wearing one." The guys turned from the TV to look. That'll get 'em.

My big-but-perky phase coincided with the bodysuit era. I acquired a collection of Lycra tops—some with unwieldy snap-crotches that made peeing a whole adventure, but most cropped at the waist. I loved these tops for their flattering, wide-scoop neckline. The problem was, they didn't look good with a bra. The straps showed. And those silicon nipple covers called "Head-lights" hadn't been invented. So I wore my bodysuit with Band-Aids over my nips. I cheekily mentioned this to Jim the bar owner, whose attention I was always after, and it worked. He spent the whole evening by my side, saying, at intervals, "I want to see Band-Aids."

From my C-cup stage onward, men felt free to comment and speculate on my new "assets." One guy, in our early flirting stage, ran his finger right under my breasts and said, "So really? These are real? I wouldn't find implant scars right here?" We were standing at a crowded bar.

One of those late nights when Jim and I were in his bar alone, he freely cupped them in his hands and said, "Enjoy these. One day they'll be down at your belly button." "Yeah, I don't think so," I sassed back. My mother's had reached that droopy milestone, but she'd always been top-heavy. Having enjoyed my blissfully flat teenhood, I didn't think I was going in her direction. As far as I was concerned, I was perky for life. I wasn't planning to age in that way or any. I ignored wrinkle cream ads the way I now ignore the ones for COPD and arthritis medication. N/A. Not applicable.

Then came a winter of too much Tasti D-Lite (supposedly less fattening than fro-yo) that outweighed my too-much-time on the elliptical. Mahfooz, the shopkeeper at the bulk candy store World of Nuts, weighed my bag of assorted gummies (fat free!) and served me my daily Tasti fix (ten calories per ounce!) with a cheerful comment on my sweaty post-gym look. "Laura! Always running and jogging, jogging and running, make a good body!" But on the words "good body," he shook his splayed hands at his sides, ten inches out from his hips, the gesture you'd make to indicate someone's getting a li'l, y'know . . . *Large Marge*. I'd gained a size all around. But the most Large Marge part was (were?) my boobs. My Anna Sui baby-doll sundresses now gaped between the buttons at the top. More hoochie-doll than baby-doll. I had to fold the button sides under and wear them open like a V-neck.

Clothes shopping becomes a huge pain when the first criterion is, "Does this work with a bra?" Spaghetti straps do not. Off-the-shoulder tops do not. Adorable backless jumpsuits do not. Unless you like that trashy look of the bra showing. When those stretchy seventeen-ways-to-wear-it wrap dresses were big, a shopkeeper tried to wrap me in one at least twenty different ways before giving up. And strapless? Forget it. Before you tell me, oh, they make some great strapless bras now, I promise you: I've tried them all. Every strapless bra, all over this great land of ours. The lady in the shop on University practically held me at gunpoint to make me at least try her favorite. "You haven't worn a strapless bra 'til you've worn *this* one. Trust me." Even she, who never admitted defeat, had to acknowledge: "I guess it does push your girls down a bit."

"The girls" is what they call them when they think you should show them off more. "Bring out the girls." "Why are you hiding the girls?" "The girls want to play!" Look: not all "girls" are created equal. They're not all showgirls. I know that when you think about a "rack," you probably picture Salma Hayek's, spilling forth like a godly offering. You picture a set of manageable, perfectly round orbs nestled inside a Victorian sweetheart neckline. Or J. Lo's pair, parting to either side of that torso-long front slit, agreeably making way. Imagine: breasts that stay fastened by tape to flimsy, silky fabric. I wish! Mine would require a system of harnesses, pulleys, and bungee cords. They're low and don't present the way you see on TV. I promise you. If they did, if they sat where a teenager's do, I probably wouldn't have minded them being more and more of a public topic.

When I went for a run on the city streets, ineffectively strapped down by two sports bras, men now ran alongside me, miming "bouncing boobs" with their hands. One—a chubster whose own moobs were at least a D-cup—did this while yelling, "Bounce, baby, bounce." More than once, a stranger approached me at a bar and said, "Excuse me, my friends and I have a bet. What cup size are you?" After I moved to my apartment in Greenwich Village, a doorman from the fancy, celeb-studded building on my block stopped me as I walked by to inform me that I looked like one of the residents: Marisa Tomei. "Except better. Know why?" Without waiting for an answer, he pulled out his shirt at the chest with both hands to make pointy nipples and grinned ghoulishly.

"Cause she ain't got none a *these!*"

"These" became my defining feature. Friends frequently reported, as though it were a compliment, that someone had described me as the girl with the {insert "big jugs" hand gesture in front of chest}.

Anytime I complained about the attention, friends asked, "Well, why wear such tight T-shirts then?" I tried to explain my anatomy: that if I wore loose tops, I looked preggo. Oh, how I longed to wear waistless, flowy things, boy-cut shirts, A-line tops and dresses—think Mia Farrow's yellow dress in *Rosemary's Baby*—and look like a pixie instead of what I did: a bosomy, earth-mama, middle-aged art teacher.

I started wearing minimizer bras, and then larger minimizer bras. FYI, there's a maximum to how minimal they'll make you. At age twenty-eight, I began obsessively researching breast reduction surgery.

In my opinions on plastic surgery, I'm the worst combo: judgy and arbitrary. I think it's fine to change something about yourself that you don't like. Your breast size, for instance. But only if you're going smaller or at least not really big. Why would you do that? You know you're in for a world of boob sweat, chafing, and hooting and hollering, right? You really want to be defined by your enormous bazungas? If nothing I've said here dissuades you, have at it.

And noses: With my little, shiksa-like upturned number, I'm in no position to tell you not to get a nose job, but don't get a nose job. Most nose jobs are a bad idea. See Jennifer Grey. If you ask me, or even Jennifer Grey herself, her star power was in her original *Dirty Dancing* schnoz.

And why would you get that Beverly Hills duck-lip look? Or anything that looks like obvious "work"? The only good work is work that doesn't look like work. Gloria Steinem, she's had good work. If the Jennifers—Aniston and Lopez—have had work done, that's good work. I say "Yikes" all through the Golden Globes. I say it about the actresses who've had their faces pulled back into Joker mouth, and also about the ones who haven't. I'm the problem.

At least one friend tried to talk me out of having a breast reduction. "Why would you change who you are?" Um, because I don't want *who I am* to be "boobs"?

I remembered a counselor at the aforementioned hippie naked camp showing us that she could keep a pencil suctioned firmly in place under her breast. In that sweaty place. Didn't fall out, even when she bounced around. No pocket necessary. *Excuse me, do you have a pencil? Never mind, I'll find my own.* At the point when I booked the surgery, my chest could hold a whole drawer of office supplies. A small branch of Staples.

I went to a plastic surgeon recommended by a friend. Looking around the waiting room for my first consultation, I felt empowered. I was doing this for freedom. For me. I announced my plans around the office. I wanted people to be prepared and not shocked when they saw The New Me.

As it turned out, no one even noticed. The doctor didn't go nearly as small as I'd asked him to. "They'll be a little smaller when the swelling goes down," he promised. "But I like them this size." Getting a breast reduction, apparently, was not a "customer's always right" situation. When I returned to work, someone squinted and asked, "Did you . . . did you do it? I mean, you look great, either way."

In a couple of years, the ta-tas grew back. As luck would have it, I am part starfish. (Unfortunately, my eyebrows, plucked in the '90s down to Razor-Point-fine lines—more "eyebrows go here" diagram suggestions than actual brows—don't boast the same regenerative powers.)

One friend who has boob envy eyes mine whenever she sees me and says, "I can't believe that's a reduction." Actually, it's two. I went back for another. But, baboom, they defy the knife. Grew right back. Again. Bounce, Baby, Bounce.

My friend Susie, who's an entrepreneur and life coach, said recently, "You can't shrink your way to greatness." So true! We've got to be bold and expansive. "Play a bigger game," as they say. So if you want a life tip here, take it from my resilient, invincible knockers: grow every day, and don't let anyone keep you small. Be the biggest version of you! They did it, and so can you. Stay tuned for their upcoming personal growth retreat at Kripalu.

And to anyone disappointed that I haven't come around to a lesson about "embracing my curves," like those women who like to stand together in the Dove ads and giggle in their bare flesh and granny panties, well—two words for you, and they come from the heart (or the general area on top of it): Tough. Titties.

How to Tend to Your Future

Hello, new graduate. Welcome to your future. Wondering how to jump-start it? Do like I did.

Step 1: Pound the Pavement

After college, I moved back into my bedroom—which hadn't had a long enough absence from me to be my "childhood bedroom"—and started grad school. By grad school, I mean bartending school. Columbia University had a well-known course. I soon learned it was famous less for its gravitas than for being a class where the coursework consisted of getting stagger-and-vomit drunk. At any rate, I felt good signing up. I was on track to my dream career: becoming a bartender.

My father was fine with anything that earned a good buck and showed industry. My mom, meanwhile, said, "Bartending! Are you sure that's what you want to do with your life?"—as though I were signing a forty-year contract to sling martinis to hookers, johns, and pimps across from Port Authority. Similarly, when my sister started going on commercial auditions (which we all know are as sure a thing as a Powerball ticket), Mom told her friends, "My daughter's going into commercials! Aaaaah!" She gets ahead of herself.

Or maybe not. Because yes, this was, in that moment, what I wanted to do with my life. In high school, when the prep school kids were all using fake IDs and going to Dorian's (where nights of scandal and tragedy, including the notorious "Preppy Murder," usually began), my big night out was seeing *Sixteen Candles* for the third time with a girl friend and sharing something too garlicky at Third Wok. Now, after college, I felt like I'd missed out on a rite of passage called "going out and meeting guys." I figured bartending would allow me to make up for lost time. I'd get paid to jiggle cocktail shakers and make out with people who looked like Rob Lowe.

Beyond that, if you asked me what I wanted to do long term, career-wise, I'd guess, "something creative?" Bartending could be the launchpad. I would earn fat cash while socializing with a colorful spectrum of humanity, jotting down their crazy, poignant stories in a notebook for later use. I had a mental vision board of myself: leaning on the bar, chin in hand, listening compassionately to someone's troubles; dancing behind the bar with coworkers who looked like The Fresh Prince and—again—Rob Lowe; organizing thick, neat stacks of dollar bills (one night's tips, wow).

I knew the job I didn't want: something with a cubicle where I'd be forced to wear shoulder pads and pantyhose. Yes, all my notions of work life came from the movie *Working Girl*. I told people, "I'm not putting pantyhose on these legs," as though I had fantastic legs. They've never been my best feature, but not the point.

In a classroom at Columbia where the class before ours had debated Kant and Kierkegaard, I and my fellow scholars learned to make (and sample) a Harvey Wallbanger, a Sidecar, and other drinks it would turn out no one ever ordered. And then I got to slap "Certified by Columbia Bartending School" on my résumé, above one summer waitressing job, a scooping stint at Steve's Ice Cream, my Phi Beta Kappa award, and some dressed-up babysitting credentials. On my mother's dot matrix printer, I churned out a stack of résumés and went "pounding the pavement."

I probably spent four days pounding said pavement, max, but that became my go-to phrase when people asked what I'd been up to since graduation. I said it to my parents. To friends. To Mr. Wagner from the fifteenth floor, who always took a cigar out of his mouth to ask, "Ya workin' yet?" Every time I rang the elevator, I'd pray he wasn't in it. *Ya workin' yet?* "Well, I've been pounding the pavement."

Even with my Columbia credentials, one bar after another told me, "We're fully staffed, but we'll call you if anything comes up." Bartending jobs were hot, hot, hot. Everyone wanted what I wanted: wild fun, a fat payday, and that power position behind the bar. Waiting tables, you lived at the mercy of impatient customers, all signaling for you at once and giving that wristwatch glance of "What the fuck, it's been forty minutes, where's my tuna Nicoise?" As a bartender, you didn't just serve the shots, you called the shots. So many hands waving dollar bills. Whom shall I make lucky first? Servers had to be nice; bartenders could be crusty and surly. It only made them more money and more revered. Crowd worship was a built-in perk, and I wanted in.

Knowing the best prospects were new establishments because they'd be staffing up, I stopped by a corner place on Amsterdam where I heard hammers and buzz saws. A sign resting against the wall outside, hand-painted in a font you might describe as Jungle Sans, said "Wild Thing." This was the one. Close to home, and not an old Irish dive bar. Those were for frat boys, and this, I could tell, would be for cool people.

Amid the sawdust, a tall, mostly bald guy and a shorter blond guy, both wearing baggy, high-waisted jeans and utilitarian fanny packs that weren't yet laughably out of style or laughably back in again, were bent over blueprints at the unfinished bar. Looking up, they asked if they could help me. I said I was looking for a bartending job and handed the blond my résumé. He raised his eyebrows, mock-impressed. "Oooh, Columbia Bartending School!" he giggled, in a way that was strangely sexy. And then, those heartbreaking words: "We're fully staffed, but you never know."

They introduced themselves. Jim and Sammy. "We're opening next week," Sammy said. He rolled my résumé into a tight telescope and flattened it in his jeans pocket. "We'd love to see you here."

"She's cute," one said as I left. That was all I needed. That, and "You never know," which I took as a strong maybe. Maybe I could schmooze and flirt my way into a job. I was going to that opening.

I did, and soon made Wild Thing my second home. I showed up like clockwork at eleven p.m., before it got crowded, planted myself at the bar, and drank Diet Cokes. Funny to want in on a drinking scene when I barely drank. Other regulars assumed I was a drunk, there to get my Long Island iced tea on. Nope. Just to get my flirt on. And, of course, to get offered a bartending job. It took patience and persistence, I reminded my parents when they asked how "the hunt" was going, and whether staying out 'til four every morning was a great strategy. "These owners need to see I'm not going away and I'm not giving up!"

An article about Wild Thing in the *New York Press* called them "the new nightlife kings." Before this, I'd never had a nightlife. I saved the article in a drawer like it was concert memorabilia and I was an early fan.

Step 2: Create Actionable Goals

My nightly goal was to make out with someone before the sun came up—ideally, a bar owner or bartender. People with power. I also wanted, simply, to be there. I wasn't just afraid of missing out, though I was, for sure, especially after I missed the night Bruce Willis came in and sang Sinatra songs with the bouncer, who was his former bodyguard.

What I was really afraid of was being missed. It felt like a crime to not show up as expected—a commitment I've never felt for any real job but somehow mustered for the job I didn't have. Someone told me Jim and Sammy called me "the manager without a briefcase." When I heard that, I thought they meant I was sexy because I carried a cross-body purse and not some stodgy satchel like my dad's. I didn't understand it was because I reported to the bar every night like I worked there, making unsolicited suggestions: "When are you promoting Jamie from barback to bartender? He's got it down!"

Fundamentally, I was there to belong, to create the feeling I envied so much in the gang on *90210* when they met at their after-school hangout, The Peach Pit. On nights when Wild Thing didn't provide that—if it was too crowded, the DJ kept playing "Brown Eyed Girl" instead of something I wanted, like Heavy D & the Boyz, and/or no one was paying attention to me—I would walk eight blocks up Amsterdam to another new bar, Buckaroo's. They had a dance floor and played better music, but it was a rougher crowd. The owner wore motorcycle gear and said rude things, like, "Those your real tits?" Downstairs, an old man known as "Toy Man" sold water pistols and yo-yos out of a briefcase in the men's restroom, as a front for the cocaine he also sold out of the briefcase in the men's restroom.

On packed summer weekends, they employed a shot girl nicknamed Bustier Michelle. She wore an artillery-style shot-glass strap diagonally across her chest, running between her boobs. Like Rambo in a leather, lace-up crop top.

When the opening crowd waned and they laid her off, Bustier Michelle and I became mutual wing women. She faithfully traipsed between Wild Thing and Buckaroo's with me, looking for my crush of the night, whoever that might be. (This was my new "pounding the pavement.") In turn, I walked the same stretch of Amsterdam Avenue with her, looking for a cop she'd slept with once. He rolled up in his cop car one night, said, "Hey, lookin' good, I'll call you." Michelle doubled over, clutching her bare stomach: "Ohmigod, I'm so in love, I'm nauseous. How sweet was that?" I felt sad for her in the way you feel sad for someone who's not that different from you.

Michelle and I made ourselves at home in our two bars, throwing our coats and purses behind the bar or in areas marked

"Employees only." We were inner circle. VIPs. Instead of dancing with the crowd, we liked to climb into the DJ booth and work our moves above the riff raff. One night, the Wild Thing DJ announced, "I need room. Bar hos out of the DJ booth." Jim and Sammy backed him up: "Bar hos out of the DJ booth." Sadly, we were the only ones in the DJ booth.

We didn't have much in common beyond being Jewish, Upper West Side bar hos who thought we were VIPs. But for that time, Bustier Michelle was the friend I needed. My sister was away at college. My high school friends were sick of my nighttime routine and no longer available for it. Something about "jobs" and "needing a good night's sleep."

My daily schedule was what we now call a "freedom-based lifestyle":

Go to bed at sunrise. Wake at noon. Eat Cheerios mixed with Special K. Let Mom know we're low on Special K. Watch all three ABC soaps. Monopolize the one stair climber at Jack LaLanne's (nicknamed "Fags over Dags" because it was popular with gay men and directly above D'Agostino's). Shop for more "going out" clothes, because when you go out like it's your job in 1991, there's no such thing as too many Lycra crop tops.

After all this business, I'd drink Diet Sunkist in my bedroom and try to avoid a "What are your plans for finding work?" talk with my dad. If he asked, I'd sigh, "I'm networking." Technically, it wasn't untrue. What is grinding with strangers at last call if not "making connections"?

My mom came into my room under the guise of collecting soda cans so she could ask, "Did you . . . make any progress . . . um, job hunting today?" She invited me to eat dinner with her and Dad, but I bowed out. Their dinner time was my nap time, so

I could be my best around midnight. I took my "manager without a briefcase" job seriously.

Step 3: Work Your First Job

In late summer (which felt like a decade into my post-college life), someone finally came across my résumé and called to offer me an actual bartending job.

The gig was at a bar named Cody's, on a stretch of the Upper East Side you might call "Broville." The regulars were dudes in sports jerseys and overly tanned sorority chicks in scrunchies and frosted lip gloss. This crowd loved Steve Miller songs and Jägermeister. They'd count heads—"You want Yayguh? You want Yayguh? Ten shots of Yayguh"—and then they'd sing drunkenly, arms around each other, to their favorite Steve Miller song: "If you want my apples, baby, shake my tree-ee-ee . . ."

Not my music, not my people, not my kind of boss. The manager was a thick-forearmed Texan named Bubba who, instead of saying "barback," would say "Mexican." As in, "Tell one of the Mexicans we're out of ice."

So much for finding my Peach Pit. But at least the money was great.

Psych—it was ass. I was lucky if I made cab fare. The bar's popularity had dwindled and I got weeknight shifts with, often, one sorry customer at the bar. I was too slow even for that. At Columbia, we'd practiced all kinds of fancy drinks, but not speed. If you asked me for a draught beer, you were in for a painful pause where I stood, as if in a K-hole, musing, "draught beer . . . draught beer . . ." before I finally moved a muscle and reached for a glass.

"Know why I hired you?" Bubba asked.

I took a guess: "Columbia Bartending School?"

"Nope. Your nails. Most girls have nice nails," he told me, "but not you. Shows you're not afraid of hard work." Truth was, I couldn't be bothered to get a manicure. Too much work. (I still feel this way. Why is getting your nails done considered "self-care" or "pampering" as though it's a treat?)

Bubba quickly found I didn't live up to the promise of my ragged cuticles. "Just 'cause there's no one in here doesn't mean you should be standing around right now," he told me. "In hospitality, there's always work to be done. Are all your glasses spotless? No? Didn't think so." I felt forlorn at this job, like I'd been sent to a mean orphanage.

Bubba fancied himself a real "operations guy." To revive crowd loyalty, he planned a "huge blowout."

"I need everyone to roll up their sleeves for this one," he said to the staff in his Texan twang. "It's how we remind our people why they came here in the first place, and the name of the game is balloons. I want balloons on the ceiling, balloons at the tables, balloons on the walls, balloons everywhere. If there's one thing I know, it's balloons."

I pictured that on his business card: *If there's one thing I know, it's balloons.* I still think of him sourly when I blow one.

The firing happened the following week, when I was busted by a professional spotter. That's someone hired to sit at the bar like a customer and snitch on the employees. This one ratted me out for pouring the barback a free draught beer after his shift.

Bubba came upstairs with the receipts and said, "I don't see the beer you just gave the Mexican rung up on here."

I grabbed my purse, got in a cab to Amsterdam Avenue, and went back to my networking. I was embarrassed at being fired, but a little relieved. I missed my Wild Thing nights and felt guilty not being there for my non-job.

Step 4: Work Your Last Job

A few months later, another bar called. I'd thought Cody's was shitty, but the next one? Shittiest bar in New York. I mean literally.

It was a punk rock bar in the East Village. And hard as I'd tried in eighth grade by wearing paper clips as earrings, I was so not punk. I didn't know where I was, except how to get there from the subway. Turn right past the Palladium, walk two blocks of drunks and junkies, arrive at shithole. Again, literally. I'll get to that.

It was now winter, so I wore my vintage black wool coat to work. It soaked up a thick stink of cigarette smoke. "I'm glad you're working," my mom would say, sniffing the air as I left for work. "But yuck." Stale smoke on clothing now reminds me of bartending. So does the odor of old beer and turned citrus. Kombucha tastes like that smell. I hate it.

I started with packed weekend night shifts—working alongside a gruff, "seen it all" bartender named Stormy who looked a little like Cher and told me to "look alive, Babe."

"I'm in the weeds here," she shouted, snapping her fingers to get me moving. My speed hadn't improved in my weeks at Cody's, and the only thing I did quickly was get demoted to day shifts. I worked these solo and had to get there in the morning—totally antithetical to my bartending dream.

When I arrived for work, I'd take the "rock-and-roll" cassette out of the tape deck and put in my hip-hop mix, even though I knew Ronny the daytime manager would soon come in, wrinkle his nose at my Nice & Smooth jam, and switch back the tape. "What does the sign say outside?" he liked to ask. "Does it say 'Space at Chase, a Hip-Hop Bar'? No, it says 'The Space at Chase, a Rock-and-Roll Bar.'"

I thought, Yeah, could use a rebrand. Of course, I was the one who was off brand for the bar, but tomato, tomahto.

My regulars were Con Ed workers who wanted a buzz before going back to work on the power grid and a bald, toothless doorman named Gus who came straight from his overnight shift. He waited outside for us to open. There was also a fully sleeved guy with a biker beard who worked at a Chelsea sex club called The Vault. He liked to drink whiskey and play darts or thumb through his *Tattoos 'n' Tits* magazine. I don't know what it was actually called, but all I could glimpse were those two things.

Rob Lowe, where art thou?

Once in a while, my friend Jocelyn would come by to say hi. Actually, she'd come by to say, "We have to get you a real job." She was a meddler. I still didn't want a "real" job. I just didn't want this (literally) shitty one.

And here comes that part. You might guess it was about the bathroom, which, yes, was the kind where you open the door and say, "Aw, hell no." Right out of *Trainspotting*. But the real shit part was something I'd discovered on my first day.

Setting up, I'd spilled some popcorn on the bar and started to pick it up and eat it. A customer shrieked, and I dropped the popcorn.

"Don't you know what happened in here last night? GG Allin played!"

He then told me what that meant. GG Allin, head of everyone's mom's favorite band GG Allin and the Murder Junkies, was the original "fecal punk rocker." Before a set, he'd eat an Ex-Lax candy bar, timed to kick in when he got on stage. Then, throughout his shouted "songs," he'd reach down his pants, pull out handfuls of his own poo, and fling it at the audience. These audience members signed up for it. They weren't expecting The Monkees. Most would run out of the club when the poo antics began, and GG would chase them. It was like the running of the bulls in Pamplona, but with a shit-covered punk rocker.

In short, the three-second rule was off. This bar, even more than Cody's, was not my scene. And I wasn't theirs. Ronny got tired of changing my cassette and hearing complaints from doormen who wanted to get drunk faster than I was capable of serving them. At least he fired me at home over the phone, a courtesy which, as I'd learn from future firings, was rare.

I wasn't sad about not going back to work there, either. I returned to sleeping 'til noon. And, of course, networking.

Step 5: Lean In (To Being a Disappointment)

No one in my life was stoked about my path during this time. Nobody said, "You're going to look back one day and be so glad you gave yourself the gift of mooching off your parents and floundering." Well, I *am* glad. Sure, the cushiness of my sitch at Hotel Mom 'n' Dad may not have fostered the best work ethic. But it paid off in other ways. My "networking"—spoiler alert—actually led to meeting my husband years later. And my job-free, loser status? That left me wide open when a friend called about a job starting that day. Which, spoiler number two, would be the most important job of my life.

So, if your parents are willing to have you at home, sleeping in your twin bed, drinking Diet Sunkist, and watching *All My Children* on the TV you got for your bat mitzvah, I say take them up on it. Be a disappointment for a while. It could be the best thing you do for your future.

Blow Jobs I Gave in the Early '90s

These days, everything's a "journey." You're not in menopause, you're on a menopause *journey*. Buying a house? Real estate journey. On *Top Chef*? "Please pack your knives and go" means they haven't seen the last of you . . . but it is, alas, the end of your *Top Chef* journey. Even while I was living it, I considered the following chapter of my life a phase I just had to work through. But it takes on a halo of achievement and purpose if you call it a journey. So let's go with that. My Blow Job Journey.

Why was I on this journey?

I have a friend who confirms fifty times whenever we have dinner plans. "Yes," I sigh. "We're still on. It's a month away, do you have some conflicting thing that night?"

"No, but you know me," she'll say, demonstrating the danger of too much therapy. "I need guarantees and safety from my friends because I didn't get that from my parents growing up."

It's hard to say "get over it" when I spent so long after college demanding what I didn't get growing up: boys liking me. This, I had decided, was my time to shine.

First, I blew Jim and Sammy. Not in that order. That's just how you'd say their names. Jim and Sammy. Jim liked to joke that everyone thought his last name was AndSammy. On Sammy's thirtieth birthday, which I had marked in my otherwise empty datebook, I put on a flattering Anna Sui baby-doll sundress and walked many times past Wild Thing, which was just about to open. I hoped to catch him outside scrutinizing the freshly hung sign or bringing in lumber so I could hand him a card and a small potted plant, which for some reason I thought made for a sexy gift. I ended up handing it to a construction worker who'd said, "You keep walkin' past here. You lookin' for someone?"

I'd been thinking about Sammy ever since he and Jim had turned me down for a job but said I was cute. Getting flirted with was almost as much a victory as getting hired.

The first night I dropped by, Sammy said, "I don't think you're really twenty-one." I showed him my ID. He giggled at my bangs in the photo. "Wow, spikey!" Next thing I knew, I was behind a door by the ice machine with his penis in my mouth. He said, "If I come, will you swallow all of me?" I nodded and "mm-hmm'd" yes, and he did, and I did. He gave me an ice cube to freshen my mouth and said, "C'mon, I'll drive you home."

I wasn't ready to go home. Even if I had been, I wanted to walk. It was a nice summer night. But I liked that he was going to drive me, like on a date. And what was I going to say—"No"?

In the car, he asked what I wanted to do with my life.

"Bartend for you," I said. "I don't want some office job." I followed with my trademark line: "I'm not putting pantyhose on these legs."

"They're very sexy legs," he obliged, ignoring the hint about a bartending job. After he dropped me off, I came back out of my building's lobby and went for a walk in the other direction.

I blew Jim on a night soon after I blew Sammy, when I was sitting at the bar hoping to become Sammy's girlfriend. I hadn't considered Jim. I'd thought he was gay. He was also crazy-old—mid-thirties—and mostly bald with snaggled teeth. But he was easy to talk to, and flattering.

"You're so sexy. I mean, you are just SEX," he told me. "When I saw you walk by the other day in that sundress, I had to go home and touch myself." He added, "I know, everyone thinks Sammy and I are gay lovers and that I've got The Virus." His face did have that trademark gauntness. Sharp cheekbones and a look medical books describe as "wasting." His jeans were tight and hiked up in a gay way, but in his case it turned out to be more of a leftover disco way. He and Sammy had met in the late '70s as roller-skating guards at the Roxy.

Jim asked me what I wanted to do with my life. People love this question when you're just out of college, as if there's a code on your diploma you can scan at checkout to get your Life Plan.

"Bartend, for now," I said. "Preferably, here."

He said I was too smart for that. What about a real job?

I told him I wasn't putting pantyhose on these legs.

He said, "Let's get out of here" and took me to China Club, where people said Magic Johnson hung out and Bruce Willis had been a bartender before *Moonlighting*. Everyone there knew Jim. He showed me how to dance partner-style and be twirled—which I did badly, twisting the wrong way and yelping "Aaaah!"—and then pulled me into a slow grind. "Oh yeah," he said, his pelvis pressed against and guiding mine in a way I'd think about later, nostalgic for this night of attention. "This is real masturbation stuff."

We had breakfast in the diner upstairs, which China Club regulars called "China Diner," and then went back to Wild Thing, where Jim let us in with his key and turned on one low light. The sun was coming up. We fooled around in the DJ booth. He said, with his hands down my pants, "You have such a beautiful, beautiful pussy," observing beauty by touch as though he were blind. Like in the movie *Mask*, I thought, when Eric Stoltz feels Laura Dern's face.

Then it was my turn, and I blew him.

I spent many nights that summer hoping for a replay of my night with Jim. He took me a few more times to China Club, but not by myself. He liked to call out, "My group!" like a camp counselor, and bring a bunch of us.

A couple of times, as I approached Wild Thing, I spotted Jim outside with his girlfriend. I knew it was her because she was wearing his Wild Thing jacket. I turned around and went to Buckaroo's instead. Jim had told me about the girlfriend. She visited regularly from her college upstate. He stayed with her, even after my blow job.

To get meta here: I once brought this chapter to a writing workshop. Most participants thought it was about sexual freedom. One woman, whose own project was a memoir about raising llamas and who was angry at all males, including the male llamas, thought the opposite. "Wow, do I feel sorry for this girl in the story! What a sad character. She's just so disempowered!" (Our teacher gently reminded her this was memoir.) To me, this "journey" wasn't about sexual empowerment or disempowerment. Even if I looked like I was on a quest for dick, it was actually a quest for success. BJs just happened to be—as it were—the measuring stick.

I blew Jason, the owner of Buckaroo's. He wore a Harley jacket, stood outside smoking a lot, and never looked at me until one night when he leaned across the bar and yelled, "Did you blow my brother?" I looked at him, confused.

"Sammy at Wild Thing."

They weren't brothers. Turned out it was their in-joke. Sammy was blond, Jason a redhead, and people thought they looked alike, with their barely-there eyebrows. Brothers or not, blowing Jason made me feel like family. I did it downstairs, where the dance floor and bathrooms were, and he went down on me back upstairs, on top of the Guns 'n' Roses pinball machine in the front window. I worried someone would see me from the street, my black jeans bunched around my ankles, which dangled childishly over the front edge. I was conscious of my bare thigh flesh spread wide on the glass surface. How did some girls have no thigh spread? How skinny did you have to be? "That was fun," Jason said, wiping his mouth. "Don't tell anyone. This girl I like, Deanna, already thinks I'm a scumbag."

One friend joked that I was so quick to give a blow job because I didn't have a better job. Yes, and: it was because I didn't have a better move. There was kissing, and then you gave a blow job. What was in between? I didn't know what to do with balls. A hand job seemed so dry and strenuous. A blow job, though true to the "job" half of its name (the "blow" part is a misnomer for the ages) seemed like an easier job. And it got the job done.

There was always sex-sex, sure, but my college boyfriend—a baseball player from New Hampshire who voted for George H. W. Bush—had never even told me to get on top. So I only knew how to receive intercourse, not how to, like, do it. Perform it. Like you saw on TV. When anyone said, "I bet you're a hellcat in the sack," I was terrified I'd have to make good on it, even if I falsely confirmed with a sexy tiger noise: "Rarrrr."

Plus, sex-sex, when avoidable, was too far to go with someone I didn't like. It was the early '90s. You could get AIDS.

A blow job—which could be used to indicate, "I'm your girl-friend now"—also seemed, simultaneously, like the best way to say, "Bye, not interested." Saying "I'd rather not" felt harsh and impolite. Women on TV rejected men with a swift "I don't think so." "This is not going to happen." "Get lost, creep." That seemed impossibly abrupt. In real life, you said no with a blow job. It was the kiss-off. A proven, if not entirely succinct, way to call it a night . . . and kick him off my journey. The undesirable guy would zip up and say, "See you later," and I could go home and eat a few bowls of Special K, ravenous from having skipped din-ner and elated to have escaped a sleepless sleepover.

I blew Chris, who had tried to go home with me the night I met him. I wasn't interested. I told him he was really hot and I was *so* tempted, but I wasn't into one-night stands. He called per-sistently for a "real date," reminding me, "I thought you said you wanted a serious relationship," and finally talked me into letting him cook me dinner at his borrowed studio apartment when he was in town from Larchmont. I ate a little of the veggie stir-fry with brown rice he called his "specialty," then let him convert the sofa bed and strip down to his Hanes tighty whities. I wanted to get this done, to blow him quickly and leave early enough in the evening to join my girl friends at Amsterdam's. I greeted them with my fists in the air like a soccer champion: "I'm free!" I felt like I'd been sprung from prison.

I blew Russ, the ex-boyfriend of my friend's friend Robin. He flirted with me, asking so many times if I was *sure* my tits were real that it became a running joke, but never took it further because he didn't want to "step on Robin's toes." "I'm not close with her," I promised. I waited for him one night outside a club party. When he came out with another girl, I told him, Hi, excuse me, I've been here waiting—like he was a cab or the fish counter at Zabar's. He said something in her ear, kissed her on the cheek while pointing her to a taxi, and went home with me, but he wasn't happy about it.

I blew Justin, a fitness trainer at Equinox. He had only seen me drenched in sweat on the elliptical machine, where he liked to stand and talk to me about how he was *making it all happen* with his acting career. "You know, going to parties, handing out headshots, doing my thing, making it all happen. Hey, how come you sweat so much but your body stays the same?"

He was lingering near the front one day, as I had hoped, when I left the locker room showered and dressed in a new belted skirt-top combo from Charivari. On my lips: Bobbi Brown Shimmer #4, lined in Mac pencil. I normally changed only my T-shirt when I left the gym, allowing it to darken with damp boob prints from my sports bra. "You clean up nice," he said. He invited me to come check out the brownstone where he was apartment sitting for some "rich cats." That's where I blew him.

Welcome or not, these encounters were a satisfying metric. Something other than my weight that I could measure and check. Wonder what meaningless numbers we obsessed over before follows and likes? Here's your answer. I kept a growing list of guys I'd been with, and how far we'd gone. I rewrote it in various notebooks, starting over occasionally to test my memory or see if I could come up with some names I'd forgotten. I thought: If shy, high school me could see me now! It was an early version of pulling down my phone screen every five minutes when I've just posted on Instagram. Hearts and comments, daily steps, monthly earnings, blow jobs: I've always loved refreshing my stats.

I blew my old babysitter. It was one of those lonely nights at Wild Thing where neither Jim nor Sammy had time to flirt with me. After jealously watching Sammy sing and semi-dance to "Ring My Bell" in serenade of a waitress from Isabella's he'd later marry, I talked to a guy with long, dark hair in a ponytail. Over a beer burp, he told me his first and last name, which I recognized. "I think you used to babysit me," I shouted over the song "Brown Eyed Girl." He asked to walk me home and see where I lived, to jog his memory.

"Oh yeah, this feels familiar," he said at my parents' front door. "I think I remember that welcome mat." He looked at his watch and wagged his finger. "It's time to put on your pj's."

"Only if I can stay up and watch *Love Boat* and *Fantasy Island*," I cooed back, even though I wasn't attracted to him.

I didn't want to bring him in. I had missed the chance to lie that my parents were home, so I took him into the stairwell, which I'd only ever used for trick-or-treating and playing on steps with my Slinky. It worked. After the blow job, he left.

Little Ricky told me he worked at Buckaroo's, where I met him. That seemed true. He went behind the bar with impunity. I later found out he occasionally handed out flyers for them, but was in no way on payroll. They just let him hang out and use the soda gun.

Along with Little Ricky's little dreads and his pretty little face—he said he did a little modeling—I liked his big swagger. He was a great dancer. At home in the mirror, I tried to perfect the Harlem Stomp, a move I'd seen him do to Heavy D's "Now That We Found Love." Just like in the video.

The night he called me to "come hang" with him at Buckaroo's, I got there too early and waited hours for him while he waited for Brent the bartender to get off work. "Brent and his girlfriend Caitlin want to hang out with us," he told me, and reached over the bar to pour me my fifth Diet Coke from the soda gun. "Caitlin thinks you're cute." I hoped that didn't mean I had to kiss her or something. No group stuff, please. I didn't know Caitlin but I had seen her. Someone said she was rich. She was skinny, with the right jeans, bodysuit, and hoop earrings, a look I desperately wanted to nail. Brent had a British accent, black spiky hair, and high cheekbones, like a rock star. They were a hot couple. They scared me.

At four a.m., we finally got in a cab to go downtown to Save the Robots, an after-hours club I had heard of but never been to. I hadn't gone to any after-hours club, much less many during-hours clubs.

We walked through the dancers, a throbbing tangle of torsos slick with sweat, mesh tops, pacifiers, whistles, glow sticks, and clenched jaws, to a room with a bar. Ricky did a tequila shot and made out with me. Caitlin and Brent did cocaine off a tablecloth next to a topless woman. I was the only one there pepped up by lots of Diet Coke and a nap.

Then, we were in a cab heading back to Caitlin's apartment on the Upper West Side, where Brent and Caitlin showed us their library of VHS tapes with handwritten titles: *Brent and Caitlin*

Fucking on the Beach, Brent and Caitlin Fucking Like Bunnies, Brent and Caitlin Knocking Boots in Riverside Park.

In his British accent, Brent said, "You've got to make a movie to watch a movie," and I said no way. But not in those words. Instead, I made a joke, something like "I don't do unpaid porn." Or maybe it was "I don't do low-budget."

"No video, guys," Ricky said. "My date's not into it." I felt protected.

I was tired and wanted to go home. I kept thinking a cute exit quip would be, "Let's table this for later," but kept missing my window to say it. As you do when you're awkwardly trying to excuse yourself from a porno.

Once we were naked on the couch, I told Ricky no unprotected sex. Since he didn't get an answer when he said, "Yo, you guys got a party hat?" he promised me, "We'll just do oral."

I pretended Brent and Caitlin weren't having sex on a chair kitty-corner to our sofa and kept my eyes closed for most of it. When I opened them, Brent was standing over us with a video camera. "That was good stuff," he said. "You're movie stars."

I found out one night that Jason had played our video over the bar at Buckaroo's while the happy hour patrons whooped and cheered. Jason assured me no one knew it was me. "It's too dark to see your face, just your tan line and body. Everyone thought you were Caitlin."

I was comforted and flattered by that, but still freaked. My heart pounded. Where was the tape?

Little Ricky promised to give it to me if I agreed first to hand out club flyers with him downtown. "Wear something sexy," he instructed. When I met him at the subway, he complained, "You dressed kinda preppy for this." He eyed my flowy floral shorts

and flats. "I said sexy. Edgy." After our flyer errand, I went with
him back to his mother's brownstone apartment, where he produced the promised VHS tape and popped it into the VCR.
It was all snow. "I guess someone taped over it," he said, eject-
ing the cassette. He pulled out the tape, tore it, and cracked the
black shell in two. "Just for safety. I swear, this was the tape." I
pretended to be satisfied, though I suspected he was lying.

I always thought of that tape as the "Why I'll never run for office" tape, which is convenient because I never wanted to anyway.

I've also thought of it as the "Who the hell was that person?"
tape and the "My parents were actually right about what I was
doing out until four a.m." tape.

And I've thought of it as the "This is what happens when you
don't know how to say *no way, fuck off* when you're uncomfortable" tape.

I blew Max, a smoking-hot anti-apartheid protester from my
college who people warned me was "a skank ho." The first time
we hung out was on a stoop near the Museum of Natural History, where we did some light making out. He explained his
activism work—and why his organization had to refuse "blood
money"—while he felt me up over my clothes.

The next date would be a real one, he said. A Saturday night.
He told me he'd swing by and pick me up at nine. Instead, he
called at midnight from the pay phone on my corner and said,
"Ready? I'm downstairs." I'd been sitting on my bed in my mini-
skirt and knee-high leather boots for three hours watching taped
ABC soaps. Yes, I was ready.

"Sorry," he said as I came outside. "I was at this dope party!"
He was wearing a Kangol bucket hat and plaid pants that were,
indeed, dope-party pants. He took me uptown to his family's

apartment, a prewar building near Columbia, where the door-man laughed and high-fived him on our way in. While it oc-curred to me that I wasn't the first girl who'd come home with him that night, it escaped me that that was probably why it took so long to blow him.

I didn't hear from him that week.

I spent the next month obsessively checking my answering ma-chine. I finally got a message: "Hey, I went to see this movie! *Friday the 13th*. It's off the hook! I'll call you later!" He did not. His message might have been meant for someone else. I'll never know.

I blew Jim again, this time at his and Sammy's new bar and dance club, Tarot. They opened it two years after they'd opened Wild Thing. This place had all the bells and whistles: smoke machines, cages for dancing, a real psychic who gave readings in the window, and membership ID cards. I still have mine, which showcases my 1993 middle-part bob, pencil-thin brows, and dark, lined lip. Jim brought me in during the day when it was closed, put on my favorite dance song, "Treat 'em Right" by Chubb Rock, and turned on the smoke machine. I no longer hoped to be his girlfriend, a shift that made me feel powerful. I had more going on now. I worked at a magazine. I knelt in front of his unzipped fly in a cloud of strawberry smoke, which is why I still get a confusing sense memory when I eat a pink Starburst.

I blew and slept with Skip, whom I guess I was dating. He looked like a Black Rob Lowe and was the manager of Lucky Cheng's, a Lower East Side bar and restaurant where the servers were all drag queens. It was hot shit. He lived above the Ear Inn on West Spring Street, where all the cool parties happened and overflowed into the street. More than once, outside Bell Cafe, I saw Marisa Tomei wearing knee-high tube socks and track shorts, and wished for Marisa Tomei legs. Point is, that's the kind of person you saw on Skip's block. (By this time, I was over the Upper West Side and only blew guys downtown, a practice I considered moving up in life.)

One morning, when I was up before him and hustling to get back uptown to a step class, I spotted a note on Skip's kitchen counter on top of a basket of receipts. In girlish pen, it said, "Went out to get cereal, Love. Back soon. Love, love, and more love—J."

Soon after, we were supposed to meet at Lucky Strike, a SoHo bistro where my friends Vic and Stephanie and I ended our downtown nights with our half-diet combo: fries and steamed spinach with mustard. The fifth time I put a quarter in the pay phone to check my messages, the manager, Dante, said, "Whoever stood you up, it's his loss."

Dante had flirted with me before, at a barbecue in Central Park called Bone Fest. He saw me getting a Diet Snapple and asked, "Are you in recovery?" I said yes, from Diet Coke. I meant it. He laughed, said I was sassy and he liked it.

While I waited for Skip, Dante invited me to sit with him and his friends, who were the Red Hot Chili Peppers. I didn't know that, but I knew they were someone from the way they griped about a *New York Times* review. "If you can't make art, criticize it, right?" The guy next to me, wearing a feather boa, told me his name, but it was too noisy to hear.

"Fleer?"

"Flea."

"Oh! Sorry. Nice to meet you, Fleet."

Skip never showed, but the night was redeemed. I started going down to Lucky Strike by myself.

I blew Dante. Well, more than that, as he had publicly predicted. He'd introduced me to some model-y girls who sat flanking him on the steps to the dining platform.

"This is Laura. We're going to joke around a bunch, and then we'll sleep together, and afterward we'll always be friends." I laughed and hoped he was kidding about the friends part, to hide that he wanted more.

He left me a message on Yom Kippur that I played over and over. "Happy High Holidays. Isn't this the day you atone? At the sound of the tone . . . I don't even know the rest of my joke. Come down to my place tonight. Norfolk Street. You can bring stuff to stay over."

In his tiny, peeling hallway, he opened the door mid-drag on a cigarette, kissed me on the mouth for the first time, and ushered me into his apartment. It was the size of my sister's childhood bedroom, which was originally a maid's room.

After we had sex, he asked, "Do you have a God concept?"

I smirked. "I'm here on the holiest day of the year, so I guess not. Do you?"

He said yes, his sobriety. "I want that for you," he added. "A belief in something bigger than yourself."

He asked if I had someone special in my life.

"Not really." I wanted to say, "Yes. *You.*" If I did, I thought, would I be here?

"Why?" I asked. "Do you?"

"I do," he said, pulling on a cigarette. "You'd like her. She's a great girl."

After a sleepless night in his twin bed, I dressed for work and got on a bus to the job I hated in Midtown.

My college friend Mike, who was visiting from Oregon, came with me to Lucky Strike the following night. I had described it as "my hang," and Dante as "the guy I have a little thing with."

"I'm sorry, Laura," Mike said when Dante ignored us all evening. "You're so much better than that."

I swung by one empty evening to find Dante holding the *New York Post* open in front of him. He told me he was leaving to catch a movie. When I showed interest in joining him, he folded the newspaper and said, "Actually, I think I need to get to a meeting."

Another night, I went with Vic and Stephanie to Dante's one-man comedy show, where he made jokes about words that sound Yiddish—*ladle, lentil*—and did a schtick about his days smoking crack. I thought, "That's why he can't be with me right now. He's focused on staying off the pipe."

I spotted him from a cab one night. A club bouncer was unlatching and holding a velvet rope wide open for him. Dante had his arm around a girl with long, golden ringlets and a perfect, soft-looking tan suede jacket. I knew that was his Someone Special.

That's when I gave up on Dante. I tapered off on the BJ quest and started looking obsessively for a perfect tan suede jacket. My new journey. Not a God concept, but close enough.

Therapy Ruined
My Wednesdays

When I was nine, I was forced into therapy. A teacher had told my parents I was unhappy and should "see someone."

Her evidence was my lower lip, which I liked to stick out and flip over—no hands required—with the inside membrane showing, so it looked like a giant fish lip. It was just a party trick, the kind of thing you're excited to master when you're a kid. Like winking, or making armpit farts.

"Please, please, please don't make me go to therapy," I begged my parents. I sobbed that I wasn't unhappy, which didn't make a great case.

My dad said, "That face you make with your lip looks unhappy." As proof, he aped it with his own lip and fake boo-hooed. "If you're not unhappy, why do you do it—because it feels good?"

Ew. I gagged at the question like I smelled poop. I hated being asked about my feelings. Unfortunately for me, being probed all the way up my asshole for feelings was a way of life. Welcome to having a dad who's a shrink.

Until his forties, my father had worked as an industrial engineer for Eastern and other airlines. When I was little, he decided he loved helping people more than he loved time-efficiency studies and tallying thefts of mini liquor bottles. He became a psychotherapist and began his life's work as Doctor Belgray. For our family, this career switch had its pros and cons.

The pros wouldn't be apparent to me 'til much later. The cons, on the other hand? Pretty glaring. For one, the tradeoff in perks. My dad's airline jobs had offered free or low-cost world travel, sometimes in first class. Hard to beat that, unless you were one of the Zabar's kids, who went to my school and got unlimited lobster salad and lox. Our family? We got . . . feelings. Incessant talk of feelings. Life with my dad was a nonstop feelings festival. An all-day, all-you-can-feel buffet.

We couldn't even go see *Grease* without it being a thing. On the way out, my dad asked how I felt about the movie.

I said, "It was good."

"Good isn't a feeling. I want to know how it made you *feel!*"

"Fine."

"Fine isn't a feeling either. What did you like about it? I noticed you sang along to the song about greased lightning." (He always referred to titles that way: "the book about the joy of sex"; "the movie about Sophie and her choice.") "What," he prodded, "did that make you feel?"

Would *you* want to talk about feelings with a dad like this? When asked if folding over your lip "felt good," would you want to do anything but plead the Fifth, lock your emotions in a steel safe, inside a vault, within a fortress, mummy-wrapped with duct tape, inside that clear plastic packaging from the electronics store that cuts you when you try to open it, all at the bottom of the sea?

Agreeing the lip thing *felt good* was my way out of therapy, but I couldn't give in. "It doesn't 'feel good.' It doesn't mean anything."

Nice try. To my dad, everything meant something.

"Hold on," he'd say if I told him to stop smothering me. "The word *smother* has 'mother' in it, so let's talk about why you chose it."

He was the one who gave everything extra meaning, with his own language gaffes.

When I was fifteen and preparing to go with a group program on my first overseas trip, he kept referring to the guidebook series Let's Go Europe as "Letting Go."

In the most spectacular Freudian slip of all time, when he got on the private bus shuttling friends to my wedding, he stood at the front and announced, "Hello everybody. I'm David Belgray, Laura's husband." But, ew, gross, he didn't deny it meant something. Instead, he laughed, "Every girl marries her father!"

And so, I and my bottom lip found ourselves spending Wednesdays with child psychologist Dorothy Bleck. (Not her real name, but close.) Wednesdays at my school were a half day, and everyone went to Burger King. Normally, I'd be with my classmates, inhaling fries, flinging pickle slices across the comfy orange booths, sucking a delicious, too-thick shake, and basking in the freedom of being sprung early. Instead, I sat in an office where the light beam from the window was choked with floating dust motes and played Monopoly with, basically, an overpriced babysitter.

For fifty minutes, Dorothy Bleck asked me dumb questions about—you guessed it—my feelings. I shrugged, moved my thimble down the board, and bought Baltic and Park Place. I think she let me win, which didn't make me hate her any less.

Want to know how I felt? Like a left-out, weirdo loser. If I wasn't unhappy before, I sure was now.

A few times, my father joined in the session. Child therapy turned into family therapy, where Dorothy Bleck instructed me to turn to my father and repeat after her.

"Dad," she prompted.

"Dad," I mimicked in my "This is so stupid" voice.

"I don't like it when you ask how I feel."

Eye roll.

She wouldn't let me go until I said it: "I don't like it when you ask how I feel."

My mom shared this objection. She was never a "feelings" person either. It's not that she's cold. She likes hugs and says "I love you" easily, at least to people she loves. But she's restrained. She doesn't vomit her emotions at you, and doesn't cry easily. She might dab her eyes a little during a movie.

Dad, meanwhile? Such a crier. He would blubber in the middle of a sentence, and then recover and laugh as he began the next one. Like a sudden sun shower in the Caribbean.

"My army buddy Harvey loved Japanese women—" *Smiling.*

"He dated scores of them, but I think he was ve-e-e-ry lo-o-onely—" *Sobbing.*

"At any rate—" *Smiling.* "What a guy. Too bad his business idea for umbrella hats didn't take off."

My mom shook her head and sighed at these outbursts. "I swear he wasn't like this when I married him."

Not that she'd trade, she reassured us. But when she said "I do," she hadn't counted on a gushing firehose of feelings for a husband—not to mention dinner talk of womb envy and penis envy, or weird colleagues at cocktail parties. "Whenever I ask these people where they're from," my mother griped, "they say, 'How would it help you to know that?'"

And then there was the most tiresome trend: my father's fixation on psychoanalysis as the only answer . . . to everything. Your restaurant service is slow? The owner needs therapy. Police violence? The commissioner needs therapy. My seventh-grade Spanish teacher who was going too slowly for me needed therapy. My mom bought a George Foreman grill to make healthy meals and hired a nutritionist to help her lose weight. You know what she really needed? Therapy. And the nutritionist, boy did *she* need therapy. Even George Foreman: Therapy. Every time he forgot his login for Facebook and spent an hour blaming AOL customer service for it, my dad hung up yelling that these people all need therapy. Beginning in 2017, he wrote to the White House repeatedly, offering his services free of charge to Donald Trump, who needed, well, you know. Actually, my dad said Trump was "probably beyond therapy."

My mom now admits she agreed to send me to Dorothy Bleck at age nine because when she objected, my dad accused her of not being supportive. Then, he'd conclude, "It's because of your issues with your father. You've never resolved them. To do that would require therapy."

My dad's only regret about being a therapist was that he, the best in the business, couldn't be ours.

Had to hand it to him, he believed deeply enough in his profession, his versatility, and himself to confidently market his services all over the Manhattan Yellow Pages. He listed these under:

- Aging and Aged Psychotherapy Services
- Anger Management Services
- Jewish Psychotherapy for the Aging
- Management Consultants in Midtown
- Therapy for Business Owners in Manhattan

You get it. All the way up to Z—Zealous NYC Head Shrink, maybe?—flip to just about any letter, any need for advice, and you'd find my dad.

If you've been on the New York subway in the past three decades, you've probably seen a poster for Dr. Zizmor, a dermatologist who, 'til retiring in 2016, specialized in everything. Cystic acne, regular acne, psoriasis, brown spots, acne scars, eczema, dryness, oiliness. You name it, he treated it. If your epidermis was showing, he could help. His placid face, unchanged over thirty years, was surrounded on the ad by a word cloud of embarrassing skin problems.

In my teens, when my dad showed me his yellow-pages strategy, I realized: he was the Dr. Zizmor of shrinks.

Finally old enough to get it, I was impressed by his business smarts. I was also entertained by the nut jobs who dialed his number. One left a series of messages in a rasping, high voice (think Gilbert Gottfried): "Docta Belgray, my bawwwwllsack itches! Oh god, it's really itchy!" I made my dad play these for me over and over, and reenacted them for my friends. Stories of Dad's wackadoodles—both patients and colleagues—were, I guess, a perk.

Doesn't take away from my bitterness about therapy. I'm not letting that go. (To do so would require therapy.) Having been deprived of both my Burger King Wednesdays and my emotional privacy, I was too resistant in adulthood to "see someone" until I felt truly stuck and desperate.

On the cusp of thirty, I wasn't attracted to my perfect boyfriend. I was depressed at work. I wasn't doing anything big. I had no more great ideas. I was obsessed with working out. I was obsessed with ice cream and couldn't stop eating it until I tied it up in the plastic Food Emporium bag and threw it down the trash chute, but, of course, first I'd untie it and eat some more before I bid adieu. A fattening goodbye party.

Had "life coach" yet been a thing, I probably would have looked into one of those. I didn't want to prove my dad right that everyone needed therapy, but I needed some way out of my rut. The therapist I chose was traditional like my dad—staring at you 'til you talked—and infuriatingly soft-spoken, like Dorothy Bleck. I saw dust floating in the window light, water stains on the ceiling. She supported every objection I had about seeing a shrink. Subconsciously, I was probably out to prove therapy sucked ass.

Although (or because) the therapist was only three blocks away, I was late for every session, and spent most of our fifty minutes talking about why. She let me babble for a while, smiled her mild, shrinky smile, and asked, "Do you want me to be angry with you for being late? To punish you?" I was, of course, being punished, by having to pay for time I didn't use. The rest of my time, I spent talking about why I didn't want to be there. I started skipping sessions, then tapered off without any real progress in my life except that I had freed myself from the chore of going. My dad and therapy hadn't just ruined my Wednesdays, they had ruined therapy.

And yet, a few years later, I decided to pick it up again. I needed some way out of my stuck misery. I still hadn't done anything "big." I'd taken the same screenwriting course three times without writing a screenplay. And, worse than not being into my good boyfriend, this time, I was hopelessly attracted to a bad one.

Relationships with men: another downside of my dad both being a shrink and wearing his emotional guts on the outside like a colostomy bag. They say we (hetero) women look to reenact the patterns we had with our daddies, but I fled in the opposite direction, toward the closed arms of unavailable dickbags. That habit culminated in two and a half years with a married serial cheater—the kind who would tell me he was flying back from Paris on Wednesday when he really came back Monday and secretly had piña coladas at BBQ, went dancing in the South Bronx, and fucked someone else, meanwhile instant messaging me, "Can't wait to get off that plane tomorrow and come straight to you, hope your [sic] naked."

My friend Ariel loved her therapist, Emily. "She's not shrinky," she promised. "She's cool. She's like us, you'll want to be friends with her."

She was right. Emily was different. She ate at cool restaurants, wore Prada shoes, kept her office nice with fresh flowers, and the biggest twist: next to the Kleenex, she put a bowl of Hershey's miniatures. *What?* I was allowed to sit there and eat a Krackel? A Special Dark? It was a wild affront to my dad's strict Freudian approach.

"If a patient comes in chewing gum," he'd say, "I make them spit it out. I tell them, in here, we deal with emotions through talking, not chewing."

People thought I was rebelling against my parents by dating the inappropriate married guy, but the true act of rebellion was seeing a therapist who let you snack.

Emily's whole style of therapy flew in the face of my dad's training, and I was here for it. She didn't simply ask me my feelings, she dared tell me some of hers. While friends constantly told me I deserved better than this guy, my therapist was the only one to say, "This man is not loving or respectful to you." Or, even more persuasive, "I think he's a sadist."

I needed that. I didn't write a screenplay during my time seeing Emily, but I did get myself out of a shit relationship. I moved forward in my life, which is what I'd hired her to help me do.

Later on, when Steven, my eventual husband, and I were dating and close to no longer dating, we went to a couples therapist. Again, I was skeptical, but desperate to fix whatever wasn't working, whatever kept him from wanting me as much as I wanted him. While Steven and I gagged at the therapist's advice to "cherish each other," she helped save our relationship with her salmon-colored suit. She wore it every session, that offensive shade of fish-flesh orangey-pink that looks good on no one. Hating it brought us closer together. And here we are.

This isn't a referendum on therapy and whether it's useful. I believe it can be—transformative, even—with the right therapist. Or, the wrong therapist in the right wrong suit. I just wouldn't say it's always good, or the *only* thing. My dad insisted, "It's the greatest tool we have for discovering who we are," and to that, I say, oh yeah? What about those online quizzes that tell you which of the Golden Girls you are? Or which pizza topping? I'm mushroom. Very helpful to know. That info is my north star.

My feelings about therapy aside, and also my feelings about feelings, I can now share some positive ones I've come around to about my dad's career.

For one, between his yellow-pages strategy and his constant networking—handing out business cards and offering help to every Tom, Dick, and Itchy Ballsack Harry—he modeled the thing we now call "putting yourself out there." His shameless self-promotion showed me there's no shame in self-promotion.

He also modeled combining your interests and skills instead of having to narrow it down to one. My friend Marie Forleo coined the term "multipassionate entrepreneur," but my dad might have been the original—weaving his first-career love of business management into his practice of psychotherapy. Some clients actually came for the business help (and stayed for the therapy). One of my dad's longest-running clients was a cheese-stick mogul. Apparently, he came to dominate the cheese-stick industry and attributed his company's explosive growth to my dad. One perk I left out: we got free cheese sticks.

And then there's the relaxed timeline. As I struggled to find work that felt like my "calling," it was comforting to see my dad's successful midlife career switch. His might have inspired my mom's as well. Though she had her PhD in musicology and had earned the title "Dr. Belgray" well before my dad, she decided in her forties that she didn't want a career in music. She took all the "What should I do?" assessments and, at my dad's insistence, read *What Color Is Your Parachute?* Discovering an interest in children's books, she got a job as a publishing intern. Imagine. Being an intern in your forties? Getting someone's coffee and fetching their Xerox copies when you have two kids, a doctorate, and probably a decade in age on your boss? Talk about brave.

Both of these pivots put in my head the idea that you don't have to figure out what you want to be 'til midlife, and probably won't. Your career story *will* go through a rewrite. Each time

I panicked that I'd never make it onto any "25 under 25," "30 under 30," or "40 under 40" list because I still hadn't found my thing, my late-bloomer roots made me feel less behind.

And finally, the blessing and curse of having a dad who loved what he did so much that he planned not to stop until the day he died. (He came close. The cheese-stick guy stuck with him practically until my dad's final breath.) On the curse side, a tough standard. Trying to find my way in the world, I rejected any work options that felt even an iota less fun than "I could do this 'til I croak." That agenda doesn't exactly open up a world of possibilities.

On the blessing side, my dad's unrelenting, nauseating, blind enthusiasm for psychoanalysis showed it was possible to be so obsessed with and fulfilled by your work that you never wanted to retire.

And when I think about that, I feel—aw fuck, don't make me say it. Fine. I feel . . . good.

Tap That Talent: A Twenty-Something Odyssey

Soon after I met my friend Vic, she dated and obsessed over a film-school guy. (I, too, was obsessed, and we almost had a threesome. That's another story.) When he slept at Vic's place, he would leave early in the morning—probably to bone someone else, but first, to get to the post office and mail off copies of his student films to festivals and zines. Vic and I agreed: he was going to be big. Not only did he know what he wanted, but he was the kind of person who mailed things. He had "the post office gene."

He's now a major Hollywood director, with some of the highest-grossing box-office hits of all time. Two words: post office.

Back then, fired from two bartending jobs and contemplating next steps, I felt cursed. I didn't have the post office gene, or any of the traits you're supposed to have to make it.

For instance, you have to *want it*. But want what? I never had that big vision other people seemed to have, with a clear path: "I want to be a Supreme Court justice. So I'm taking the LSATs." Or, the film guy: "I want to be a big-time filmmaker. So I'm going to the post office."

You have to be hungry. Not for snacks. I mean *true* hungry.

You have to overcome struggle, but I didn't want struggle. My friend Jocelyn boasted that, to pay for her three-hundred-square-foot studio on West Tenth Street, she "didn't take a dime" from her rich, fucked-up father who'd "never been a real parent." Why wouldn't you want a bad parent to compensate with money? I'd have taken *every* dime.

Speaking of dads: every time mine entered my room and said, "Can I have a moment of your time?" I braced myself. Either he was going to show me the stock listings and try to teach me investing (something I probably should have listened to, but the topic made me float above my body), or he was going to ask about my progress finding a job.

"I'm looking for something," I told him. "But there's nothing good. I don't want to sit at a desk all day."

"Tell me what you'd like to sit at, then. Where do you imagine yourself sitting?"

He wasn't being sarcastic, as in: "What do you *think* you sit at for work? A swim-up bar at the Four Seasons?" Another dad might say that. Mine was trying to shrink me. He wanted me to dig down and reveal my deepest career daydreams.

I didn't know where I'd sit. Maybe in a circle of comfy sofas? Or around a white, midcentury-modern table, spitballing ideas. Or like Tom Hanks, in that movie where he works in advertising. His character sits around with colleagues, chairs tipped back, cranking out ideas, throwing pencils at the ceiling. The setting was too corporate for me, but I wouldn't mind sitting like that.

I also liked the idea of not sitting at all. Of being on a TV or movie set, peering into a video monitor and making suggestions while doing lots of pointing. This fantasy largely came from TV ads for Tylenol or Advil. "I'm too busy in my exciting, creative career to get a migraine."

I knew one thing: I didn't want to sit alone, writing long things. I'd pulled all-nighters and agonized writing every paper for school. I usually faked sick the next day, so often that the class joke was "Laura has AIDS." (It was the '80s, our jokes were problematic.)

I had once loved writing. At ten, I scribbled day and night, penning a novel that was a shameless rip-off of *Huck Finn*. My characters rolled in the dirt of the town square and said things like, "Don't you talk about my pa!" I was my own biggest fan, until I met that cruel voice called "the inner critic." God, I missed that drive that comes from blind confidence. Now, I didn't feel suited for the obvious writer's path of Author or Screenwriter. Typing away in a garret, a wastebasket spilling over with crumpled drafts and tears of self-loathing—No thanks! I wanted a job that harnessed my creative gifts while avoiding all that pain.

I looked through the job classifieds every day, circling anything that said "advertising," "creative," or "entertainment." Usually, the description included "Must be detail-oriented"—deal breaker!— or "Looking for a self-starter"—nope, not good at starting myself. And then there was "Lucrative opportunity to make own hours and earn commissions," which, I quickly learned, meant printer sales or phone sex.

The latter actually didn't sound bad. Holly, my camp friend from Vermont, did phone sex and said it was fun. She'd segued into it from handing out event flyers on the street while on roller skates. Her boss liked her style of asking "Wanna come to a party?" and promoted her to dirty talk and moaning. She then moved on to stripping and go-go dancing. Her stage name was Holiday.

Other friends' jobs, more in keeping with their parents' expectations, sounded terrible.

Chris moved to DC to find work at a think tank, which meant, ew, politics.

Leslie did paralegal work for a giant, white-shoe law firm. She got up early and worked late at night. In a skirt and, ugh, pantyhose.

A few friends temped, which seemed worth a shot. You don't like it? You don't go back. And you never knew, you could end up in a cool, creative company and be so well liked that they'd ask you to stay on—as the person who stands behind video monitors and points and has no time for a migraine.

To temp, you had to type a certain number of words per minute. I bought *Mavis Beacon Teaches Typing* on floppy disk. It was a video game, à la *Space Invaders*, where you'd shoot the letters on the screen by typing the corresponding keys. I played it on my mother's gigantic Apple II Plus and got proficient. No skill, by the way, has ever served me better. If you take away one actionable tip from this book, it's learn to touch type. I put on a dress and earrings, passed the tests, and got accepted into the temp pool.

The first temp job was in a lawyer's office, a far cry from the slick, modern digs I'd seen on *LA Law*. Where was the polished wood and glass? Where was overpaid, flirtatious divorce attorney Arnie Becker and his red sports car? All this place had was buzzing fluorescent lights, dusty accordion files, and beige metal cabinets from the '70s.

The next job was in a public-housing agency. With no Thursday-night NBC drama to set expectations for that gig, I had none. I forwarded calls and took messages from people disputing evictions or complaining about roaches.

I wore pantyhose, just like in my nightmares, rode the subway during rush hour, and ate salad bar lunches alone at my desk. After those two jobs, I stopped answering calls from the temp agency and took what I considered a well-earned break.

One day in May, a full year into my "job search," my phone rang at ten a.m. Okay, it might have been eleven. "Sorry to wake you," my friend Jody said.

"No, I was awake." Total lie. I'd been out 'til four and had planned to rise at the crack of noon.

"Well, good," Jody said. "Are you dressed? I'm here working with Lisa Birnbach." I perked up. I knew they were family friends, from temple. Lisa was author of *The Preppy Handbook*, which had been hugely popular during, well, the preppy years. Now, Jody quickly explained, Lisa was working on the second edition of her guide to colleges. Jody was fact-checking, and they needed more people to come in and help. Like, in the next hour.

Here was a chance to work with someone famous. Still, I desperately wanted to go back to sleep and enjoy my day as planned. Now, I would have to skip my favorite four p.m. step class at Equinox. I'd have to get on a subway to an office in Midtown.

"You can wear whatever you want," Jody said. So there was that. "It's at her husband's office. He's a filmmaker." So there was that, too. Maybe this could lead to something entertainment-y. With standing, pointing, no time for migraine.

I went. The job lasted several weeks and led to everything else in my life.

If I hadn't spent the year pounding the pavement as a would-be barmaid and doling out BJs instead of working a decent entry-level job as expected, I never would've been available for this stroke of luck.

A group of us fact-checkers spent all day calling the colleges listed in the book, asking questions like, "Would you say that your student body likes to party hard?"

We sat around a table. Not brainstorming, not throwing pencils, but it felt collaborative and fun, down to the group sushi orders. And it was entertainment-y! Sitcom and movie stars came and went. There was talk of availability: "Robin Williams is a strong maybe." Because we fact-checkers tied up the phones, Lisa's husband's production assistant frequently yelled, "I need a line!"—which I considered a thrilling, Hollywood touch.

I enjoyed the work. Sometimes, more than just checking facts, I got to write little nuggets for the book. Little nuggets, I discovered, were my forte. What an epiphany—writing, without the agony. Or, as my dad had always called it, "bellyaching."

Lisa saw promise in my little nuggets. When my father came to meet me for lunch, she told him, "We love Laura here." And then, the sentence that spoke right to my soul: "We've got to find a way to tap her talent."

That. *Right there.* That's what I wanted, what I'd been waiting for: for someone or something to come along and Tap. My. Talent.

Maybe I loved this expression because it made me think of maple syrup, which I will eat straight from the spoon with no shame. I'm a sucker for those ads where the syrup pours right out of the tree and onto the waffle. I've always wanted that to be my career: a spigot through which my genius would gush forth in a powerful torrent. Someone get a bucket! Lotta talent coming out over here!

I guess it's what everyone wants. To access their full potential, step into their greatness, and unleash their awesomeness. That "unleash" stuff smacks of rank bullshit and, also, it speaks to me. I always loved the idea of someone unclipping the leash on my awesomeness and letting it run loose in the park. Go, awesomeness, go chase that squirrel!

Now that I've achieved it, I can confirm, getting paid to express yourself is nirvana. On the other hand, when you're starting out, settling for nothing less than work that aligns with your soul purpose and provides a valve for your greatest gifts can make finding a job somewhat tricky.

I was fortunate. While the fact-checking job wasn't a full-on talent spigot, it eked out some promising first drops.

And then, as good things do, it came to an end.

The good news? Now I had a mentor. Someone who'd already carved a path I wanted, in a way that looked doable for me. Lisa was funny, she made a living writing, she had gotten married and had her first kid super old: at thirty and thirty-two, respectively. Like my mom. *Good*, I thought. *That gives me time.*

Once the book was turned in, Lisa hired me to come to her apartment and help sort through clutter. Honey, I *am* clutter. Not my strong suit. She was short on ways to tap my talent. But there was an exciting prospect. She'd been offered a post as deputy editor at *Spy* magazine and said she could get me an internship that fall.

Spy was a hot downtown satirical publication described as "snarky." It took aim at celebrities, sacred cows, and whatever you'd call Donald Trump. I hadn't read it much, but I knew an

internship there would be the kind of job that made people wonder, "How'd she get that job?"

I had thought about working in magazines, though I wasn't
sure doing what. I didn't want to be a reporter and go out on a
"beat." I now knew I liked writing short, funny things, though—
and *Spy* was full of short, funny things.

For the rest of summer, I went back to my non-working life.
Sleep late, work out, watch TV, eat, buy crop tops, nap, go out 'til
four a.m., repeat. All without the nagging thought, "What am I
gonna do with my life?" My father no longer asked if I was "making any headway." The only thing better than a great job? A great
job on the horizon.

On my first day at *Spy*, I arrived eager, right on time, and
slightly damp in my magenta Merino wool V-neck. It was 80 degrees out, but I'd wanted to dress for a season I thought of as Fall
at a Magazine. The head assistant set me up at a desk, where I
pictured myself writing reams of short, funny things.

And it was at that desk, in that seat, where I showed the world
what *Spy*'s newest intern could do: Xerox.

My main daily task was a thing called the Gossip Pack. It fell
to the newest intern. I'd get the *Post*, the *Daily News*, the *Ob-
server*, and the *Wall Street Journal* and create a roundup of all their
gossip or gossip-adjacent pages. Copy, collate, staple, distribute
to all the editors.

A more driven intern would have gotten to work early and had
those packs waiting on editors' desks when they arrived. Mine
were juuusssst a little late, because so was I. I'd had great inten-
tions of being a New Me and always showing up on the dot, but
I remained Old Me. My lateness with the Gossip Packs didn't

cause complaints, at least none that got back to me, but I doubt it helped me make that splash I'd imagined, either.

Gossip Packs weren't my whole job. They wanted us interns to become contributors and editors. I was to come up with story ideas, pitch them, and write them. I knew inspiration would probably take a while to strike—and when it did? Watch out. Geyser of talent. Syrup city, baby.

For the time being, I did the tasks in front of me. Not super well or anything. I was never a master of things young go-getters are supposed to do, like "anticipate the boss's needs" or "be a quick study."

My first week, one senior editor asked me to haul a box of books to the nearby used bookstore, The Strand. He'd received them for free from publishers. "And then," he instructed, "just bring me back the money."

"So, wait," I said, confused. "What money? Is there a receipt for the books? How do I get them there?" I didn't understand the scheme. He crossed his arms, tilted his head, and sighed. "Let's try this again. You. Bring. These. Books. To The Strand. You sell them back, and you bring. Me. The cash."

I felt hollered at and incompetent and wanted to cry, but I managed to hold it back. Crying on your first week as an intern was not the path to success.

While waiting for my talent to align with the job and gush forth, I enjoyed working at a verifiable "cool company." This was what an office could be! We hung out and joked. There was a skateboard. Even if nobody used it, it added an element of "funky." So did the neighborhood, Union Square. Seedy but up-and-coming, teeming with models on go-sees.

My job at *Spy* was probably the best social life I'd ever had. We got to go to the legendary *Spy* parties. We flirted. The hot art director said he'd had a dream about me. One of the writers I had a crush on asked me out.

We had in-jokes. Office characters. A pervy older man with a white mustache and monocle was the face, though not the writer, of the movie reviews. He showed up to parties and hit on the interns. The mailroom guy had a Christian rock band and an identical twin. An ex-cop reporter came in just to collect pricey gifts sent by Martha Stewart, whom he'd interviewed, and to make phone calls. He wore so much cologne, his phone smelled of it when he'd been away for weeks. We called it The Cologne Phone. Outside in Union Square, a street musician named Squid played the same tuneless earworm day in, day out. We all came back from lunch, humming it against our will, like it was the office anthem.

I now brag a lot about working from home. Everyone in the online world does. (Or did, pre-COVID.) "I just empowered five hundred women . . . in my pajamas!" Still, I'm sad for twenty-one-year-olds who become bloggers or influencers and skip working around other people. Other people often suck, but that's the fun part.

And don't forget group lunch. We interns blew through our stipends down the block at Coffee Shop. *The* place to spot known party promoters and supermodels back when either category had cachet, it was always packed, but I had an in with the maître d'. If I was rigorous about anything at this job, it was being a regular at Coffee Shop. Having a job made it unfeasible to turn up every night at Wild Thing, so I transferred that loyalty here.

Whenever a bunch of us wanted to go to Coffee Shop, I'd say, "Lemme call Sid." My superhero trick. Sid always saved us a coveted round booth. We had internships at *Spy* and a booth at Coffee Shop. We were big, important, fifty-dollar-a-week stars.

My dad, who didn't get the whole internship thing, shook his head at my wages. "Your talent is worth so much more," he said, slathering his toast with Country Crock Shedd's Spread. "What if you were to sit down with the chief of finance there, and show him how much money you make for the magazine? Show him how you're responsible for the profits."

My dad's calculations were never all that data based. He bragged often about having earned Eastern Airlines "mmmilllions and mmmillllions" of dollars during his tenure there in the late 1960s. He leaned on the first syllable in *millions* like a Muppet in a *Sesame Street* bit brought to you by the letter "M." In his mind, the company had never acknowledged his contributions or paid him his due.

I told Dad my work wasn't worth much. He thought I was being hard on myself, but I knew I was falling short.

In fact, the managing editor had taken me and my co-intern to sushi. "You know," she said, blowing on her miso soup, "as interns, you *can* take initiative. In fact, we encourage it."

Oh no, *initiative*. That thing where you do something without anyone making you. Not in my DNA. Though I gladly would have shown initiative if I'd had any ideas. I couldn't think of anything I wanted to write about. I was running out the clock. As usual, I was behind.

My co-intern Debbie took her cue and researched a piece on prison. A few times, she was so excited to reach someone at a correctional facility, she pumped her fist and squealed when she hung up the phone. When would I feel like that about a project? Lucky bitch had initiative.

Then, one day, I finally got a lead I thought might be something. Maybe even . . . something big.

A woman started calling to report that musician Don Henley was trying to kill her.

The switchboard forwarded her to the interns. This was how you make it, right? You take the call others are too important to bother with. You discover the next great novel in the slush pile your busy colleagues have given up for garbage. I eagerly picked up the phone and listened to the woman's daily rants.

"Don Henley broke a glass bottle in his apartment. I can feel it twenty miles away, he's in Malibu. And get this, Laura—" She'd learned my name and now asked for me. "I'm walking barefoot in *my* apartment, and I'm not kidding you: my feet begin to bleed! It's voodoo. You can't make this stuff up."

"No," I agreed, scribbling notes:

Don Henley.

Voodoo.

Broken glass, bloody feet.

Finally, I felt like that go-getter who was *on to something*. A bombshell. Maybe I was a reporter, after all.

"Yeah . . . I don't know," an editor grimaced when I pitched it. The story, he pointed out, would be making fun of a crazy non-celebrity who was paranoid about a has-been celebrity. Of course, writing this now, it's clear as Don Henley's broken glass that the editor was right. But I was shocked when he told me, "It's not really *Spy* material."

Dreams dashed, I wondered: Did I really want to be *Spy* material? I wasn't cut out for it. Plus, the older editors didn't seem like they were having much fun or making much money. Did I want an income I'd have to supplement by selling free books to The Strand?

As it became clear I wasn't going to "crush it" in my internship, I prayed the perfect job would land magically in my lap before the six-month buzzer sounded and some bushy-tailed, more success-driven new intern got my desk.

As luck would have it, I got wind of a heaven-sent, temporary gig as a "clipper" for Comedy Central. I took a few sick days and filled in for a staffer on maternity leave, doing my absolute dream job: watching standup comedy routines and finding bits under thirty seconds that could live on their own. I thought I was exceptional at it.

Now that I'd found my thing, I couldn't bear the prospect of returning to the magazine and being useless. And *hallelujah*, the creative director told me they had an opening for a full-time clipper. There were a lot of people going for this job, he said, but not people who'd already proven themselves. I had this one in the bag. I wrote the world's cleverest, LOL-filled letter about why that clipper should be me. I added a reco from Lisa to put it over the top. It felt so good to know my future.

One friend, Jocelyn, was always telling me I needed a job when I didn't have one and that I needed a better job when I did. She now called every day just to say, "Hey, Clipper." She bought me an LA Clippers hat.

"It's nice to see you passionate about your career," my dad said. "I'm kvelling! I hope it pays better than the internship."

A couple of weeks passed without a word from the creative director, which was strange. He had said the position was starting soon. It was like waiting for a guy to call after I'd slept with him.

(And we know how that went.) After a month of constant dialing in to my machine, I got a message.

"Hey. I'm finally, finally, getting back to people. Give a call."

Also, the usual from Jocelyn: "Hey Clipper! You hear anything?"

"So . . ." he said when I called back. I already knew what he was about to say. "We went with someone else."

I was one of the top two candidates, he explained. The other was male. "I put it to a vote with the team. They definitely liked you, but we have a company b-ball game going, and everyone wanted a guy who can shoot hoops."

So, another rule of success: have a penis. At least it wasn't me, just my genitalia. But I still hung up with the about-to-cry lump in my esophagus.

Lisa was in the office that day. She worked mostly from home, hugely pregnant. "I didn't get the job," I sobbed, running to her like I was telling her someone we both loved had died. She didn't reach out to me, so I threw my arms around her swollen middle in a consoling (to me) hug. She said, "Aw, that's too bad."

I was hoping she'd have some other idea to tap my talent. She didn't offer one. She had a meeting.

Soon enough, a new lifeline appeared. Its name? Julia Roberts. Apparently, she was looking for an assistant.

This was it. I was almost glad I hadn't gotten the clipper job. Sitting in a tiny room all day with a TV and tape deck, watching comedians in front of brick walls? How many times could I laugh at bits about "the thing about"? *The thing about dieting, is . . . The thing about old people is . . . The thing about Pudding Pops is . . . Here's the thing about men. Am I right, ladies?* I would have been consuming and recycling, not creating.

This job with Julia, on the other hand—who knew what it might unleash in me? I imagined myself helping her run lines in her trailer. Asking people to give her some space. Sitting on set, in a chair with my name on the back, offering insights between takes. "What if we changed this line a little?" I might say, pointing at the script. "Y'know, play around with it, swap these two words?" She would turn her head to stare at me with narrowed eyes you might mistake for anger until you realize it's wonder: "Who even ARE you and how are you such a genius?" There'd be no time in my day for a migraine.

I bought a crepe pantsuit with shoulder pads, as you did, and lined up an interview. Fully expecting to meet with Julia, I met with her manager, who warmed me up with her Julia Roberts story. After *Mystic Pizza*, she said, she had told Julia to lose fifteen pounds. Then, everyone wanted Julia. "And every day I came to work," she said, "was a 'Julia day.' I made calls, fielded offers, made her a star."

"I think you did okay," I winked. I was nervous, but also encouraged. She was selling me on Julia. She wanted me to want this job.

"So." She clapped once. End of storytime. "She's shooting in DC, and she'll need someone to drive her around. You drive, right?"

"Not super well?" I said (understatement of the decade). "But probably with more practice . . ."

She laughed. "I love the honesty! You're a trip."

Why lie? If I was going to get this job, it would be based on my personality. Me being me. And then, no more would be expected of me than that.

"Are you detail-oriented?"

"Well, it's not my forte, I'm more creative than organized, but I can be."

"Noted," she said. "What do you want to do for a career, long term?"

"I'm figuring that out, but I've always thought something entertainment-y?"

"Ohh . . . kay . . . and why do you want to work for Julia Roberts?"

I flipped my hands out, palms up. The "duh" gesture. "It's Julia Roberts!" I said it like I was in a commercial for Julia Roberts and Julia Roberts was a hamburger chain. "I mean . . . What's not to want?" That's the part where I'd bite into the hamburger. *Yum!*

Let's not kid ourselves. Even I knew I was the world's wrongest person for this job. I didn't hear back.

At the magazine, editorial and publishing were all on one floor. I had spent most of my time sauntering in circles, doing schmooze laps, so I had friends in both departments. As the last grains of sand poured to the bottom of my internship hourglass, the publishing side said, "We'll take her."

They even had a salary for me: twelve thousand a year. The mercy of it, from fifty dollars a week to a thousand a month. Quite the reward for sucking as an intern.

They gave me an assignment no one on the editorial side wanted: writing a full-page advertorial for Dewar's Scotch as if it were a "real" page in *Spy*. I got to write short, funny things—a one-paragraph essay on being a grown-up (I'll leave that there) and a quiz called "Do You Party Like Your Uncle Marty?" It was to determine whether you were an old-fart loser. If so, you could remedy that by drinking Dewar's.

When it came out, I had a whole page in *Spy*. Mine. My friend Tim—a member of the "brain trust," as the new editor in chief called his all-male group of young, favorite writers—said the guys on the editorial side were talking about how funny my writing was. Me. I was a funny writer. Not to mention, an official, professional "copywriter." Decades later, when people ask how I got into copywriting, I trace it back to the Dewar's piece. It was my first. Still in a binder in my old bedroom.

I worked on the ad side for a year. I didn't always get to write short, funny things. Some days, I proofread ad proposals or re-typed letters. Other days, I bought plastic cake plates for someone's birthday. But now, I knew what I could do professionally: write copy. And I still had all the perks of *Spy*—fun friends and long lunches at Coffee Shop, a loose morning start time, lots of CDs sent to the office for free. Jamiroquai, Crash Test Dummies, Blind Melon. Some didn't even have a hole drilled in the case to mark them for promo use, so I could exchange them at Tower Records for hip-hop. No one dressed up. I could save that crepe pantsuit for funerals and wear baby tees to work. Life was good.

Then, the Italian racing-car heir who owned *Spy* started coming around a bunch. People said that wasn't good—that he was bored, and probably selling the magazine.

Corporate sent in a guy named Jonathan. He wore a dark suit and roamed the office, ominously taking notes. Soon, he was coming in jeans shorts and packing up boxes. His rhythmic ripping of packing tape had the ring of something I'd heard countless times from bartenders at four a.m.: "You don't have to go home, but you can't stay here."

Staffers who didn't want to go down with the ship began an exodus. "You're so proactive," I said jealously, watching a friend zhuzh up and print out her résumé.

It's probably clear by now that I was less proactive. I was me: the person in the burning building saying, "I dunno, I don't smell smoke, I think I'm gonna stay." After all, if I jumped, where would I land? I still didn't know the job I wanted, just the feeling (talent: tapped) and pay (beaucoup bucks) I wanted from it. Everyone else, meanwhile, moved on before they had to, to bigger and better, because they *knew* what they wanted. Like Vic's seductive filmmaker boyfriend, they had the post office gene.

When I think of their next steps, I picture the end credits of *Animal House* or a season finale of *Real Housewives*. Freeze frames with a brief success epilogue over each character.

Meredith got a marketing job at Marvel. Thirty-six thousand dollars a fucking year. She was going to be a titan.

Rick started working for an activist documentarian, who called him in on weekends and made him feel guilty if he left before eleven p.m. Next, he went to Letterman, where he struggled to get any jokes on the air. I was glad not to be him. "My days are numbered," he told me. Now, he's a sitcom showrunner, and his days are rich.

Rob went to a big ad agency as a junior copywriter. "Do you throw pencils at the ceiling?" I asked. He said all his ideas were shot down by an exec still milking one claim to fame, which was coming up with the army slogan "Be all that you can be."

Tim had been faxing daily jokes to a famous comedian on basic cable, and got hired. He'd later tell me about the comedian's masturbation habits. "All day long, the guy fucks pillows." Tim went on to be head writer for the best late-night show, then a top dog at

TV's longest-running animated series. He has Emmys and makes a fortune. He told me in the early 2000s, "Write a spec script and submit it. You'll get a job here." Spoiler: I didn't write one.

Finally, Mindy went to my favorite magazine, one we'll call *Gotham*. The job didn't match the glamour of those glossy pages. She almost never had time for lunch, even at her desk. The office was in Midtown. It sounded like hell. Still, when she called to tell me they needed a talented copywriter, I applied and got the job.

I took it because if I didn't, it was a matter of weeks before I'd be jobless again, my dad on my case to read *What Color Is Your Parachute?* The writing was on the wall.

Sorry I'm Late

One of my top embarrassing memories: in my mid-thirties, busting into a work meeting ten minutes late, having walked from home to Times Square in the summer heat, and then being asked by my boss if, "before we get started," I needed some tissues or paper towels. She was looking from my face to my feet, which were in flip flops. All parts of me, dripping with sweat.

I hate my lateness. I hate anyone's, because, as we all know, we loathe in others what we most judge in ourselves. I have one friend in particular whose lateness enrages me. The only time she's ever on time—early, in fact—is when we meet at Japonica, a sushi place on University. Each table has one cozy seat on the inside of the wooden booth and one seat on the outside, its back to the drafty door. Guess where she's always sitting when I show up?

Otherwise, late. If I swing by to meet in her lobby at a certain time, she waits for me to get there and have the doorman call up. *God forbid she should spend a hot minute waiting for me downstairs*, I think, knowing I'm almost as bad. I watch the elevator, which I can tell she doesn't call for at least five more minutes, and then that plodding, 1960s beast takes five minutes to reach her high floor and another five to come down. "Sorry," she says. "The elevator stopped on every floor." No it didn't. I watched. And no one got off the elevator with you, either. It's a bad lie. I've used it myself.

According to many articles online, we're no longer supposed to say "Sorry I'm late." Instead, we're told, we should say, "Thank you for waiting." No apology. At least not if you're a woman, because women apologize too much. Well, sorry not sorry, I think showing up late deserves an *I'm sorry*. It's more respectful, if not one bit less annoying.

"Sorry I'm late": I say it as I show up to the Zoom call. The dinner party. Worst of all, the recovery room, where I'd wanted to be *before* my husband was out of his anesthesia from having a melanoma sliced off his arm. He waited half an hour to see my face because I'd insisted on walking and timed it poorly. Not my finest.

There are different theories on lateness. The one I've heard longest is that it's a form of arrogance. If you're late, you think your time is more valuable than the other person's. Not in my case, I swear. For me, it's delusion. Clock dysmorphia. Magical thinking that stretches time in my head. In an hour, I think I can take a ninety-minute walk. In fifteen minutes, I think I can shower, watch a little Netflix, dry my hair, pick an outfit, reject it, pick another, and get somewhere fifteen minutes away. Or maybe it's a special time metabolism. They say, "You have the same twenty-four hours in a day as Beyoncé." True, I guess, but I soak up time like eggplant soaks up oil. Time to leave already? Where'd that hour go? Cue text: *Running 5-ish late. So sorry!*

I've said "Sorry I'm late" so much, it could be my catchphrase. Like Fonzie's "Ayyyy"—except nobody claps. Nor should they. That said, I can't be a hundred percent sorry I'm a late person, because, as my best friend reminds me, it's the reason we met. It was 1992, the summer between working for Lisa and my internship at *Spy*. My friend Susan, from the fact-checking job with Lisa, already had a new job, in development at a film company. I went to meet her for lunch, and, surprise, I was late.

Her assistant greeted me. "Hi! You must be Laura! Susan was mad you were late, so she went to Bendel's to look for stockings, to punish you."

"Shit," I said, fanning myself. That sounded like Susan. Good at life, and judgy of anyone who wasn't. The assistant, Victoria, introduced herself, offered me a Diet Coke, and invited me to sit with her while I waited. "I'm late for everything," she said, "so I don't judge."

While Susan punished me at Bendel's, Victoria and I talked like two friends who haven't seen each other in a year. The kind of conversation where you send the server away five times, saying, "We're so sorry, we still haven't looked yet, but we will."

We moved from *where are you from, where'd you go to school?*, to *ohmygod, do you know Vernon? let's call him right now and tell him we're together.* Which we did, then on to *what's better, fro-yo or Tasti D-Lite?* and *let's face it, muffins are really just cake*, to *who do you like, are you dating anyone?* and *I'm waiting for this guy to call and of course he hasn't*. Vic—I'd already shortened her name—stood up to show me how much weight she'd lost since breaking up with her boyfriend. She didn't say *my boyfriend*, though, she said his name, Steven Gold, which made me feel like I was already part of her life. "Believe it or not, this is actually really skinny for me," she said, doing a twirl in her jumpsuit. Black rayon with flowers—I still remember it. A Cindy Crawford lookalike, Victoria was, and is, the most stunning person I've ever known.

By the time Susan came back with her tiny, striped Bendel's bag, Vic and I had exchanged numbers and I was like, "Susan who?"

That night, Vic and I met up and sat on a bench outside the restaurant Amsterdam's, on a girl date that never ended. From then on, we stalked each other's crushes at bars together and met each other's friends. My high school friends. Her Columbia ones. Her beautiful friend Stephanie, who made things happen. Stephanie attracted celebrities, got us into clubs, scored us free motorcycle boots, showed us how to be warm-but-icy to win back the interest of a guy who was blowing us off. (I never mastered it.) We cohosted parties. Went to each other's birthdays. (Hunan Cottage. Free plum wine.) We flew to South Beach, where we ogled models and Victoria plucked my eyebrows into oblivion. I had sex with a guy in a youth hostel while she marched at an anti-neo-Nazi rally, which was par for the course.

She came to my parents' twenty-fifth-anniversary-slash-Clinton-inauguration party, to my father's funeral and burial twenty-five years later, and to every birthday and Jewish Christmas in between. My sister became her honorary sister, her son my honorary nephew. Our husbands are best friends.

If I were a naturally on-time type, there would be a Vic-shaped hole in my life. And I'd probably have lasted longer in my least favorite job, my one and only nine-to-five. It's another flaw that worked out in my favor, as our flaws often do. It's infuriating when people get ushered through security or even upgraded to business class because they showed up late for their flight. I hate those people. And yet, I guess I'm one of them. I haven't had that kind of luck at airports, but thanks to being late to meet Susan, I got the unfair upgrade of all time.

Still, I'd gladly trade my lateness for being pathologically punctual. One of the times I showed up late for dinner with my mom and dad and said, "Sorry for being late," my father said, "Don't be sorry, Laura. That's just you! You're not being late, you're being you!" Damn, Dad. That's some cold shit!

I'd love it not to be me. I'd love to get to the restaurant and not have sweat cascade down my face like a waterfall at a shopping mall. Whenever I get together with my friend Susie, she texts, "I'm here, no rush," about thirty minutes before we're supposed to meet. She'll then shoot me a photo of her journal and prosecco. It drives me crazy, mostly because I want *that* to be me. I've improved a bit, especially once I started to realize that being rushed and late is cruel to myself, and being on time or even early is kind. (Consistently Early Susie is the very essence of self-love. She'll tell you so. Sometimes she'll text, "Having lunch with my favorite person . . . ME!!") To my fellow late person, I'm here to say: if you can trick yourself into it, earliness is the tits! Five stars. I love getting to be the smug one. So scratch what I said about apologizing—if you show up late and I'm already there, no need to be sorry. That's just you!

Bad at Corporate

In 1994, *Spy* magazine closed and I reluctantly took a copywriting job at a more buttoned-up magazine in Midtown. I rode two subways, the 1/2/3 to the 7. Switching at Times Square during morning rush hour, carried by a riptide of grim nine-to-fivers, made me feel like one of the faces in stock footage on the news. "Millions of employees returned to the workforce today . . ."

I got out in the bleak East Forties and trudged two painfully unremarkable blocks. The only commerce near the magazine's office was Au Bon Pain (three of them) and The Gap (two). Fashion that year was all about neutrals, so factor in wall-to-wall beige in The Gap windows and on the streets. I wore it, too. Even on my lips. The summer of no color.

My new boss liked to dial my extension at nine a.m. on the dot and leave a voicemail making it official that I wasn't there yet. We'll call her Evelyn to protect the identity of someone whose office stank of sauerkraut. Her voice, permanently congested, sounded like she was holding back a sneeze or trying not to breathe you in. Her daily message went: "Hi Laura. It's Evelyd. It's after dide o'clock. I guess you're dot here yet. Dot good. You're jeopardizihg your Friday Subber Hours." Beep. End of. New messages.

Summer Hours. Not the treat they sounded like. Instead of coming in at ten, we started at nine and put in an extra hour Monday through Thursday so we could take a half day off on Fridays. For me, being on time for a ten a.m. start was struggle enough.

Evelyn had hired me despite the obvious red flag: I showed up late for the interview. Just a few minutes, which I thought was no big deal, but I now cringe. After making me wait fifteen extra minutes in reception, she asked, "Did you have trouble fihdihg us?" Because it's hard to find a good writer and my test project was good—Evelyn said it "knocked her socks off"—I guess she ignored her misgivings.

Evelyn was only thirty-six, but as I write this, I picture her as cruel, shrewish Aunt Lydia in *The Handmaid's Tale*. That's how twenty-four-year-old me saw her. (I guess it's fair punishment now when the barista calls me "ma'am.") I felt Evelyn was always reprimanding me, making me do it over, hunting me down. Everything was an emergency. If I didn't pick up on the first ring, she'd march out to my desk and say, "I was trying to call you. Were you id the bathroob?"

She always thought she was right. Holding up a draft of my copy, she pointed to a word circled in her awful red pencil. "'Restaurateur,' Laura? You left out the *n*." (She pronounced it "ed.") I told her the word didn't have an *n*, but she wasn't having it. God bless the Internet and smartphones for coming along to help you prove you're right, and, therefore, superior.

Evelyn's office smelled. She kept leftover party platters on top of her mini fridge "to nosh on." She hoarded one plastic tub of sauerkraut for a week. Also, old wine, with Saran Wrap as a makeshift cork. "It stinks like old salad in there," a friend said. "Or hot dog."

She threw people under the bus for her mistakes and took credit for their ideas. When my friend Mindy went with her on sales calls and proposed a marketing campaign the client loved, Evelyn would lie, "Yes, I'b glad you like that. It was my idea." Not a good look, but one you might chalk up to corporate culture. From what I've seen since, a lot of execs, terrified of losing their jobs and/or determined to be moved up to a better one, act this way. They design by committee, second-guess your work, and steal your ideas. Mindy, the world's most generous, gracious human, told me she fantasized about quitting and tucking a piece of fish into Evelyn's radiator as a parting gift. "But would she even notice the smell?" we both wondered. We agreed that, with the sauerkraut, it would be gilding the lily.

Was Evelyn the worst, scariest boss? Looking back, I can confirm she wasn't a good one, but there were way worse. My friend Margaret had applied to work at *the* number-one, top, top fashion magazine. (Same one as in *The Devil Wears Prada*.) At the interview, a senior assistant looked at Margaret's skirt and said, "Hmmm. . . . We have to change you." Her hem length was "last season" by at least an inch, and, if left on for the interview, would enrage the editor in chief. My friend didn't get the job, but if she had, I'm sure her "mean boss" stories would have easily trumped mine.

"Would you like some suggestions to get along better with Evelyn?" my dad asked when I complained at home. Psychotherapy plus management consulting—this was right in his wheelhouse. I told him not really, thanks, because I hated her.

"Oh!" he said, raising his eyebrows—same face he made when offered a hot brownie. He loved a paradox of the subconscious. "That means part of you loves her."

Ohhhkay, Dad. Whatever you and Freud say.

It wasn't just me who thought Evelyn was The Worst. Her last name was Hall-Dickersen, but the ad sales team called her Evelyn Hall-Dickhead. I felt seen!

Her assistant, Suzannah, got the worst of it. All day long, you could hear Evelyn calling out for her. "Suze-addah! I deed you!" "Suze-addah, I'b huhgry, where's by lundch?" "Suze-addah? Suze-addah! Has eddywud seed Suze-addah? Where is she? This isn't Club Med!"

Nope, it sure wasn't Club Med, even if I dressed like it was.

I favored shrunken, belly-button-baring baby tees (my favorite brand was "Tee's Tees"). Great for going out dancing, less fitting for a publishing department where most staffers wore power suits. These were people who didn't just "have" meetings. They "took" them. To take a meeting, you do things like "put your best foot forward" and "dress for success." I dressed for something else. I wanted success, but not here. There wasn't anyone whose job made me say, "I want to do *that*" or "I want to be *her*." Certainly not second-guessing, idea-stealing Evelyn.

My baby tees were thin. The office was freezing. I heard a couple of guys from ad sales agree, "It's nippy in here." I knew what they were referring to, but I stuck with my baby tees. I thought they were flattering. And, unlike silk, they hid pit sweat—still more embarrassing to me than visibly sprung nips. Evelyn said nothing about my wardrobe verbally, but her glances spoke volumes. They expressed every passive-aggressive comment you could make about an outfit. "That's what you're wearing?" "Wow,

I wish *I* were brave enough to wear that." Or, the ultimate back-hand: "You look comfy!"

Like my attire, my style of sales copy didn't fit the tone Evelyn was looking for. She said my ideas needed to be "more elegant, more up here." She illustrated "up here" by waving her downward-facing palm over her head. Ironically, the universal sign for "over my head."

She hated my concept for promoting the Year End Double Issue, aka the YEDI. I'd had the illustrator mock up a cute prehistoric creature with a multiple-choice quiz, "What's a YEDI?" I thought it was a home run.

With a facial expression normally reserved for telling someone their dog died, Evelyn handed back the piece. "This isn't elegant edough. Maybe if it were a Dickelodeon piece, but this is a sophisticated magazeed. It needs to be *up here*." Nickelodeon—I wished! "Also, I need you to be on tibe tomorrow to fix it." She warned, "That means nine, not ten. Don't forget about Subber Hours."

I tried to be better, but not hard enough, and Evelyn revoked my Summer Hours. Instead of leaving early on Fridays, I was to stay late and work on the company's internal newsletter. Basically, detention. At two p.m., everyone else filed out, jackets hooked on thumbs and slung over shoulders—the universal sign for "gettin' outta here, let's hit the Hamptons." Not me. That's when Evelyn would hand me a list of news items I had to report or celebrate: The sales team's Florida retreat. Chad's promotion to beverage and tobacco manager. The engagement of two people who'd met in the marketing department. I did my best to be subversive. Headline: "Is That a One-Sheet in Your Pocket, or Are You Just Happy to See My Added Value?" Had it not been assigned to penalize me, I might even have enjoyed the task. I was too pissed off to realize that, with this stupid exercise, I was doing the work I was born to do—inject humor and personality into something expected to be stiff and boring.

People from ad sales complimented me. "We love the newsletter! It's actually fun to read!" "Oh my god, the part about hookups at the HR offsite, I died." Evelyn didn't spot most of the sarcasm or innuendo I slipped into these two-page missives. She'd undo a few sentence fragments, cross out slang, and say I could "go edjoy the weekehd." She acted like she was letting me go early, but this usually happened after six, the office humming with silence. She stayed late to see my punishment through.

After I'd been there six months, Evelyn called me into her hot dog–scented office and asked me to shut the door. She made her trademark "your dog died" face and said, "It's dot working out." I asked if there was anything I could do to change her mind, but I was relieved at her answer:

"I'm afraid dot."

Who can blame her? I wasn't punctual, detail-oriented, or eager to please. I didn't want to conform to the tone of the magazine, I wanted it to conform to me. I thought everything should be cheeky and funny. I still do, which is why I get replies to my newsletter, usually from guys named Bob who found me on LinkedIn, saying, "Unsubscribe! Very unprofessional!" When it's your own business and you're the boss, you decide what's professional. When your boss is Evelyn, not so much.

I skipped out of her office with my pink slip. Okay, I didn't literally skip, but it was literally a pink piece of paper saying I was terminated. I might have sashayed. But with my head down. I felt at once both liberated and stung. It's embarrassing to get

fired. The essence of "disgraceful"—leaving in disgrace. Especially with the word "terminated." You're not just out of a job;
you're dead. It's so corporate.

In my mind, corporate is a culture (or ring of hell) that ob-
sesses over structures and policy, where people say things like
"chain of command" and "run it up the flagpole." Corporate isn't
inherently bad, it's just not for me.

You rarely hear the term "nine-to-five" without the modifier
"soul-sucking" in front of it. "Ditch your soul-sucking nine-to-
five." Then, there's "Stop working for The Man!" And, a Pin-
terest favorite, "If you don't build your own dream, someone
will hire you to build theirs." Is it so bad to build someone else's
dream? What if you don't have one of your own? Or, what if
you do, and it's to help with someone else's? Here's the thing.
Not everyone finds it spirit-crushing to be an employee. I know
people who are happy as clams—clams with stock options and
free dental cleanings—being told what to do and what time to
clock in. Some people are wired for it. Turns out, I'm not one
of them.

Lucky me that I had Evelyn for a boss. I didn't know how
blessed I was to work for someone I didn't like. If I had admired
her and felt supported by her, I might have tried harder to please
her, to "go the extra mile," to excel. When you shine in corporate, you're likely to get stuck there, whether it suits you or not.
Like the friend's girlfriend I mentioned at the start of this book,
who rose up and up and up. At each *up*, she worked for a more
abusive boss. One threw a stapler at her head. (She stuck around.
Daddy issues.) If I'd risen up and up and up, I might have gotten
to "top-brass" level, or "C-suite," and found myself one day in the
same fried state as so many of my clients. They call themselves

"recovering lawyers" and "corporate escapees," which hints at nothing if not PTSD.

As soon as I was out the door for the last time and in the hot September air, I felt like myself again. I didn't know what I'd do next for work, but I knew what I wanted to do that night: go to Lucky Strike with my friends Vic and Steph, stay out late, wake at noon. Now *those* were Summer Hours.

I'm Writing on This Thing Called the Internet, It's Hard to Explain

Easy money. Is there such a thing? Does it ever last, or come without a catch? When you see people suddenly rolling in easily made cash on TV, you know a downfall is close at hand. Cops at the door. A market crash. A devastating commercial flop after a quick-cut montage of nonstop successes. And/or that first sniff of coke, which leads to daily sniffs, which leads to our newly rich hero selling off assets, starting with his Patek Philippe and ending with his mother's Hummel collection and 1982 tube TV. And still, the song "She Works Hard for the Money" always made me sad for her, whoever "she" was. *She works hard for the money, so you better treat her right!* Wasn't there a job she could do more easily, and still deserve to be treated right?

I had a taste of easy money in 1994. Not big money. Not enough for an epic demise where I forgot who my real friends were and surrounded myself with mooching "yes men." But still—easy. During my unemployed time after being fired as a Midtown magazine copywriter, a former colleague from *Spy* named Michael called and offered me a gig. He was now at an Internet startup. What that meant, no one really knew. We all used big finger quotes around the phrase: *"Internet startup."* We got what email was, though we still used the hyphenated term "e-mail." But what else did you do with the Internet?

Michael explained. His site, called The Transom, would provide a thing called "content." It had a "bulletin board." This was the *Flintstones* version of a forum. I guess the *Jetsons*-age version of a forum is Facebook, which is now for *Flintstones*-aged people: we're prehistoric, or grew up watching *The Flintstones*, or same/same.

Michael would pay me to be a plant. A ringer. My job was to post once a day or so, to help the forum look like—and thus become—an active, thriving community. A "fake it 'til you make it" business model (before you could buy followers). Any topic I wanted, Michael said. Just get the conversation going.

I was thrilled by the invitation to write about what mattered in the world: *Melrose Place* and *Beverly Hills, 90210*.

On *Melrose*, these were the cliffhanger-heavy days of Alison (Courtney Thorne-Smith) becoming a drunk and Kimberly (Marcia Cross) destroying lives and—in the big reveal—ripping off her wig. On *90210*, Dylan McKay (Luke Perry, RIP) was in a thrilling drug-addiction spiral, even doing the hard shit like heroin, which he smoked off of aluminum foil. This is called "chasing the dragon," and, like all addicts on TV, he did it while driving on the side of a mountain. Brandon, Brenda, Kelly, Steve

Sanders, and the gang staged an intervention. They brought in a drug counselor played by famous recovering addict and *One Day at a Time* star Mackenzie Phillips as sort-of-herself.

And me? I got paid to discuss this stuff!

Had I known Mackenzie Phillips would one day reappear on *Celebrity Rehab*, I'd have had even more material. Not that I was lacking, between David Silver learning to curb gang violence with two words ("squash it") and Kelly getting trapped and burned in a fire at Steve Sanders' rave. I wrote as passionately as any cub reporter you'd see in a movie, rushing back to the desk with a scoop. *Type-type-tippy-tap-type.* Pounding out my findings and thoughts. This was what it felt like to be absorbed in your work—to experience being a workaholic, that elusive disease I wanted almost as badly as I wanted a tapeworm. (Who doesn't? Free calories, no? Or does that not really work?)

The engagement my writing got was off the charts. By "engagement," I mean a lot of back and forth with one flirtatious guy named Geoff who also liked to talk about *Melrose* and *Bev Hills*. Every time I posted, I spent the rest of the day refreshing the Netscape browser to see if Geoff had commented yet. (So this was what you did with the mysterious "Internet"—gin up input from strangers to stabilize your self-worth. Genius!) I met up with Geoff once in real life, at a place downtown called Temple Bar. He brought his fiancée, which—from his hostage-y discomfort in saying, "Laura, this is Heather"—didn't seem to be his choice. So, my engagement was with the newly engaged. And by "off the charts," I mean there were no charts for engagement back then. Few people even knew how to get on the Internet, much less measure it. One ongoing conversation about a couple of prime-time soaps was considered viral.

I earned a weekly retainer for this work. I was still living at home with my parents rent-free, so any money was gravy—or, more accurately, lipstick money. (MAC Twig and Bobbi Brown Shimmer #4 FTW.) And, the best part, I made it doing something I gladly would've done for free. It wasn't a real salary, and it only lasted a few glorious months, but it was the easiest buck I ever made, and a little taste of what I wanted in a job.

It was my first time earning an income for writing in my own voice, as myself. Being paid for self-expression became, and remained, my definition of bliss. Work bliss, anyway. There's work bliss and then there's bliss-bliss—which, to me, is stepping off a plane into the warm bath of 80-degree Caribbean air with a light wind in mid-January and being handed a glass of punch with a piece of pineapple on the rim. (My template for happiness, if you haven't noticed, comes from the show *Fantasy Island*.)

It probably should have occurred to me as soon as blogging later became a thing that I should do that. But it would have required that unattainable quality called "initiative." *How do you make money from a blog? How do you even set one up?* I wasn't ready to look into any of it until long past the moment to cash in. There was a decade or so when you could become a well-paid Internet star by writing about your hateful boss, your bets on who would win *America's Next Top Model*, your daily bowel movements—and I slept through it. Even though I'd already gotten my start at The Transom. Late to the party as usual.

The one other time I was handed work that didn't feel like work happened over fifteen years later, in 2010. An ex-Disney-lawyer using his severance dough to open a game-night-themed restaurant in West Hollywood wanted my creative help. He flew me to Las Vegas for a team retreat. My only job there was to try different restaurants with the group, take notes on the menu descriptions, and brainstorm names for snacks. What to call the tater tots—or, rather, the chef's *take* on tater tots. There were no deliverables. No homework. All that was required was my presence and my spontaneous input on a variety of "lite bites" at jalapeño-happy places like the Pink Taco and YOLÖS. Like going back to coach after your first upgrade to business class, it was hard to give up on this kind of easy-money gig being my life. I'll probably spend the rest of my career waiting for another assignment to fly somewhere and sample the artichoke dip. Due warning: my fees have gone up! (But remain negotiable. DM me.)

It's rare and lucky for someone to offer you money to show up and be you. "Love what you do and you'll never work a day in your life." Yeah, duh. Give me something to do that I love, and I'm there. It's what I've spent my whole career looking for and—fine, with varying degrees of effort and initiative—working toward.

Star Fuckers

My husband thinks I'm the "biggest star fucker." I'll admit: I try a little too hard with anyone famous or semi-famous. D-list, even. My laugh gets loud and high-pitched around so much as a series regular from *Law & Order*. At a friend's dinner, where I sat near a cast member from Bravo's reality show *Million Dollar Listing*, Steven said in my ear, "You're funny." I asked funny *how*, but I knew. I knew I was beaming laser "like me" eyes at that TV real estate agent—famous for doing a Karate Kid–style high kick and squealing "Wheeee!" whenever he sells a condo. I was talking just to him across other guests and their chicken parm.

Yeah, I want celebrities to like me. If someone known by millions of people appreciates me, I am special.

But am I special in *feeling that way*? Am I the "biggest" star fucker?

Well, I'm not the only one who kicked into star-fucker mode when my friends Victoria, Stephanie, and I encountered a true giant of Hollywood—a big, big star—in 1995. We were on a trip to London, having brunch in a neighborhood where he famously lived and worked.

"Oh. My. God. Don't turn around," Vic said. "But that's Martin Scorsese."

She didn't really say "Martin Scorsese." It was a different filmmaker—one on that level. If you Google "greatest film directors of all time," you'll see his face right up top. But for legal purposes, we'll pretend that's the name: Martin Scorsese.

"He's my favorite filmmaker of all time," Vic said. "I'm taking a class on him in film school right now!"

"Go meet him," we nudged. "Get his autograph."

"He's in the middle of ordering. I'll wait 'til the waiter goes away."

She began the Double Dutch dance of waiting to jump in. *Shoot, the waitress is taking his order. Now he's eating. I think he's with his mother, I feel rude barging over there. Maybe when the plates are cleared.*

And then he was gone. He probably had a house tab there, or never got a check, simply because he was Martin Scorsese. (Again, he wasn't Martin Scorsese.)

Vic punished herself through the rest of her omelet.

"I'm the biggest moron! It goes to show you, when you have a chance, you have to take it."

Well, we agreed, the next time it was "now or never," she'd be bolder. She'd pick "now."

And then, as we left the restaurant, there was Martin Scorsese, right across the street on a park bench. Sitting, taking in life. As great filmmakers do.

"This is it," Stephanie said. She herself never hesitated. "You're gonna say something to him. NOW."

We went with Vic, standing just slightly behind.

"Excuse me. Mr. Scorsese?"

He looked up.

"Hi. I'm so sorry to bother you. I just wanted to say, I'm sorry we were staring at you all through brunch. But I've been studying you in film school and I love your work SO, so, sosososo much."

Marty raised his eyebrows.

"That's funny," he said. "Because I was staring at the three of you. I wondered where you were from, and whether you two"—he eyed Victoria and Stephanie—"were sisters."

"We're *like* sisters," Stephanie said, giving her throaty, toothy laugh.

She and Vic don't really look alike. Stephanie's features are lush and outsized, made for giant sunglasses, like Sophia Loren or Julie Christie; Victoria's are demure, symmetrical, and delicate like Cindy Crawford (who was on her fridge as thinspiration). But they both had a sister-like, model-y beauty and matching, pencil-thin eyebrows. With my rounder face and straight hair, no one mistook me for a third sister, even if I had my own set of those brows. Victoria had taken a tweezer and eyebrow pencil to me and turned my natural, thick 1980s-style caterpillars into a pair of flying seagulls in a plein air drawing. (I've spent hundreds of dollars on serums trying to grow them back, but those '90s upside-down V's were a must-have accessory and made me feel like I had a "look." Almost worth the current patchiness.)

"Your company is right near here, isn't it?" Vic asked Martin.

It was. He asked if we'd like to see it. *Um, yes?* Holy crap. This was the kind of magic that happened when you "went for it."

We walked with Martin past Italian cafés whose owners called out to him: "Buongiorno, signor Scorsese." A legendary actress running with her dogs called out to him from the park. "Yoo-hoo, Marty!" We mouthed "Oh. My. God." to each other behind him.

At his landmark building, he held the door open and ushered us upstairs. His top floor workspace was painted with frescoes of iconic scenes from his films.

Our afternoon plan had been to visit a friend and her parents who'd moved to London from New York. We wanted to ogle their fancy new pad. Instead we spent the whole day at Marty's, talking about life, playing the biggest versions of ourselves, all auditioning to be his favorite.

Victoria identified scenes in the frescoes—even the obscure ones from Marty's box-office bombs.

Stephanie had taken up acting and kept using the language of the craft. "She's so open and raw on the screen." "I love how he uses his instrument." And, most of all, "He makes such powerful choices."

For my part, I tried to be funny. I, too, wanted Marty to spot something in me. I'd recently started landing gigs that let me point at the TV (mostly during commercials) and say, "Hey, I wrote that!" But I still hadn't done work that would harness my talent and make me a wunderkind. At twenty-five I felt the wunderkind window closing. I wanted Marty to turn to me and say, "You know what you should do with your life?"—and then give me the answer: something creative and fulfilling that involved a team laughing and slapping their heads at my brilliance. (*At such a young age. Unfair!*)

Plus, with Vic and Stephanie, I sometimes felt like "the third one." On a recent night at Lucky Strike, Dante, whom I still loved, had told Vic, "My god, you're stunning." Then he'd swiped fries off Stephanie's plate and told her, through gritted teeth, as if in pain, "I'm obsessed with you." To me, he said, "Another soda?"

Now, with Marty, I wanted to stand out as the hidden gem, the sleeper hit. The one whose sizzle is less obvious than her friends', but sneaks up on you and leaves you wondering, "Why can't I stop thinking about this quietly beguiling creature?"

"So." Marty leaned back on his leather sofa. "What do you think of Leonardo DiCaprio? Is he a star? Should I cast him?"

"Oh my god, yessss," Stephanie said, closing her eyes and inhaling through her nose as though breathing in fresh-baked cookies. "I loved his choices in *Gilbert Grape*."

"I loved that movie as a whole," Victoria said, and, in her film-school-articulate, rapid-fire style, explained why.

"I liked Leo's work on the sitcom *Growing Pains*," I joked. "But I preferred Kirk Cameron—and *his* choices."

Marty nodded thoughtfully, missing my irony.

"You know what we don't have anymore?" he pointed at the air. "Real female stars, the kind who are true pretty girls. Like in the '50s. Someone soft. Feminine. A *girl*."

We giggled girlishly. He was out of touch, but it kind of suited him—a legend from a bygone "golden era."

He had us gather around his tape recorder, where he played us an opera he'd had scored for an animated project. We danced to it awkwardly, like your mom's friends at a wedding to "Thong Song."

He asked our ages. Stephanie, almost twenty-seven, was the oldest.

"You know the perfect age for a woman?" he asked, looking right at her. "Twenty-seven."

Stephanie laughed: "Hahahahaha oh my god I love you."

Next, the subject of pot came up.

"I haven't smoked marijuana in twenty years," Marty informed us. "But I happen to have some." He also happened to have a rolling machine. We moved to a round table, where he expertly rolled a joint.

The sun was going down. "Vic," I pointed at my bare wrist. She was the only one with a watch. She shrugged. We couldn't leave now. My friend's number was back at the hotel, so I couldn't call to adjust our evening plans. I was now in hot water, manners-wise, but cared more about milking every minute of our audience with Marty. He still hadn't offered a way for me to tap my talent, but I knew it was in him. And none of us wanted to break the spell, pop the bubble containing us and this show-business god.

Marty lit the joint and took a drag with his thick, wet lips. (Remember, this wasn't Martin Scorsese.) Vic and Steph each took a drag. They looked at me.

I'd never smoked pot before. I hated the smell. A longtime Just Say No nerd, I was scared of drugs. Though I no longer believed pot was a dangerous "gateway drug" that led straight to mainlining heroin, it made me nervous, and I didn't know how to inhale. I'd never even tried a cigarette.

But here, one of history's most revered filmmakers—an icon of '70s counterculture, a contemporary of Jack Kerouac and Hunter S. Thompson, no less—was handing me a joint he'd rolled himself. If not now, when?

I knew not to expect a real high from my first joint. Smoking it with Martin Scorsese—that was the high. The story, the buzz of all this having happened would last long after the stinky weed.

We'd been there for hours. "Hold on," I realized out loud. "Marty, you don't even know our names."

"How about that, you're right." I now contemplate the mind of someone who asks three new friends their ages and not their names. Was he sitting there all day thinking of us as One, Two, and Three? Was he embarrassed like a regular person is when too much time has passed to say, "By the way, what's your name?"

"Before we tell you," I said, in a way I thought coquettish, "you have to guess."

"Okay," he said. "I like this. So, you"—he looked at Victoria— "would be something young and feminine. A true *girl*. You'd be a Barbara."

I snorted. Barbara was, and still is, an aunt's name. *Kids, come out and say hi to Aunt Barbara. Did you send a thank-you note to Aunt Barbara for the sweater? I just got off the phone with Aunt Barbara. She said Uncle Mel needs a pacemaker.*

"And you . . ."

It was my turn.

"Well, Diana's the goddess of knowledge. So I think you're a Diana."

Great. The smart one. Cue flashback to the seventh-grade spin-the-bottle party where Vince Gold's spin landed on me and we went in the closet and shook hands. I wasn't the one you kiss. Just the one you cheat off in math. Now I wanted "Barbara."

"What about me?" Stephanie purred.

He studied her. Her long, dark hair was fastened at the crown with a barrette in East Village hipster style. (The trend: "little-girl chic.") She stared back.

"You, for some reason, strike me as a Francesca."

"Francesca"—as we'll call her here—was the name of his teenage daughter, whom he had cast in a few sexy rom-com roles. She
was the apple of his eye, as they say of daughters whose fathers
seem to find them attractive.

Marty bit his lower lip, holding Stephanie's gaze. She could
keep "Francesca." I wanted to be the favorite, but not in an
incest-y way. (If any part of you wonders, "Wait. *Is* this Martin
Scorsese?" I swear on my life, it's not. I've never met Marty, and
have heard only wonderful things about him.)

It was now 6:10 p.m., and we'd been expected at my friend's
parents' house at 5:30, before dinner. They were probably wondering if we'd gotten lost. Marty swallowed a yawn. Time to go.

He asked for our contact info, which we took turns writing on
his coffee-stained notepad, figuring we'd never hear from him
again. But maybe he'd remember Stephanie if she ever auditioned
for something of his? We hugged him hard at the door and drove
back to the hotel, where I called my friend and apologized for
blowing off her parents to spend the day with someone famous.
"My mom put out a whole cheese platter," she said. "We thought
something terrible had happened to you." My face still prickles
with embarrassment about it.

We returned to New York and regaled everyone we knew with
our Cinderella tale.

Six months later, my phone rang after midnight. I was home in
bed. Caller ID hadn't been invented yet but I took a gamble and
picked up, thinking it was the latest guy who'd promised he would
call and still hadn't.

"Laura?" the phone line crackled. "It's Marty."

He was on his car phone, on the way in from the airport. And
he'd called me! Of all of us. Maybe I was the first one on the list,

and he'd forgotten who was who. Maybe he thought I was the most secretarial, the likely point-person dweeb. *The Diana*. Or, hey, maybe he felt a unique kinship with me. And why not?

He said he wanted the three of us to meet him at two a.m. for "a late dinner" at Il Mulino.

Wow, I thought. *Dinner at two in the fucking morning?* It was such "famous person" thinking. At age twenty-two, we'd have been up for it. But come on—as grown-ass adults over twenty-five? (Never mind that I was, at that moment, in my childhood bedroom, my parents watching Leno on *The Tonight Show* in the next room.) Of course, I was tempted to say yes, suck it up, and put on an outfit. This could take us from "We once met Martin Scorsese" to "We're friends with Marty."

"Aw, I wish," I told him, "but we're all in our pj's."

No doubt he pictured us together, wearing teeny silk nighties and having a squeal-and-giggle pillow fight. Like three soft, feminine Barbaras.

"Okay then. How about another night this week?"

Phew. I hadn't blown it.

He made a reservation at Raoul's, a SoHo institution known for celebrities and steak frites. Raoul's had been there since the '70s, when artists lived in illegal lofts without electricity or plumbing and the neighborhood's cobblestones were smeared with dogshit. It was exactly the kind of old-school place you went with Martin Scorsese. (Or, *not* Martin Scorsese.) We met him at the lobby of his fancy Upper East Side hotel, and he took us downtown in a limo. It felt very *Pretty Woman*.

Over the course of dinner and several bottles of red wine (which I passed on in favor of my no-calorie staple, Diet Coke), Vic and Stephanie worked Marty into a frenzy of sexual possibility. He made frequent references to his apartment "back at The Carlyle." You'd think, when you want to lure someone back to your hotel, you'd mention champagne and chocolate-covered strawberries or the Jacuzzi. Instead, Marty kept dangling SpectraVision, his hotel's cable service provider. "You know, I have three hundred channels," he'd say, refilling Stephanie's wine glass. When Vic mentioned one of his films, he looked at his watch. "Even at this hour, bet we could catch that movie right now on SpectraVision!"

"You know what we should do?" Stephanie said, putting her hand across the table on Marty's forearm. He raised his eyebrows in anticipation. "I think, later tonight, the four of us should go back to your hotel . . . and have a fun . . . sexy . . . crazy . . . hilarious . . . genius . . . all-night . . . *platonic* sleepover."

Through this thought, Marty's expression was like a balloon with a smiley face, inflating breath by breath, the smile and eyes getting bigger and bigger, until Stephanie got to the word "platonic." Then all the air went out and the balloon face went slack.

But he nodded, likely imagining "platonic" was negotiable. "Let's! We can go back and watch SpectraVision." His face brightened again.

I refrained from protesting. Who wants to be the buzzkill and call it a night? I had work due in the morning and I dreaded sleepovers. You wouldn't have guessed it from all the guys I went home with, but I hated sleeping with someone else in the bed. If it had to happen, I at least wanted to know in advance and bring a bag—with underwear, toothbrush, and sleep clothes. If you wear a thong, you can't just go to sleep in your underwear. Could *you* sleep with fabric up the crack of your ass?

There was still time for Marty to get tired and drop the idea. Steph had gotten us on the list for a hot Fashion Week party, so we went there next, excited to walk in with a show-biz deity as our shared date. Linking arms with Marty, we wove through models and famous people and found a spot. The music was kicking: a remix of A Tribe Called Quest. We half-danced, pressed in by the crowd and surrounding Martin Scorsese. He was wearing a black beret, closest thing to a bomber jacket and bullhorn to telegraph "famous director." But among the crush of tall beauties and hipsters in sneakers and Kangol bucket hats, he just looked like some grizzled old guy. It felt like we'd brought our uncle to a mosh pit. We grooved around him with the same joyless tether as when you dance around your purses on the floor.

After that, we hit Bowery Bar, where Marty resumed his full-court press to get us back to The Carlyle. "You think the people-watching *here* is entertaining?" he said as we commented on everyone's outfits. "Wait 'til you see SpectraVision."

I was panicking about the time. It was clear I'd have to be the one to break up the party.

"I wish I could," I said, pouting for effect. "But I have a writing deadline."

I had to write a Top 20 Countdown for VH1's Moon Unit Zappa, famous for being Frank Zappa's daughter and the voice and creator of the valley girl in the song "Valley Girl." I supplied her with lines like, "With another week at the top, this next artist has plenty to crow about. It's Sheryl Crow, and all she wants to do . . . is stay put at number one with 'All I Wanna Do.'"

Marty suggested he could help me with that "back at The Carlyle."

"While they watch SpectraVision, we can knock out your scripts. You know, I helped a certain gal write a certain screenplay for a little movie called . . . *ET.*"

"Oh, wow," I said. "That would be awesome." I didn't mean it. Even if he had come up with the line "Phone home," writing a VH1 countdown was a solitary art, in which you probed that raw, emotional place deep inside yourself for new puns on Hootie and the Blowfish.

Of course, it would've been something to say "Martin Scorsese and I cowrote a script." But this was like having a Michelin-starred chef offer to help you heat SpaghettiOs. Also, I knew once we got to the hotel and turned on SpectraVision, no countdown was getting written. I'd be screwed for my deadline.

"I admire you so much," Stephanie told me. "You're so driven. I love it."

What she meant was, *Shut the fuck up about your scripts. This is my acting career. We're going to The Carlyle.*

Back at Marty's suite, he turned on the TV as promised. "Here we go. SpectraVision." He backed up with his hands out as if he'd just made the perfect fire and clicked it to CNN. Or something in Korean. I only remember being disappointed in the selection. It was the same channel offerings I had at home, except ten of everything. Ten CNNs. Ten MTVs. Ten QVCs. You could buy a ThighMaster or a set of chip clips in any language.

Marty had us all lie down on the bed together. Stephanie, the smart one, popped back up. "I'm going to roll us a joint," she said, and busied herself at the narrow hotel desk near the bed. "I have to go to the bathroom," Victoria said, and popped up as well.

"Don't be too long," I said, as Marty spooned me.

"I have a message for Laura," he whispered, suddenly taking up nautical talk, "coming in at 150 knots."

And then, he blew in my ear.

No one had ever blown in my ear. I'd seen it on *Happy Days*—I think it was one of Richie Cunningham's turn-ons?—and wondered, why does anyone like that? He had a wet mouth. There was sea spray. "I'll be right back," I said. Vic came out of the bathroom, and I got up. It was my turn not to be next to Marty. We had gone from vying for his attention to vying for escape.

"Come here, Victoria," I heard him say as I closed the bathroom door. "I need a girl to hug."

And that's how the next few hours went. Stephanie busied herself just far enough away on other furniture, rolling that joint that would never be complete, while Vic and I took turns on the bed, gritting our teeth through cuddles with Marty. I stressed about the passing hours and diminishing returns. I think we all wondered what our ultimate goal was at this point.

Marty drifted in and out of sleep, but never lost complete consciousness. Every time we left him solo on the bed for more than a second, he would stir and cry out, "I need a girrrrl to hug!"

I know how creepy it all sounds. And sure, it was yuck-o. I don't really know why we even stayed there but it never felt like a threatening situation. It was more ridiculous than anything. "I need a girl to hug!" became our favorite in-joke. At any mention of Marty: "I need a girl to hug!" A guy was lech-y: "He's very 'I need a girl to hug.'" I never felt in real danger that night, except for the danger of insulting Marty or him no longer liking us. And what would even be the consequences there? He hadn't dangled one indication that he would cast us, open doors for us, or even get us into the next *Ninja Turtles* premiere. Plus, let's face it: we'd pursued the guy from a park bench across the Atlantic, where

he was minding his own business, all the way to this moment—
each, in our own way, expecting him to shower us in significance.
To hand us the keys to ourselves, like he was the Wizard of Oz.

Once Marty started to snore, we looked at each other and
mouthed, "Let's. Go."

You'd think that was the end, but Stephanie invited him
months later to one of her loft parties. These were always full
of downtown people. Stylists, DJs, famous yoga teachers, Madonna's baby daddy, and Tabitha, the leather-pants maker to the
stars, who'd designed the chaps Stephanie was wearing at this
very party. Tabitha adopted Marty and left with him. He had a
new girl to hug.

He never gave Stephanie a role, opened film-world doors for
Victoria, or solved the puzzle of tapping my talent. I still had
no idea how to make a lot of money from being my brilliant self
while doing something "entertainment-y." I can't lie, though.
Having this story to tell made me feel a little extra special, even if
it never would have happened to me on my own.

Being a star fucker isn't necessarily about wanting something
tangible from the star. Sure, a premiere invite is nice. A selfie
together can go a long way, especially on your website. (I'm awesome! Famous people agree to stand and smile stiffly with me!)
Mostly, though, it's about thinking certain people have an extra
supply of sparkle and significance they can donate to you, like a
kidney. (Of course, when I say "you," I mean me.) Maybe that's
why everyone wants to meet Oprah, or even just Gayle. It's about
wanting them to *see* you. To single you out and confirm that big
hope: you, no matter how quietly, are a star.

I've heard that when you dream about being friends with
a celebrity, it means you see something in them that exists in

yourself. If so, I share many traits with Beyoncé. Also with Amy Poehler, my old boss, Big Bird, and, yes, Marty. Marty, a man of extraordinary talent and loads of power in Hollywood. But still, in the end, just some man with a thing for soft, feminine, girlish girls . . . to hug. He was no Oprah, and maybe Oprah's no Oprah if you hang out and watch SpectraVision with her. Even so, at least once after that night, I dreamt of Marty picking me up in his limo, this time alone. "You're one of the greats," he told me in one dream. "And I didn't want to say it in front of the others, but it's *you* who's the Barbara." Maybe that's all I ever wanted to hear from Martin Scorsese's thick, wet lips.

. . . Again, it wasn't Martin Scorsese.

Next-Level Dream Job

A popular T-shirt on the Internet says, "My greatest talent is watching 5 years of TV in 1 week." I'm way ahead of you, I can do ten years in two days. Before streaming was a thing, I was doing it old-school, taping and consuming hours and hours of my favorite shows on my combo TV/VCR. (Called a "TVCR." It was the future.) TV: my talent, my passion.

Which brings me back to the saying, "Love what you do and you'll never work a day in your life." Also, "Do what you love and the money will come." In my mid-twenties and unemployed again, I was down for all of that. The problem? What I really loved was watching TV.

Who was gonna pay me for that? "Good work watching *General Hospital*, here's your check. And there's plenty more where that came from. Keep it up, and you're going to be one very rich woman."

Where was *that* job?

I got my answer—or something close—when Adam, a friend from *Spy*, told me about his new job: writing promos at VH1.

"What are promos?" I asked, already feeling a buzz of something good.

"I watch a bunch of TV and come up with those little spots during the commercials that are about the shows."

"Oh my god. THAT'S A JOB?"

He might as well have said, "I live on a cloud made of ice cream."

Here's the thing: It wasn't so much that I didn't want to work. More like, I wanted to be so absorbed in my work—like I had been during my brief stint writing for The Transom—that, rather than work, it felt like watching TV. And, ideally, that work that felt like watching TV would involve watching TV.

I didn't know it, but I was looking for what the Japanese would call my *ikigai*, my "reason for being."

A few months after Evelyn fired me, Adam told me VH1 wanted more promo writers. He brought me in to 1515 Broadway, home of MTV Networks, to meet with the editorial director.

I'd been to the building before, for a few informational interviews with friends of friends. I'd come away with no new career ideas, but when visiting the cafeteria, The Lodge, I had been seduced by its TV-themed food stations (e.g., Stimpy's pizza) and employees in jeans and Doc Martens eating fro-yo. I knew I needed to be there. And finally, here I was for a real interview.

Normally, for an event like this, you'd bring a VHS reel of your spots. But I'd never written one. So I brought my Dewar's advertorial from *Spy*, a few less-funny, more straightforward pieces I'd done for Evelyn, and printouts of my online chats on The Transom.

The editorial director, also a *90210* fan, thought my observations about Brandon Walsh's psycho ex-girlfriend Emily Valentine were funny enough to take a chance on me. She assigned me my first promo. I guess this was the stone-age version of getting hired based on your tweets.

The promo, a "12 Days of Christmas" sweepstakes campaign, was supposed to be a quick, low-budget clip spot. But I didn't understand, and instead wrote a twelve-spot campaign that required a shoot. Since this was the '90s and money came out of the soda machines, the director okayed my high-budget, twelve-spot idea. It was jam-packed with corny gags and wasn't going to win any awards, but I now had a reel and an in at VH1.

I became one of their go-to promo writers—and then some. I got to write for their video countdown shows. A lot of puns, and not my music, but for sure a "How'd you get that job?" kind of job.

My friend Mindy, still at the magazine where I'd been sacked, said, "When I told Evelyn how much you got paid for a single promo, her jaw dropped!" Nothing could've made me happier—except, maybe, working for Nickelodeon, the place Evelyn had suggested my work was more suited for.

I'd grown up on Nickelodeon. Well, if you can count watching a children's network during your high school years as "growing up" on it. Now, I loved Nickelodeon's evening segment, Nick at Nite. They had my favorite old sitcoms, like *Leave It to Beaver*. They also had the best promos. Their spots had attitude. They put a fresh, funny spin on old shows, picking out a detail you might not have noticed, like about Reuben's toupee on *The Partridge Family*. "The Reuben Hair Shift. It's part of our television heritage." Their promos made you feel like an insider for loving old TV. And I wanted to be one of the insiders who wrote them.

And then it happened. In 1995, about a year into my work with VH1, Nickelodeon called. They needed someone to write trivia questions for a radio promotion of *The Munsters*. It was the off-air department. Not on-air, but a small step away.

From a beanbag chair at Nick, I was watching my stack of borrowed *Munsters* tapes—living the dream—when a tall man wandered into the media room looking perturbed. His eyes narrowed at Cousin Marilyn on the screen. He picked up one of the black, pebbled VHS cases and inspected it.

"Oh. So it's you who took all the *Munsters* tapes."

He asked if he could watch them with me, and lowered himself to the other beanbag chair without waiting for an answer.

His name was Bruce. He kept asking me to pause so he could take notes. "Hold on, rewind to that shot of Grandpa Munster. Keep going, keep going . . . nope, missed it. Forward a little."

I asked what he was doing.

"Writing a chapter of the Nick at Nite book. It's a synopsis of every episode."

"They're paying you to watch every episode and sum it up?"

Bruce nodded and finished a note. "Yes, of *The Munsters*. That's my chapter. Okay, you can take it off pause."

This sounded like the job I'd been looking for. Watching old sitcom episodes in close detail, on a beanbag, and then writing short, funny things about them.

"Are there any chapters left to write?"

He said there might be, and led me down the hall to his boss, Tom, who was the editorial director of on-air. *Hello!* He said that yes, there was one chapter left: *Bewitched*. Was I up for watching every episode?

Bewitched, about an ordinary housewife who was also a witch and could make magic by twinkling her nose, was one of my longtime favorites.

"I'm so happy it's *Bewitched*," I told him. "So much better than *I Dream of Jeannie*."

"Careful," Tom said. "Around here, those could be fighting words."

I imagined working in a place where you debated *Bewitched* vs. *Jeannie*, *Jeffersons* vs. *Good Times*, *Brady Bunch* vs. *Partridge Family*. I'd been training for this my whole life.

Tom liked the work I sent him and hired me. I crushed that *Bewitched* chapter. No procrastination, no writer's block, no deadline extensions. It would be my first book credit and, more importantly, my doorway to the hallowed halls of Nickelodeon On-Air Promos, or, as the cool kids called it, Nick On-Air.

Tom gave my name to producers, who started calling me with work. Normally, to be a writer there, you had to start as an intern or production assistant. For once, this late-to-the-party slowpoke had managed to duck under the ropes—albeit without knowing the ropes. My show notes were terrible. Half the soundbites I picked were either off camera or had music playing over them. My scripts clocked in at thirty-five seconds when they needed to be thirty. But I kept getting work.

I was writing spots for *Ren and Stimpy*, *Tiny Toon Adventures*, and other cartoons. I had arrived . . . almost. What I really wanted was to work on the grown-up stuff, for Nick at Nite. I wandered often into Tom's office to hint as much.

One day, he handed me a piece of paper. "Ever watch *Drag-net*? We're doing a goodbye marathon. Why don't you write the promo?"

It's one of the few times in my life I remember thinking, "This is it. This is my shot!"

That's what they say in movies or TV. It's always the plucky, overlooked go-getter waiting to show their stuff. The understudy prays the star will get sick. The rookie cop wants in on the big murder case. The editorial assistant wants their own column. Alexander Hamilton—you know that one. Point is, they all know they can do it, better than anyone. All they need is a shot!

Normally, I was the one told, "You know, you *can* take initiative." But this time? Mmm-mm. Watch out, world.

From the tape library, I took out and watched every single episode of *Dragnet*. I could have created the spot watching three, but I was going all the way. I piled tapes into my tote bag and schlepped them home to the Upper West Side. Walking up Broadway from Times Square, both hands hooked under the straps on one shoulder, I felt like a soldier with a duffel bag, coming home from war.

I read my spot in the writer's meeting. People laughed. An exec looked at me and said, "Who *are* you and where did you come from?" I felt like I was in a movie. About success.

I started getting more Nick at Nite assignments. My first big one was *The Odd Couple*. I watched every episode, sitting at a borrowed desk with headphones on, scribbling show notes on my legal pad, laughing 'til I cried. Sometimes, Bruce, an aficionado of anything made before 1975, sat and watched with me.

On their way out, people asked, "Do you ever go home? Take a break!"

Who was I? I was the me I'd wanted to be, that's who. The me with a work ethic. I had unlocked the secret to my best, most committed self, and it's this: I'm not lazy, as long as I'm obsessed.

My *Odd Couple* spots were a hit. I was offered a regular weekly rate, more than I'd ever earned before, and made part of the team.

I made work friends. We went to The Lodge together and saved each other seats at meetings. I showed up at noon when I wanted to, and sometimes even early, but only when I wanted to. I was assigned the big show launches. *I Love Lucy. Laverne & Shirley. The Bob Newhart Show.* (Though, full disclosure, Tom ended up writing most of that campaign after Bob Newhart read my scripts and sent a note: "Maybe another writer?" They can't all be winners.)

Tom and I spent a boring staff meeting trading a piece of paper back and forth, coming up with scatological names for ice-cream flavors. Stench Vanilla. Who Cut the Cheesecake. Vanilla Fudge Let One Ripple. I was friends with my boss! I alternately thought of him as "my friend Tom, my boss," and "my boss Tom, my friend." Or just, "my mentor." (My first mentor, Lisa, had mostly disappeared. Not for any reason, just, you know, life.)

I loved sitting in Tom's office. As a joke, when I handed him scripts for approval, he'd take out a gigantic red marker and pretend to cross the whole thing out. He taught me rules of comedy and promo writing. "It needs a callback at the end," he'd say, working something out with his pen. Or, "The triple needs to pay off with a bigger surprise."

When he did reject a script, he'd explain why, and even if I fought him, I learned. Sometimes my comedy logic was flawed;

other times, it was simply too absurd, too in-joke-y, or—often the case with my work—too dirty for Nickelodeon. He'd say, "Let's put it in the Fuckelodeon file," which was his binder of scripts that would never fly.

I went on shoots, worked with classic TV stars. Over the years, I taught Sherman Hemsley, aka George Jefferson, to moonwalk. Adam West, TV's original Batman, told me he loved my scripts and—pervy, but thrilling—whispered in my ear, "I'll see you in the Bat Cave." Kelly Ripa, a more contemporary personality, used my name a lot. "Laura, tell me about your job." You could see why she was a star.

My spots were showcased at Promax, which is like the Oscars of promos. I got to go to recording sessions and give "light direction." You couldn't give a read, but you could say, "Can you put more smile into it?" or "Can you lean on the word 'was' instead of 'impressed'?" I got to order lunch from a big binder of menus. Editors at editing houses got to know my work. When I showed up they'd say. "I *thought* this was a Laura Belgray spot."

I bought an apartment. Tom wrote the recommendation letter assuring the board that I had "long-term employment," and I invited all my coworkers to the housewarming.

Entertainment Weekly named Tom on its annual "Hot List" for his work in promos. Promos were hot. I got to tell people, "I write promos for Nick at Nite." When my dad came to take me to lunch, he looked around and said, "Wow, is this place creative! In the '50s, you would've all been blacklisted by McCarthy!"

Most memorably, and touching, the department brought in Tasti D-Lite for my office birthday party. I was known. I was seen. I worked in TV. I was tapping my talent. No one said "We have to find you a better job." I had the coolest job ever.

Sure, I wasn't exactly writing for Letterman like my friend Tim. And someone in the office did say, "This is a temporary job for me. Promos are the lowest form of entertainment." A Hollywood writer friend had told him that. And there was an old-as-dirt (probably forty) producer named Charles who inspired a pact among us young promo people: "Shoot me if I ever become Charles." He stared at the women's chests and lurked behind you for way too long before saying "Hellooooo . . ." but our derision was about him still doing promos . . . at his age! Promos were a stepping stone. You weren't supposed to do them into your golden years, like Charles. (Again, he was probably forty.)

I knew I was supposed to move on, or up, one day. But I didn't want to. I didn't want to become my boss. He had to manage people. I certainly didn't want to be my boss's boss, or anyone whose job was to present graphs of prime-time ratings spikes in the Midwest. But I didn't want to leave, either.

In her 2021 book *Unfollow Your Passion*, my friend Terri Trespicio quoted me saying, "I love stasis." I'm not the person who, when things are good, gets antsy for them to be even better, to "level up." I like *this* level. And back then, at Nick at Nite, I liked *that* level. My late-bloomer, change-fearing self wanted it all to stay the same.

Of course, we know it couldn't and wouldn't. Eventually, there would be reorgs and corporate shuffles. I'd be assigned new bosses. Friends would leave, and I would stay. I'd start getting writer's block and be seen crying in the bathroom because I couldn't think of a good idea to launch *The Jeffersons*. I'd be told I was "bad for morale" with my weird hours and missing paperwork. On a shoot in my early thirties, I would spill a bottle of Wellbutrin in front of Roseanne Barr and feel like an insane hot mess. My personal stock would go up and down, I'd get fired and be brought back. Years would pass. I'd ask a brilliant colleague, "Why aren't you writing TV shows, or your own stuff?" He'd ask, "Why aren't you?"

No good story ends, "Everything was great, and then nothing ever changed. The end." But for right then, it was awesome.

Part III

Commitment-Phobe: A One-Act Play

At twenty-seven, I was sick of sleeping with assholes, thinking I would reform them and get to hear them say, "You've made me a better man." Shocker: no one said that. Clearly, I was doing something wrong. So, when I met Dylan through a work friend and really liked him, I bought *The Rules*, a popular mid-'90s dating book, as an experiment. On the cover, an engagement ring floated above the subtitle: *Time-Tested Secrets for Capturing the Heart of Mr. Right*. Not normally one to abide by rules, much less a book called *The Rules*, I surprised myself and actually followed them: don't be too eager, don't make the first move, no sex before the third date, etc. The basic premise was, don't be a giant ho bag. The only rule I broke was telling Dylan about it soon after we met. He said, "*The Rules*. Isn't that where you can't kiss 'til the second date and the third date is, what—I give you a toaster?"

The Rules worked. Dylan asked me out. Called when he said he'd call. Expressed his feelings. Made me feel like me. He called me "Fireball," a joke about my terrible driving skills. In the middle of Twelfth Street, he stuck a coin to my forehead and doubled over laughing when I kept walking with it stuck there. I could bounce promo ideas off of him. He had hobbies I wanted to copy, like digging up random people's vintage Polaroid photos at the Twenty-Sixth Street flea market and framing them. My friends and family loved him.

I now had my own apartment on Twelfth Street, a great career in promos, and a committed relationship with a brilliant, kind, funny guy.

LIFE: Welcome to adulthood!
ME: Oh wow, no thanks! Pull over, please, I think I'll get out here.

Hmm, said my subconscious, what can we torch? How can I gum up my path into grown-up-ville? Is there a snooze button on this thing?

The apartment, that was safe from self-sabotage. (I'd bought it at twenty-six, only by the grace of my parents' help and '90s real estate prices, so low that if I told you what I paid, you'd walk off into the sea.) I had put maintenance fees on autopay so I wouldn't lose the place to my deranged fear of paperwork. Although, come to think of it, I would later jeopardize my good standing in the building by throwing myself a thirtieth birthday party with lots of dancing on the bare parquet. I got a strong warning for violating the rule of 80 percent covered floors. What else: Slow down the career? That could be arranged later, too. Patience! One fuckup at a time. The relationship—that seemed like the best place to start.

I first felt the stirrings of not-longing one summer night when Dylan and I had talked about having dinner. Semi-forgetting but not really, I worked late screening *Mary Tyler Moore* episodes at the office and then took my time walking home, stopping at Barney's on Seventeenth Street. (RIP.) I spent two hours trying out Bobbi Brown lipsticks and Clergerie slides and got home to a series of "Where are you, I thought we had plans" messages on my answering machine.

I called back and asked, "Would it be okay if we didn't get together tonight?" Dylan said, "No, it wouldn't be okay." I thought, *He* needs to read *The Rules.*

Another evening, on the way to dinner, I looked at his vintage plaid sports jacket and asked, "Aren't you going to be warm in that?" It was 80 degrees out. He rolled his eyes and shook his head to himself. "I think what you mean is, 'I hate that jacket.'"

I denied it, but of course he was right. It made him look like Rodney Dangerfield. It did look warm, though.

I started feeling really tired, all the time. He'd say, "What do you want to do tonight?" and I'd say, "I don't know. For some reason, I'm so—"

"I know," he'd finish. "You're tired. Maybe you should see a doctor."

Something was off, but I didn't admit it to myself until Dylan was in LA for work and my friend Dana and I went to his apartment to feed his cats. Dana's eyes went right to something I'd always ignored—a whole shelf of classic black-and-white composition books. Dylan's journals. All lined up, pages puffed by his diligent ballpoint scribbling. A shelf of private thoughts, probably some about me.

Dana asked if I'd read them, and gasped when I said no. She had a long rap sheet of reading her boyfriends' journals to see if they were cheating or liked someone else.

"Look at them," she said, ducking as Costello the cat jumped over her head from a bookcase shelf. "There must be thirty there. You're not even tempted to peek?"

"Nope," I shrugged. Not because I was a good person who minds her business. On the contrary, I'm the nosiest bitch around, which made it all the more worrisome that, truth be told, I had zero interest. And that's when I realized Dylan didn't make me feel the way I wanted to, which was clingy and desperate. I needed a guy who made me feel obsessed, who drove me to act insane and violate his privacy.

Instead, this one made me feel safe, yuck. He was—shudder— loving and trustworthy, which made me feel itchy and crowded. Reciprocity: overrated! I didn't have it in me to break up, so I stayed the course but kicked him out of bed. Not figuratively. I mean for real.

We'd been talking about marriage, but I wasn't there yet, nor sure if I ever would be, because I never got a good night's sleep with him in the bed. I've always slept better alone, still do; and, let's face it, no matter how madly in love you are, there's no better, dead-to-the-world sleep than a night solo and starfishing on a hotel-room king. That said, Dylan was a big guy who snored and consistently found his way to the center of the mattress. Throughout the night, heaving with all my might, I would nudge and nudge him toward the edge so I'd have some room.

Sometimes, I did this in my sleep, which is how I woke up one night to find Dylan out of bed, limping around the room and collecting his clothes.

"What are you doing?" I croaked. I was so annoyed, being woken up. Didn't he know I was so tired?

"You pushed me off the bed," he said. "I have a huge gash in my knee."

Oh.

I turned on the light. He was really bleeding. I'd been aware that my metal bed frame was dangerous. I'd nicked myself on it countless times while making the bed. The thing had so many sharp edges, it was like sleeping on a giant steak knife. A real adult would have gone out and bought a bed skirt six blocks away at Bed Bath & Beyond.

Dylan hobbled down the street to the St. Vincent's emergency room and got stitches—by himself. I, meanwhile, went back to sleep, grateful for more room to spread-eagle. Not my proudest moment as a girlfriend. *The Rules* had worked, all right. So well, *I'd* become the asshole.

We tried making it work. Started swing lessons, which he hated. I used up the book of lessons he'd paid for, by myself. For work, he spent the winter in Nova Scotia, and I meant to visit him. Instead, I sent him Swiss Miss hot chocolate packs, a gesture I somehow believed super thoughtful. What says "I love and miss you" better than mini marshmallows? He sent me a Valentine by fax, and I had to go to a copy place to receive and pay for it, which felt laughably unromantic. Secretly, I was thrilled. For once, he was the one who'd screwed up, not me. You know things aren't great when you're stoked your boyfriend screwed the pooch on Valentine's.

One day, when he came back and the weather got nice, he suggested we go for a walk.

Hashing out the meaning of "taking a break"—the status we agreed on only because "breakup" sounded too harsh, and maybe my going back to therapy would help?—we walked fourteen times around Washington Square Park, until Dylan announced that his corduroy pants were chafing his scrotum.

After taking a break faded gently to breakup, Dylan partnered with a writer/actress friend and produced a two-person play called *Sleep Sack*. A one-night engagement at a theater in Greenwich Village, it was about a woman who can't get a good night's sleep with her bed-hog of a boyfriend, so she makes him start sleeping in a confining sack made out of sewn-together sheets. Spoiler: while in the sack, he falls off the bed.

Watching from my seat, as the actor playing Dylan rolled and thudded to the floorboards in a pool of stage light, I was filled with both guilt and pride. Pride because I couldn't not feel a touch giddy with importance, seeing my own life played out in front of a paying audience. Guilt because . . . I was a total fuckface. I wondered, for the millionth time, "What's wrong with me? Why couldn't I be more into him?"

Successful, devoted, endlessly curious, disciplined about turning his life into art: Dylan was what anyone would call "a keeper." One that I, for a change, actually could have kept. And yet here I was, with commitment issues so deep, they were being acted out on the fabled New York City stage. I'd turned an easy boyfriend into literal relationship drama.

I knew parting ways was the right move for both of us, though. It goes without saying that he deserved better. And I wanted, maybe even deserved, to feel crazy about someone in a way I couldn't summon for him, and I never truly wanted him back. Plus, I loved having the whole mattress to myself. Maybe that's why the next time I shared my bed, it would be with someone I couldn't keep in it. And *The Rules* could suck it.

He's Never Going to Leave Her

"Don't fall in love with your dance instructor," an old man warned as I came out of a ballroom lesson. He'd been watching through the studio window. "Don't worry," I laughed. "I won't."

It was 1999 and I'd continued the lessons Dylan and I had started before we broke up. When we'd first enrolled, the movie *Swingers* had come out, and everyone was swingin'. (Not to mention, quoting the line "You're so money.") At a wedding, a couple from our table rocked a few moves they'd learned at Arthur Murray, and my mind was blown. I said, "We need to do that."

Dylan was game to try, but quit after two lessons. He said it reminded him of "being on the boat and getting yelled at" by his dad. In other words, not so money. I, on the other hand, caught on fast and was instantly hooked. I wanted to get great at it. I started taking lessons every week, and then, because I'm Queen Obsesso, every day.

I was already known for coming to the office late. Now, I was also the one who left early. "Bye, see you tomorrow," I'd say at the elevator bank, scripts left unwritten at my desk, black Mary Jane ballroom shoes sticking out of my bag. And then I raced downtown, to dance.

At work, I was starting to worry I'd peaked. Promo ideas had once flowed out of me like an uncapped hydrant. Now, coming up with something fresh felt like squeezing that last nub of toothpaste from the tube. I was stuck and frustrated with myself. On the dance floor, meanwhile, I got to see progress every day, same feeling as learning to bike or swim as a kid. Even though I was far from graceful—still the case, I'll trip over so much as a Q-Tip—I had a hidden talent for following steps. It made me feel like a natural genius. Just the high I'd been jonesing for: *Look Mom, I'm doing it!* Plus, being led and twirled by a strong partner? Nothing beat it. Like a ride at Six Flags. Best of all, it burned calories and I could skip the gym.

At first, I took privates with Fred. Only Fred, had to be Fred. I'm a one-teacher gal. I spent every penny I earned on lessons, after maintenance fees and toilet paper.

Fred told corny jokes and slapped his own knee. He wore a blousy patterned shirt tucked into black rayon pants, the kind you'd call "slacks." He made theatrical faces and ballroom-y flourishes when he danced, and insisted I learn the rhumba, foxtrot, and waltz, when all I wanted was swing and salsa. He performed an embarrassing showcase at The Duplex, a local gay bar. It was a one-man history of dance that included a routine to "Night Fever" where he pointed up and down like John Travolta, and one to rap that today would be the top GIF of "white man breakdancing." I had dragged Vic, who said, "I loved it, it was so comprehensive!" She could always find a positive spin. "And he's so dorky, it's almost cool?"

Emphasis on *almost*. Fred was not my type. Still, I thought about him way too much, and, I guess, had a little crush. Was I "in love with him"? Fine, okay, maybe the old man was right.

Because it happens. You fall in love with your dance instructor. Or your therapist. Your heart surgeon. Your plastic surgeon, your professor, your boss. Your contractor. You fall in love with the person who holds the key to the person you want to be. That's why it's a cliché: because it happens all the time.

An even bigger cliché—again, a true one—is dating a married man, losing yourself in his life, and crying that he still hasn't left his spouse.

Could I nail two clichés at once? Why yes, I could.

One Saturday, as I stood at the front desk to re-up my lessons with Fred, the door of the main ballroom opened. Inside, a crowd of young people were spinning in their sneakers and rolling their hips and shoulders, hunched low and sexy, to a catchy salsa beat. And yes, I know "catchy salsa beat" makes me sound like a 1980s news anchor talking about what's hip and hot. Regardless, it was a world apart from the ballroom-y style Fred had been teaching me, which I suddenly realized was stick-up-the-ass. I didn't want to dance like him. I wanted to dance like *these* people.

I asked the desk person, "What's that in there?"

"They're a salsa school called Razzle Dazzle," she told me. "Here every Saturday."

The next weekend, instead of booking a lesson with Fred, I went into the main ballroom and handed a twenty to a large, middle-aged man with an '80s mustache. And that's when I entered my next relationship.

Antonio liked to say I "approached him." I'd call it an acciden-
tal signal. I'd been attending Razzle Dazzle classes for a couple
of weeks when, one day after class, I found him sitting at a sticky
cocktail table counting money. It was the first time I'd spotted
him by himself that day, an opening to thank him for the class.

He was like a big teddy bear, if teddy bears had mustaches and
sweated profusely. And look, I'm not one to judge about sweat.
Once I got good enough to spin many times, my sopping-wet ponytail sprayed everyone in a ten-foot radius. I was a human lawn
sprinkler. But Antonio was always sweaty, even sitting still. There
was something about him, though—the way he led his classes,
counting out the beat in his booming voice: "Two three four, six
seven eight"; the way he made me feel whenever he picked me to
demonstrate a turn. I was a beginner, but in his strong, guiding
arms I felt like a gliding, twirling ballroom diva.

"Hi, sweetie," he said, glancing up at me from his fistful of
bills. "You moved great today."

"I did? Thank you!" He'd forgotten my name. And I'd heard
him say the same thing to many beginners who I didn't think
moved great at all. But I blushed at the compliment anyway. And
sat on his lap. Still don't know what I was thinking. I just did it. I
wasn't meaning to flirt. It was more like sitting on Santa's lap. Or
a fluffy sofa. Platonic.

He blinked in surprise, patted me on the back, and stood up
with me. "You know my wife Astrid, right?"

I looked where he was looking, to the statuesque, curly-haired
dance instructor I'd seen teaching the more advanced students.
I had not realized they were married. And I'd never really reg-
istered the design on his T-shirt: a silhouette of a fat man dancing with a thin, curvy woman. Above the couple: the words,

MR. AND MRS. RAZZLE DAZZLE. Below, in quotation marks: "ADD A BIT OF SPICE TO YOUR LIFE." And that's exactly what I did.

I emailed Antonio to ask whether there would be class Memorial Day weekend, and he wrote back.

> **HI SWEETIE YOUR REALY STARTING TO MOVE MUCH
> BETER:) I LIKE THAT SEXY HIP ROLE
> ALSO WHEN YOU SAT ON MY LAP. WOW:)**

I'm judgy about spelling and was horrified both by his typing and the realization I'd given him the wrong message, sitting on his lap. The next class, I decided, I would be all business.

When I got there that Saturday, I went straight to the back of the studio to fill my water bottle. Antonio was sitting alone in a booth eating soup. I could smell it. Beef and vegetable.

"Hi, sweetie." His deep voice carried easily over the salsa music.

"Oh, hey." I said it like I hadn't noticed him there, and stood at the water fountain, nervous to go closer.

He smiled like he'd seen my worry and thought it was silly, and beckoned with his head.

"Come over here." I obeyed. He slid over and I sat down.

"Now let's do this for real," he said, and kissed me on the lips, opening his mouth. I was too startled to pull away. I felt the mustache and tasted the soup. I didn't know whether to be turned on or repulsed. It was a combo of both. Plus terrified. What the fuck? What about "Mrs. Razzle Dazzle?" I'd seen her on my way in.

He read my thoughts. "Astrid and I don't talk, you know. We have no relationship."

As usual, my window had closed to say "Beat it," "This can't happen," "Get lost, motherfucker." The sensible person would have stopped coming to this class after reading his one suggestive email. Not me. I could not miss dance!

Right then, Astrid rounded the corner, all limbs and Lycra and hair. "Hi. I'm getting ready to start the class, so . . ."

Her tone was brusque, no warmth. She folded her arms.

"Yup, I'm finishing up," Antonio told her, spooning up soup.

"Sorry to interru-upt," she sang, mock-polite, turning on her heel—which she did literally, in actual four-inch dance heels. Straight as a pin. Zero wobble.

Antonio turned to me. "That's the most we've spoken all week."

He tilted his head back and poured the last of the soup into his mouth from the container. He tapped the bottom with his finger to hasten that last chunk of beef to his waiting tongue, and then plunked down the carton, satisfied.

"See you inside, sweetie."

He stood, shaking cracker crumbs off his shirt, then winked, walked off, and left a pile of garbage on the table. Empty soup pint, paper bag, crackers, banana peel, plastic spoon slick with or-ange beads of grease. As I would come to do many times, I cleaned up his shit. My knees trembled and my hands were icy cold.

No way. Not doing this, not with him.

But of course, I was. He gave me no choice. I mean, that's a lie, I wasn't sold into human trafficking, I was wooed with private salsa instruction. Antonio started meeting me before class to help me learn to spin, get the rhythm of dancing on 2 (the second beat, harder to catch). And, Antonio said, "to move sexy and get rid of all that awkwardness Fred taught you." I couldn't believe

I'd been into Fred. I wasn't into Antonio, either, but even while I was grossed out by him, he grew on me.

We started IM-ing each other every night on AOL. I both dreaded his messages and sprung to my laptop for them. He'd start:

> **RZLDZL:** WHAT ARE YOU WEARING
> **RZLDZL:** SOMETHING SEXY I HOPE HAHAHA
> **ME:** NOT UNLESS YOU CONSIDER RATTY SHORTS AND A T-SHIRT SEXY
> **RZLDZL:** YOU CAN DO BETTER OR I'M LOGING OFF
> **ME:** OK, OK I'M WEARING A TOWEL
> **RZLDZL:** THAT MORE LIKE IT
> **RZLDZL:** I WANT TO TAKE A TOWEL OFF
> **RZLDZL:** BE WITH ME LAURA
> **ME:** SORRY, I HAVE THIS LITTLE RULE, ABOUT NOT BEING WITH GUYS WHO ARE MARRIED.
> **RZLDZL:** GOOD NITE LAURA
> **RZLDZL:** THATS ENOUGH! LETS NOT TALK ANYMORE
> **RZLDZL:** I HAVE A RULE!
> **ME:** HUH? ARE YOU MAD NOW? LET'S TALK ON THE PHONE.
> **ME:** HELLO? WILLING TO TALK ON PHONE?

That's how it always went. Push, pull. He'd go away and come back.

> **RZLDZL:** I LOVE YOU LAURA
> **RZLDZL:** YOUR MY FINAL DESTINATION

RZLDZL: I WANT TO TAKE A TOWEL OFF

RZLDZL: IM POLE VAULTING OUT THE WINDOW

ME: WHAT DO YOU MEAN?

RZLDZL: MY HARDON

RZLDZL: SO BIG I CAN POLE VAULT ON IT

RZLDZ: BE WITH ME

(SILENT GAG.)

ME: NOT LIKE THAT, YOU'RE MARRIED.

The married thing was a ruse. If I'd been into him, that detail probably wouldn't have stopped me. I'm not proud of it. I thought if someone's marriage was in trouble, they were up for grabs. Especially if they were as old as Antonio and Astrid, forty-five and thirty-five. Ancient, why even bother? Astrid would later tell me, "One day when you're a wife, you'll understand." Now that I am, I very much do.

"Life is simple," Antonio said during one of our lessons, leading me in a klutzy spin. "Shoulders back, that's better. You make me happy. But I can't keep doing this friend shit. I want to take a towel off and make love to you. It's what adults do, my heart."

"I know, it's just . . . I'm still getting over Dylan," I lied. "I need to take this slow."

"I understand. And I need to take some time for myself, so our little dance lessons will have to stop."

No, no. I needed my lessons. Everyone else was ahead of me. They could double-spin and had so much style. I was desperate to look like they did. Plus, he made me feel special and wanted. I loved being with him. I just didn't want to *be* with him.

Maybe it was missing him during a week in Cape Cod with my family. Maybe it was a summer of him wearing me down and holding my private dance lessons hostage. Maybe it was the alcohol. I'm not sure what made me cave, but somehow a night out with him and his friends Frank and Joey got him what he wanted—behind a diner in New Jersey.

First, we drove to a place called Club Drama. On the way, Ricky Martin's "Livin' La Vida Loca" blasting on the car stereo, Frank and Joey passed deodorant back and forth, jamming it up their shirts and then offering it to Antonio. He did the same, while I asked myself, "What is my life right now?" A summer ago, my boyfriend and I were sharing popcorn at Film Forum, and here I was in a car with three guys sharing a Mennen Speed Stick. When we got to the club, after plying me with vodka tonics and making out with me at the bar, Antonio danced with me and said, "Oh boy, we've got work to do." Several hours later, we hit the diner. As soon as we'd settled into the booth, Antonio asked Frank and Joey to excuse us while we went "to get some air."

"Take your time," Joey winked.

"Yeah," Frank said. "Really breathe in *that air.*" They laughed and high-fived.

It was three a.m. He took my hand and led me behind the diner, where the dumpsters were.

"Good," he said, sniffing the air. "The garbage isn't out here yet."

There was no one around. After a little making out and finger action, Antonio pulled me behind a Jeep. I faced him to kiss, but he turned me around and raked his hands over me from behind.

"Bend over," he ordered, already pushing me lightly.

I put my hands on the car. It was filthy.

I asked if he had protection. Though I was thinking, *Not now, not here behind a diner. I can't believe this is me, doing this.*

"Don't worry. Just three strokes."

I heard his zipper and felt him hiking up my skirt. I wondered how much of my ass was visible from the street, even with his massive form behind me.

Antonio thrust himself inside me. It was more than three strokes. "Oh shit, you feel good!" he yelled.

He pulled out just in time and, I hoped, for the last time. Usually, if you let someone fuck you behind a diner, it was a good way of not seeing them again. Like when you blew your old babysitter in the stairwell.

Antonio zipped up and said, "You made love to me beautifully."

Which part of it had *I* done? Unclear.

"Shouldn't we have used a condom?" I asked. "I mean, we haven't discussed sexual history."

"My sexual history, my heart, is ten years of marriage." He was annoyed. "You know how many girls approach me? I turn them all down. Except you." He was forever making a case for what a hot ticket he was. I had to admit, I had seen his female students ask to walk out with him, join him in the park for yoga, help with his website, anything they could do to be around him after class. In marketing, it's called "social proof," and I was a sucker for it. I'd started to see him as kind of . . . I dunno. Hot.

Inside, we rejoined Frank and Joey, who were eating cheese fries. Frank was telling how he'd gotten some girl's number and was planning to take her out for lobster.

"Oh yeah! My man," Joey said, high-fiving Frank.

"I love lobster!" Antonio said. "And fried shrimps!"

He leaned in to me and whispered, "You felt so good. I can still smell your scent on me."

Two choices: revisit that night forever with a shiver of disgust and shame—that time I let a middle-aged guy with a wife stick it in me behind a New Jersey diner—or replay it in my mind as a dirty, sexy adventure.

I chose option two and let Antonio become my boyfriend. To make it official, he bought me a beeper. So I could call him, not anytime, but anytime his wife wasn't around.

Soon, I was faced with coming out to my friends. I staggered the process, telling some I'd only kissed Antonio, some that I'd fooled around with him, and a select few that we were sleeping together and practicing turn patterns in just our skivvies and tube socks (his).

Soon enough, they were all clued in. The scent on my clothes alone gave me away: a combo of Antonio's military-grade cologne and his favorite restaurant, BBQ, which he called BBQ's. He invited everyone after class, and I'd have to share him and pretend we weren't together. He'd palm a ten-spot to the manager for his favorite table like it was Windows on the World, and then order a piña colada the size of his head, vegetable tempura, barbecue, and a Caesar salad that was 98 percent dressing. Forking through the glop, he'd say, "Dig in, guys! The best part is, it's healthy." On the way out, I'd sniff my sleeve. Chicken and rib combo.

My high school crew stopped inviting me to dinners. They got used to me blowing them off for dance and no longer bothered trying, plus they didn't approve. I saw them exchange looks as I went to call Antonio when my beeper went off, like I was a doctor. Or when I told them about Astrid's latest threatening phone message, warning me to stay away from her husband. Dana would say, "She's not a cartoon character. She's a woman trying to protect her marriage from an interloper."

"They're separated, though," I kept saying. That's what Antonio maintained, and what I told everyone, including my parents.

It was a tough story to stick with when they lived together and
Astrid referred to Antonio as her husband, and he to her, publicly, as his wife. In front of me, he'd stumble. "Astrid, my w—
my dance partner." He promised Astrid would be moving out
as soon as she found an apartment and could "get on her feet."
I couldn't see that if that day came, we'd still be all secrets and
beepers. Being a couple was their whole brand image. With me
and Antonio out in the open, promoters might drop them. Even
their most loyal students would go to Antonio's rival, who was
known as "The Mambo King."

Victoria didn't love my situation, but she came to Antonio's
salsa and hustle classes, even brought friends. "When I get to
dance with him, I totally get it!" she said. "He's such a good
dancer, it's actually really sexy." Stephanie said, "I love seeing
you have a crush on your man." My sister came to his classes and
laughed at his jokes. When he taught, he was at his most compel-
ling. Thank god a few people understood his appeal.

My parents tried. When my mom first met him, she said,
"There must be something . . . you like about him . . . very much!"
Her voice got higher and higher throughout the sentence. It was
the same way she'd say, "Oh! You . . . got . . . a haircut!" when she
hated my haircut. Beyond Antonio being one and a half times my
age and wearing a wedding ring, he called my mom "sweetie."
Having worked in the recording industry and politics during the
Mad Men era, she'd spent her whole adult life recoiling from men
who call you sweetie—as they eyeball your tits and ask you to
fetch their coffee.

My father looked for common ground, in the same way each
time. "Antonio, you were in the military, yes?" Like anyone who's
served, Dad liked to bond on this topic, even though, for the

Korean War, he'd been stationed in Hawaii, after the fighting. He hadn't had to do much more than take hula lessons on the beach.

Dad would ask, "Antonio, remind me what you did in Vietnam."

The Marines, Antonio would say, doing recon.

"And what did that consist of?"

"Well, there were two groups. One was there to search, and the other was there to destroy."

"I see. And which were you?"

"*Destroy.*"

Antonio articulated the word with extreme mouth work, as though to someone lip reading across the street.

Sometimes, he added that he had "fifty-two kills" on his belt.

My dad would nod, a smile forming to let us know a good one was coming: "Have you seen *my* belt? It's a lanyard belt Laura made for me at camp."

When my family went out to dinner, Antonio ordered every side. "Let's get the potatoes, too, for the table, just to taste." He always said "for the table" and "just to taste" in the spirit of someone who's paying, but he never did even though he could have. (He had an all-cash business and a lucrative nonprofit that seemed to me to operate only right before an audit.) Which was fine, just don't act like you're paying and order the whole menu on someone else's dime.

I wanted them to be proud of him. "Antonio's salsa school is one of the best known in the country," I said more than once. One time, he told me, "Tell your parents to watch Maury Povich tomorrow. Razzle Dazzle is going to be on." They dutifully tuned in, excited to see my boyfriend dance on TV. Instead, it was his wife who came out, dancing with one of the team members as part of an episode called, "Is It a Girl, or Is It a Guy?" "That's a guy, Maury," the crowd yelled. "I can see her Adam's apple!" Afterward, on the phone, my mom said, "That . . . was . . . interesting!" She also verified, "So that was, uh . . . Antonio's, um . . . separated . . . wife, ex, something or other?"

I fantasized about quitting promos and running away with Antonio, maybe to Italy, where they loved salsa, didn't care about monogamy, and wouldn't ask what everyone else asked when we turned up at dance things together: "Where's Astrid?" In the beginning, we did run away, to Orlando. Spent four days at his favorite getaway, Universal Studios. Rides and fried food—not my bag, but being alone with him was. I was in the middle of a work project I had no business leaving, and called in from a series of pay phones throughout the park. Tom, my boss, said, "I can't hear you over the noise in the background. It sounds like . . . dinosaurs?" Career tip: Don't call work from outside the Jurassic Park ride.

My life with Antonio lasted two and a half years. In the beginning, before he started screwing other people, he stayed most nights at my place. He had a key, but I left the door open at all times. I liked it when he walked right in and said, "Honey, I'm ho-ome," in a Ricky Ricardo accent. He kept his favorite limoncello in my freezer. I made sure he had a banana and sandwich to fuel up for class. I guess I was playing wife where I could.

I inserted myself into his business, spying on his rival's class (which, honestly, was better). I brought back turn patterns and solo footwork, or "shines," to add to the Razzle Dazzle syllabus. I was great at learning shines and wished that could be my job. I became Antonio's co-teacher and part of the team, even though I still moved awkwardly and had no style. For someone who loved to belong, I sure wedged myself into a scene where I didn't, at all. The students and team members who were loyal to Astrid didn't like our closeness and called me "Dirty Girl"—because I was sweaty, and probably because they thought I was a whore. They didn't even know that inside my dance bag, dirty dance T-shirts moldered with a rotting banana. Perfect metaphor for my life at the time.

At work, I got (sort of) fired, demoted from permalance, with its guaranteed pay and sweet health plan, to independent contractor. They were tired of chasing me for my timesheets and my ever-shrinking hours. Tom said he'd wanted to defend me, but had to ask himself, "When was the last time Belgray wrote a great spot?" I did redeem myself, scripting a sales tape that won Best in Show at Promax, the industry's top award. It was a rap, which I poured myself into writing at the height of my Antonio misery, surrounded by rhyming dictionaries and Kleenex.

I cried all the time. Months, then years, had gone by, and he was still with Astrid. Worse, he was often withholding, and didn't pick up my many, many calls in a row. Victoria patiently explained, on repeat, that Antonio was living a "bifurcated experience." She also quoted *When Harry Met Sally*, where Carrie Fisher's character keeps realizing, of the married man she's seeing, "He's never going to leave her." And Meg Ryan—Sally— tells her each time, "Of course he isn't."

Antonio lied constantly, about everything. Once, he told me he was in Rome 'til Friday. I checked his itinerary with an airline agent, convincing her I was immediate family, and found out he'd already come home Tuesday. At a salsa conference in Puerto Rico with me and the whole team, he told me he was tired and going to bed. When I learned he'd gone down the street for dinner with a bunch of people, I stormed over to the restaurant and screamed at him in front of two old guys known as "The Kings of Cha Cha." As one does. He told me he had the two thousand dollars I'd loaned him to make instructional salsa tapes, ready to pay back, all in cash. Next thing I knew, he'd, quote, "lost the money," and it was my fault. "I left it in the fucking cab," he said, "because you called with some bullshit and distracted me." He blamed anyone but himself for his messes. He often shook his head, looked upward to God, and asked, "Why me?" When he was late and missed a flight: "Why me?" When his team members quit after he consistently blew off rehearsals. "Why me?" When I was upset he'd lied. "Why me?" Like it was all just rotten luck.

My therapist, Emily, told me, "He sounds like a sociopath." She might have said it in response to a story of him lying, or it might have been when I told her he made sure no one blocked his view at the movies by pouring Coke on the seat in front of him. In her non-judgy way, she noted that this all-consuming relationship had dragged on for quite some time. She reminded me of things I'd wanted to do, like write a screenplay. "I'm not here to tell you what to do," she said. "But I do believe in timelines."

I was an obsessed, clichéd mess. Everyone had theories about me: I liked the challenge and misery of unavailable men; it was secretly about exercise and weight; it was another of my weird phases; I was going through some kind of late rebellion.

I'd say E, all of the above—though the "rebellion" part wasn't about dating someone to upset my parents and thwart their expectations. I hated upsetting my parents, hated when my mom asked, in that halting, rising voice, "Are . . . you . . . um . . .

happy?" What I was really rebelling against, and thwarting, was myself.

In the end, I will say, I got pretty damn good at salsa. A few times at socials, with a good enough partner, I even had a crowd form around me. Unfortunately, they would back up when my ponytail sprayed them with sweat. Other than that achievement, Antonio and all the drama he brought were an effective way to sideline my life, put everything on pause. Writing, friendships, growth, success. In a way, our relationship was a break, a vacation—if perhaps the world's worst vacation. The kind where, instead of your luggage, you lose yourself.

How I Met My Husband

My husband and I first met at a birthday party on a boat, sailing around New York Harbor on a perfect summer night just before 9/11.

That's the wedding toast version.

The real story of how we got together defies every nugget of self-help and dating advice on the Internet, on the newsstand, or on the shelves of Barnes & Noble. You know the deal:

"You have to radically love yourself before someone else can love you."

"If you stay with the wrong person, your life won't have room in it for the right one."

And what about this nonsense—

"Making out with strangers every night and giving blow jobs isn't the path to success."

Okay, so that's not in any book, but when I was living at home in my early twenties and out 'til four a.m., I used to tell my dad

I was "networking." He didn't buy it, didn't think walking from bar to bar in Daisy Dukes and a Lycra crop top, looking like—in his words—"an Eleventh Avenue hooker," was getting me anywhere. Well guess what, Dad? It got me a husband.

Not on its own, mind you. There were other key ingredients to attracting The One—like being a fucking mess in a sad, low place. I was thirty-one years old, I'd been with Antonio for over two years, and he was cheating on me. I wanted him to be mine alone. I didn't want to marry him, but I wanted *him* to want that. My clothes always smelled of BBQ, sweat, his cologne, and obsession. Not by Calvin Klein. Just literal, "where've you been and why didn't you answer my seventeen calls" obsession. That was my scent.

The final key factor? Going out to find a good time on one of the darkest days in our nation's history. Worked for me! Who's to say you can't do the same? Here's how.

During 2001, the third year of my relationship with Antonio, I reconnected with my old friends Jim and Sammy from my "lost year" (excuse me, *networking* year) a decade before, when I thought bar owners were gods.

Sammy had now opened a restaurant in Chelsea. We'll call it The Purple Squirrel. ("The Squirrel" for short.) Jim and I met up there whenever Antonio was traveling or "with his daughter"—his favorite ruse for fucking other people. You can't pester a man who says he's having dinner with his only child. You don't ask why you're not invited, either. Especially if they're supposedly at Teriyaki Boy, where you won't set foot after you ate ten of their seaweed salads in one meal because it was half the price of most seaweed salads, and spent the night vomiting seaweed. But I digress.

Unlike most of my friends, who'd faded out during the crying-over-my-shitty-boyfriend phase, Jim liked hearing me talk about Antonio. He understood the attraction. I told him how powerfully Antonio steered me on the dance floor, how he would say, "Sit on my dick," how every boyfriend before him now seemed as alpha as an overcooked noodle in the rain. Jim was a dirty bird. He got it. Spending time with him, I felt more "me" than I'd felt since my first mambo with Antonio's moustache.

Jim invited me to Sammy's fortieth, at the restaurant and then a chartered boat. It fell on a dance-class night, so I was torn. I jealously pictured Antonio demonstrating the cross-body lead with some cuter, more rhythmically inclined girl. "Do that hip roll again so everyone can see how you move," he might say, eyeing her tight, rhinestoned jeans. Plus, if I missed a night, I couldn't get better at salsa. And if I got good enough, Antonio was going to take me as his dance partner to Paris, Milan, wherever promoters flew him. If I skipped class, how would I reach that level?

But then one night at Antonio's favorite BBQ, after a joyless horror movie about evil nuns, Antonio sucked down a piña colada as big as a hot tub and declared, "The scary rosaries shit was so well done." We had such different taste. I pushed down a wave of gloom.

"Babe," he said, "you could write something like that in your Oscar-winning book."

"Oscars aren't for books," I reminded him.

I decided I would skip dance for the first time in over two years and go to the party. I wanted to meet people who got me.

The first person I met at the party was sharp and funny and looked like Flea from the Chili Peppers. We leaned against the bar and discussed 1980s after-school specials about drugs, a topic on which I could hold an impromptu TED Talk. It turns out Steven, whom I hadn't met, was watching jealously. It's now part of our lore. Steven tells friends, "I saw Laura talking, talking, talking to him and said to my friend Alicia, 'Who's that? I want to fuck her.'" (*New York Times* Vows section—you taking notes?)

I wouldn't have guessed fucking women was Steven's bag. Why? Let's start with his actual bag: a minimal, canvas tote. "Do they make that for men?" friends ask him, but he doesn't care if it's femme. He shakes his head sadly at their cluelessness. "It's Japanese." I've tried buying the most girly umbrellas I can find to deter him from stealing and losing them. Butterflies, flowers, vaginas (not really vaginas, but I'd give it a try). He still steals and loses them. He doesn't mind girly.

A smaller group of us from the bar moved on to the next leg of the party, boarding a vintage sailboat in the marina downtown.

On the polished wood deck, Steven squeezed in next to me and introduced himself, and I was instantly at ease. A couple of times, as we chatted, he replied, "Cuu-u-ute!" in a feminine cadence that matched his architect-y glasses and dark jeans. I could tell they were the right jeans, cuffed in the right way. His whole vibe was gay BFF.

He told me he was helping Sammy open a restaurant in Tribeca, and they'd just gone on a team retreat at the Delano in Miami. I'd stayed there once, and joked with him about the slick hotel's green-apple sconces—a single Granny Smith perched in avant-garde glory on the wall of each bedroom.

"Whimsy," Steven stage-whispered, making a mock-dazzled face, hands splayed around his chin. Picture a '60s teen screaming at the Beatles. I laughed. *Exactly.*

Boogie Nights, we agreed, was the best movie in years. We re-viewed the porn star names: *Dirk Diggler. Chest Rockwell.* When I told him I'd gone to naked sleepaway camp—natural segue from *Boogie Nights*—he wanted to know everything. Were we naked all the time? Or just during swim? How old was I? Twelve?? *No way!* As our conversation turned to families, he begged me to repeat an impression of my cousin, with her earnest, NPR voice, describing a favorite tofu dessert and her "cuddly, cuddly cats."

Anytime I talked like this with Antonio, he'd shake his head and say, understanding none of it, "That is so wild." Hello, empty feeling.

If I were to make a chart of life's loneliest moments, I'd rank them as follows:

Number Three: The sound of NASCAR racing on TV on a Sunday.

Number One: Hearing from someone in your boyfriend's inner circle, "You know your man fucks anything that moves, including his own wife." No matter how deep your denial, that one's hard to top.

Between those, a devastating Number Two: Having all your favorite stories and best lines meet the blank, robotic response, "That is so wild." It was Antonio's go-to when I said something funny. Excluding racing on TV—a memory from childhood—my life at that time had been topping the loneliness charts.

The loneliness hit me in the contrast of this one balmy eve-ning, spent talking to Steven. After two years with Antonio, I'd nearly forgotten: compatibility is the tits! I kept thinking, this was the kind of guy I should be with, *if only he were straight.*

As the boat cruised around the harbor, Steven and I looked out at the city, our arms touching.

"I know it's corny to say," he told me, "but the Manhattan skyline is pretty beautiful. Look at the Twin Towers. They're so 1970s New York."

That was the best New York, I said. Crime, scumbags, and porn. I told him about sneaking to video arcades in Times Square when I was ten, how perverts would rub up on me while I played *Space Invaders* and *Pong*.

He said he used to come in from Jersey during high school and go to SoHo and Studio 54. "That's when I knew I had to move here," he said. As gay youths do, I thought.

When we got off the boat and dispersed, I didn't get to connect with him. Back then, there was no social media where you could secretly stalk a person and say, "Hey, great night, hope our paths cross soon," or some other coded version of "I want more of you and how you made me feel—and even though I'm in my shit relationship and you seem to play for the other team, I wouldn't mind running away together. In short, I would like to wear you like a skin suit. Let's have coffee."

Twelve days later, the Towers came down.

On that terrifying day, after trying over and over to reach my married boyfriend and repeatedly hanging up on his wife—this moves up to Lonely Feeling Number One—the next call I made was to Sammy. Ever since I'd emailed to say thanks for the party, we'd been trading messages that had reignited my crush on him from 1991. Maybe I was trying to reconnect with my old self and went a hair too far, like when you rewind your DVR and keep missing the right moment. I wanted to be flirted with. Maybe Sammy felt like an antidote to the hollow not-me-ness that was my life, especially on this day, after Antonio finally rang back and demanded, "Why'd you hang up on my wife?"

"That's so sweet that you called," Sammy said. "I'm fine. We closed The Squirrel and we're just having friends stop by. Why don't you come down?"

A New Yorker looking for a good time on 9/11 sounds all kinds of wrong, even psycho. Before you judge: It's not like I was calling around asking, "Where's the party?" It's that my sister and I had been cooped up all day watching the horrible footage with our mom, and then with our dad when he finally made it home from Midtown. We wanted to be around people. Parents didn't count. We cabbed it down to Chelsea, and when we walked in, there was Steven.

"Oh, hi!" he said, his arm around a pretty young woman. "This is my girlfriend, Allie."

This is the moment in the rom-com where you hear the record scratch of dashed dreams. *Girlfriend.* *Rrrr-RRRIPPP!* To me, the sound effect was the "ding" of epiphany. *Girlfriend . . . not gay!*

After that, on my long, daily walks, I started popping by the Tribeca restaurant space Steven was helping Sammy open. I had to leave the Hudson River path anyway. It was closed below Chambers for barges hauling out wreckage from the Towers.

Steven, who came outside to talk to me, would take in my sweaty upper lip and say, "You're glistening." "I know," I'd say, wiping my face with my T-shirt sleeve. "It's gross!" And he'd insist, "No, I like it." He actually hates sweat. "That's how much you liked me then," I now tell him. "I must have," he says, gagging at my drenched bangs after dance class.

We exchanged emails. I wrote him long, imaginative, hilarious messages—some of my best work—with pop culture references I knew he'd get. Sometimes I got a quick reply, sometimes nothing for weeks. I didn't read into it, didn't neurotically refresh my AOL. I was too absorbed with how long Antonio stayed out after he said he'd be at my place. "I'm having one piña colada with my daughter, then coming straight to you. Have your panties off." I learned to keep my panties on. How long do you really want to sit on your own furniture without them?

Once the new restaurant opened, I went in a lot. I brought friends—who'd started talking to me again now that I was interested in something other than Antonio or salsa—so they could check out Steven. We secretly called him "Not Gay, Not Jewish Steven," because he was neither but could pass for both. Victoria rated him "so appealing." When I went with my sister, he brought over a dish of beignets, which are basically ball-shaped jelly donuts. "They're like cum gum," Steven said. "Remember cum gum?" Of course we did—Freshen Up, the gum from our childhood with the squirty liquid center. "I like him," Marian said as he walked away. "Yeah, me, too." I really did. How do you not fall for "cum gum"?

On one visit, Sammy greeted me at the podium, "Hello Laura Belgray," and then read from his monitor, "Make that: 'Laura Belgray who Steven Eckler loves, *really* loves, like the kind of love where you want to run away together, to an island or maybe Paris or London. . . .'"

"Wait, what? What is that?" I asked, excited and confused.

"It's Steven's notes about you in OpenTable. Here, look." On the monitor, where restaurants put guest notes like "allergic to monkfish," "bffs w Michael Bloomberg," or "shitty tipper," was a long diary entry from Steven on how much he liked me.

He soon asked, shyly, if I wanted to do something after the holidays. We had our first meetup at one of his favorite restaurants, Lupa.

"I got you something," Steven said, reaching into the fancy Paul Smith shopping bag he was using as a tote and handing me a paperback. "Have you read Dennis Cooper?"

I admitted I hadn't and flipped through it, intrigued.

"I can't believe I gave you that book," Steven says now. "So dark."

But he knew his audience. Under the covers that weekend, reading a scene involving anal sex and a colon jammed with petrified poop, I thought, "This man gets me."

Before our next friend date, he said he'd make a rezzy for brunch. "And, um . . . remind me to tell you about my stuff."

He kept saying that. "Shit, I still have to tell you about my stuff."

I wasn't worried. I had my stuff, too. Antonio stuff. In fact, I was relieved Steven hadn't gone in for a real kiss yet. Just a peck on the cheek. I didn't want to be the one to bring up "stuff."

At brunch, as he signaled for the check, Steven finally spilled it. "Oh yeah," he said, as though it had skipped his mind all through our lemon ricotta pancakes. "My stuff. So, I'm sort of with a girlfriend."

"Okay," I said. "I kinda knew that. The one I saw you with on 9/11?" Yes, he nodded, and promised, "Things aren't good." I suppressed a smile. Different wavelengths, he explained. She was super young: twenty-four to his forty-one. (I'd later learn his friends called her "Baby Date.")

He added, "Our whole dynamic is fuck or fight." The level of passion this implied made my heart sink, and the thud surprised me. Antonio and I had the same frisson, though—with an added twist: We were *dance*, fuck, or fight. "You used to want to all the time," I would say to him about the first two verbs. That was one of the fights.

On our get-togethers, Steven and I started sitting side by side in the booth, scanning the paper to see what was playing. We saw *Y tu mamá también* (sexy!) and *Trembling Before G-d*, about shunned gay Orthodox Jews (not sexy). We pronounced it as it was written. Trembling before gih-dih. Our first inside joke.

After a movie in February, at a coffee place on my corner he never would've picked—an empty chain eatery with sticky laminated menus and a needless velvet rope after six p.m.—Steven said, "So . . ."

"So!" I echoed. My coffee tasted of hazelnut even though I'd ordered house roast.

"I'm working on ending it with Allie." He slid his oversized mug an inch on the table and straightened the napkin. "I thought you should know where I am with that stuff."

"Oh, that's fine. Same sitch here, with my stuff." This was perfect, like getting a term-paper extension.

He smiled. "Okay, phew."

We sipped our terrible coffees and made matching poopoo faces at the taste.

"Let's agree that we like each other," I said, "and if we were both single, we'd be a thing."

"Agreed." We held hands.

Maybe it wasn't the most ethical, honest, advisable way to start a relationship, but the great love of your life might not start as ethical, honest, or remotely advisable. If you ask me, Antonio got what he deserved, even if Steven's girlfriend did not. But that was *his* stuff. Plus, all we'd done was hold hands—unlike *some* people.

Antonio had recently left his email open on my laptop. I'd discovered messages from Gabby, a young graphic artist on our dance team—and Antonio's recent excuse for coming over late. "Gabby's helping me design the team T-shirts. Wait'll you see them, Babe." Or, "I have to give Gabby a private lesson. She dances so awkward, worse than you when you started," he'd snort. "And then I have dinner with my daughter."

Gabby's email said, "When you pressure me to have sex and I say I don't want to, I wish you wouldn't get so angry." They were that far into the relationship: having banged so routinely, she'd crossed into the "I have a headache" phase. No wonder Antonio was always too tired now. I felt my dinner of mu shu vegetables rise in my throat. "What's wrong with *me*, why aren't I enough for you, what does she have that I don't?" I wailed on the phone, the typical cheat-ee. He assured me it had been a one-time thing, "just one fuck, from too much piña colada-ing," and would never happen again. I pretended he meant it and hung up on him, but then hung *onto* him.

They say to "create space for what you want" in your life. Whether it's your closet, your friendships, your love life, your vegetable crisper, you're supposed to get rid of the clutter (now Marie Kondo–branded as "anything that doesn't spark joy"). As long as you're crowding yourself with the unwanted items or relationships that don't serve you, happiness won't find a way in—to your sock drawer, or your bed.

"Create space" is probably the advice I'd give *you* if you were in a shit relationship and wanted a better one. No one's going to say, "Hey, keep the cheating sack of pus you're with until someone better comes along, and then remain consumed by the old person so you don't present to the new person as a ravenous blob of need."

It worked in my favor, though—all that psychic space Antonio took up. What if I'd respected myself enough to get rid of him when I should have?

Say, when I first found out he was shtupping Gabby.

Or when he erased his wife's voicemail on my phone—"He's fooled you, the girlfriend, and me, the wife"—before I could hear the rest.

Or the time he left a message for a divorce lawyer in front of me, and when I later hit redial, it said, "This number has been disconnected."

If I'd given Antonio the heave-ho at any reasonable juncture, I probably would have been clingy and obsessed with Steven, and he'd now be married to someone else. So take that, all you who pitch yourselves as "the Marie Kondo of dating." Sometimes, clutter is your friend.

Steven often canceled our plans at the last minute. "Working late," he apologized. He probably had to see Baby Date, but I didn't think about it. My thought was: *Bummer, but easier. Now I don't have to lie about who I'm out with.* Antonio had become suspicious and jealous. "You fucking that guy?" he asked, after seeing Steven's message on my laptop. I cried. Partners who accuse you of cheating are usually cheating themselves.

Looking for fresh evidence, I guessed Antonio's email password on the first try. The only book I'd ever seen him read was *Who Moved My Cheese*, which he raved about. I typed in "Cheese" and presto. The new emails between him and Gabby, right at the top, delivered less of a gut punch than I'd steeled myself for: "You said you loved me . . . don't want to fight like this . . . you pressured me when I just wanted to be held." As my eyes moved over the words, I felt something unexpected . . . and that something was relief.

Here was my chance. I could break up with Antonio in righteous fury, rather than working up the courage to say, "I'm not happy."

When I called, teeth chattering, to tell him it was over, he begged and bargained and cried. I was surprisingly unmoved. My numbness felt powerful, like in the rare, shocking moments when I've looked at ice cream and thought, "Nah." I was free.

I called Steven, who had asked if I was available that night. I'd originally told him no. I had a work trip the next day and had thought I'd want to spend my last night with Antonio.

"Still free for dinner?" I asked. "My other thing got canceled."

We met at a corny neighborhood place (my pick), which he pretended to like, and had a wonderful dinner where he said he'd tied things up with Allie. I told him it was over with Antonio. We were both done with our "stuff." We looked at the dessert menu, which featured a plum tart, and said, in unison, "dropping a plum tart." *Dropping a plum* is when your balls hang out of your underwear or shorts. What were the odds of us both knowing that and saying it? It felt, to use a Hebrew phrase my more Jewy friends love, *b'shert*. Meant to be.

We made out a few doors down from my building, out of view from my doorman. Fine, maybe he'd seen me making out lately with other people who weren't Antonio: a younger, hotter salsa instructor; Sammy, on his motorcycle. Those were just fun distractions, though my therapist pointed out they'd devastate Antonio if he knew. She didn't think revenge cheating was healthy. This, with Steven, wasn't that, though. This was something real. With him, I was home.

It would be nearly six years, a few commitment issues, and some sessions of couple's therapy before Steven became my husband. Is it annoying and smug to say I have a crush on my spouse? That I love the sound of his voice and feel a rush when he walks in the door, even if he's only been gone a few hours? If so, skip ahead! Steven makes me laugh all day. He always smells great and knows it. "Ew, my gym shorts stink," he says, sniffing them, and then says, "I'm kidding, they don't. They smell like mint." He holds doors open for everyone, overtips, picks up friends from the hospital. He makes our social plans when I can't deal. He cooks, cleans, buys fresh flowers, rearranges books and objects into beautiful tableaus. (I swear, not gay!) He actually reads all his art books, and knows more about art than most dealers. The guys at Casa Magazines (New York's best magazine store) have his hard-to-find Spanish *AD* set aside and waiting when he comes in, and, like the people anyplace else he goes, they light up when they see him. Even so, he has social anxiety (we call it "stranger danger"), and will concoct a lie on the way to a party just in case he wants to leave. "I'll say I left sauce on. That works, right?" Everything he buys is a limited edition— T-shirts, Birkenstocks, beer—and if you call him pretentious, he'll say, "Thank you." He watches Criterion films and shitty Lifetime shows. A perfect high-low split.

On the downside: He talks over my *Real Housewives*—like they're trashier than his movie where the husband is murdered after screwing the nanny? He throws out the milk before we go away for a weekend, as if it's going to go bad. I remind him, "Food doesn't miss us when we're gone." We will argue 'til the end of time about air conditioning. He wants it on, I want it off. Other than those few points, I give life with him a Yelp rating of five stars out of five, and if I could, I'd give eleven.

So now you know how I met him—through friends I'd made ho'ing away (excuse me, *networking* away) my first year out of college, during a phase of rock-bottom self-esteem, while ignoring romantic complications on his end, and clinging to a desperate relationship with a cheating sadsack on mine. I did it all wrong, and I wouldn't do it any other way.

Steven and I still say "droppin' a plum" in unison whenever we come across a plum tart, hear the word *plum*, or see a plum. Or, drop a plum. We might yell "Jinx!" Forget what Dr. Phil says. If you want to know the secret to a happy marriage, that's it right there.

Self-Help Night Near the Midtown Tunnel

The workshop took place in the basement of an Armenian Orthodox church near the Midtown Tunnel. Taped to the massive front door, a flyer with a photo of an older couple whose heads leaned together lovingly told me to go inside for Spontaneous Metamorphosis . . . with the Spears! Descending the stairs, I heard the hum of mingling voices. I could already smell the industrial-strength urinal cake scent that would one day trigger memories of these weekly gatherings.

"Oh good, you're here!" my friend Gina said. She got everywhere before me. "Why don't you go get signed in and pay. I'm gonna say hi to some people." I watched her hug a burly older man with a full head of white hair. She brought him over to me. "This is Bob," she said. "He gives the best hugs."

"Want one?" Bob asked, opening his arms and leaving me little choice.

He maintained the hug for so long, I thought he might be counting to ten. He ended it with an "Mmm" sound.

The woman who took my twenty at registration asked if I wanted to buy a copy of the Spears' best seller, *Stop Doing, Start Being: How to Live an Instantly Perfect Life.* A sunset and a hummingbird graced the front.

"Uh, sure," I said, even though I'd have to hide it at home.

Steven wouldn't tolerate a glossy self-help paperback in full view on our shelves. New-Agey–script font personal development covers, which people now send me unsolicited for review, were and still are a "no." When he unboxes them for me, his face crinkles in mock sorrow. Plus, he'd worry if he saw me come home with the title. While he was all for me finding my thing, he distrusted anything that might take away my "edge." When I went on antidepressants, he claimed I didn't seem like myself. "I like you crazy," he said.

We sat in the back with Gina's other first-timer friends, Ryan and Sadie. I was nervous this would be some kooky thing for losers, but their presence put me at ease. They were pretty and stylish with cool jobs. Sadie was a TV producer, actress, and sometime model. Ryan hosted a daily MTV show that I and everyone else in the room were too old to recognize him from. But I appreciated that he was probably mobbed by teens every time he stepped out of 1515 Broadway.

What made me feel most in my element, despite the backdrop of church basement and obligatory hugs, was Ryan's skepticism, which matched mine. Agreeing it was only a matter of minutes before these people had us all naked in a drum circle, we each pretended we'd been dragged there. "She wanted us to do this together," he said, tilting his head toward Sadie. "Gina keeps talking it up."

"I know," I said as the room hushed. I lowered my voice. "Gina's been trying to get me here for years."

Gina, a friend from my salsa-dancing days, had called me out of the blue. We'd lost touch. Since I'd last seen her, I had gotten married and then segued into a post-wedding rut. The feeling of moving forward in my life that came from getting engaged and planning our Big Day had shut off as soon as I finished sending out thank-you notes.

Gina, meanwhile, had it all going on. I'd heard she'd gotten engaged, scored a book deal, quit her corporate job, and started making big bucks as a paid speaker. She was doing something that worked. So when she called and said, "Do you want to come to this thing with me?" I was open to it, even if it sounded a little squishy and self-helpy for my hardened New Yorker taste.

The room looked expectantly at the Spears, Annie and Ira, who sat at the front in twin director's chairs, higher than ours. Annie paired cropped, no-nonsense hair with dangly earrings, a style women seemed to submit to at a certain age. The two wore clashing tropical print shirts, like a couple on a Caribbean cruise whose clothes started bickering before they did.

"Hi!" they said in unison. Ira said "Welcome to . . ." and Annie finished: "Metamorphosis Monday."

"One thing you should know about us," Annie said.

Ira nodded. "We finish . . ."

"Each other's . . ." (Annie.)

"Sentences!" They finished together.

Ira, in a Jewish Bronx accent I found both comforting and discrediting, explained the concept of listening, truly listening, with your eyes *and* your ears. I was listening with all my listening holes. I was eager for him to get to the meat of the workshop.

And I was there to solve the questions that plagued me:

Is there something bigger I could be doing with my talents? How do I tap into them, into that "me" who comes up with lightning-in-a-bottle brilliance? How will I make the tens of millions I need to live the way I want and only fly first class and hire tons of help if I have kids? And *should* I have kids? Will I ever want them instead of just wanting to want them?

I was thirty-eight and knew I wouldn't feel like a grown-up until the questions stopped following me down the street.

Just after Annie and Ira started the session, a short, stout woman barreled into the room.

"Sorry," she stage-whispered.

"Karen!" Ira said. "You're here! Karen has been using Metamorphosis to thrive amid *allll* the chaos, while the economy collapses and everyone around her on Wall Street is laid off. Karen, what are the three principles of Spontaneous Metamorphosis?"

As she wriggled out of her coat and plopped her overflowing office tote on the floor, she rattled them off.

"What you resist persists; no two things can occupy the same place at the same time; and anything you see without judging it dissolves and completes itself in the moment."

The first one, I'd heard before. Jennifer Aniston had said "What you resist persists" about paparazzi hounding her after her split with Brad. *People* magazine. At the time, I thought it was her own wisdom: *Hey, that Jennifer Aniston is a smart cookie. I might have to steal that.*

The second principle, they unpacked in a way that made some, if not complete, sense. What it added up to, though, pissed me off.

"You see," Ira or Annie would conclude, "this moment is absolutely perfect. Your life is perfect, because you couldn't have done it any other way."

I didn't come here to be told my life was perfect. I came to *make* it perfect.

The third one, about problems dissolving when you see them, always got someone raising a hand to challenge it. Usually an actor.

"Does that mean that if I *see* my getting rejected for a part without judging it, I'll start getting cast more?"

"Aha," Ira would say, unwrapping a Ricola from a pile on his chair's flat wood arm. Occasionally, he knocked one to the floor. A volunteer from the front row would pick it up and place it back on the chair, and then he'd knock it off again. Like a toy a baby keeps throwing out of the crib.

"See, here's the thing. If you get okay with something with the intention of making it go away, you're not really okay with it. It doesn't work that way."

Annie gazed at his face admiringly as he continued. "You're in such a hurry to *get* somewhere. You think getting a part in a play will make you feel better, man." He said "man" a lot, which made him sound like a narc in the 1970s trying to infiltrate a gang. He also called smoking pot "doing dope." He continued, "You think whatever you're waiting for will make you feel better. You think, if the weather is nice, life will be better. But it won't! You'll still be the same person."

Oh really? When I'm freezing and then get warm, I *do* feel better. When I get an upgrade to business class, I *do* feel better. Sometimes, getting the things you want does change everything. But I never said that. I quickly learned not to disagree with the Spears.

All the regulars knew not to disagree with them, too. Instead, they'd say, "Hmm. Okay. I see that." Or "Wow. That's so kewl."

Those who didn't know better but wanted to sound agreeable said, "I'll have to think about that"—to which the Spears replied, "That's you disagreeing instead of listening."

They'd often add, "You're disagreeing because you're incomplete with your mother/father."

If the person disagreed with Ira, they were incomplete with their father. If they disagreed with Annie, it was the mother.

They named that same root cause for a whole grab bag of problems. For example, when a beautiful waif named Angie on my first night asked why she couldn't book more modeling jobs, Ira told her, "It's because the people you're dealing with are men, and you're not connecting with them because you're incomplete with your father."

Angie smiled slightly and looked upward, her collarbone hollowed like a set of empty twin swimming pools.

"Ahhh ha. Is that a smile of inconvenience I see?" Ira said.

Wow, how did he nail that? I wondered. How would he know she has daddy issues? Now, I know better. Show me a single underweight wannabe-model who doesn't have daddy issues (which, by the way, I recently heard we're now supposed to call "father hunger"). Easy guess.

That first Monday, I wanted some brilliant insights about my life. I kept thinking, "Do ME, do ME!" I half-raised my hand many times, as you do when you want to be called on but don't really.

That's how the workshop worked. You raised your hand and went up to the front to talk. You could have a problem you wanted to work out, or, like one regular, Arlene, an urge to say, "I'm just so glad to be here."

"Arlene," Ira asked, "would you say your life has transformed since you started coming here?"

"Oh," Arlene shook her head with wonder. "Absolutely. I used to talk a lot about quitting work and writing songs. Now, I have five songs on iTunes. And I bring so much passion to my bank-telling job. I do every task like it's my idea."

"You're a gift, Arlene."

"Kewl. Thank you."

Silence. Smiles.

"Thank *you*."

Brad went up. He was having trouble nailing auditions.

Annie cocked her head, inspecting him.

"Brad, right now, I have my attention on your hair."

Brad nodded thoughtfully. "Cool. Um, yeah, I just got a haircut."

"Show of hands. Does anyone else notice having their attention on Brad's hair?"

Everyone, including me, raised their hand. It did look like he had cut it drunk, with nail clippers. Floppy in some places, spiky and tufted in others.

Ira said, "See, here's the thing. You're using that silly haircut to hide your brilliance. I'll bet my brand new boat on it."

"Oh. Okay. I guess I see that."

"Well, don't 'guess' you see it, simply *see* it."

"I see it."

"Good!" Ira said. "And Brad, you just became infinitely more hirable. Do you all feel that?"

Heads nodded. Annie said, "I would cast you right now, in any commercial."

The next week, Brad had a uniform buzz cut, if not any parts in commercials.

That first night, because I hadn't fully raised my hand, Gina encouraged me to line up and meet the Spears at the end. They remained in their chairs to receive people.

"Hi, I'm Laura. I'm here because I'm in a rut at work."

"Well," Ira said, "you're in a rut because you work in a culture of complaint."

Annie nodded. "Second principle: No two things can occupy the same place at the same time. So you can't be simultaneously complaining and creating."

"Huh." We did bitch a lot in the editing room—about the project manager who called meetings about meetings about meetings; about the clueless new VP who struck down our ideas; about the unwatchable reality show we were trying to promote as a "must-watch." But that's what made work fun: complaining.

"Yeah," I said. "I guess we do complain."

Annie said, "Oh, you definitely do. Ira has a gift for seeing these things. Hey, I hope you'll think about joining us for next year's Costa Rica trip. It starts working . . ."

Ira chimed in with her. ". . . As soon as you sign up."

They were just back from that year's retreat.

"Romesh," they'd said to a guy who stood to talk about his IT job, "would you say your life transformed in Costa Rica?"

"Oh, absolutely," Romesh said.

"Will you do that movie scene you did in the talent show?"

Romesh obliged, yelling in an exaggerated Indian accent, "YOU CAHN'T HAHNDLE DE TRRUTH!"

Annie and Ira slapped their thighs. "Oh, we had fun there, didn't we?"

They loved fun. "Is it okay if we have *fun* tonight?" they'd ask, like everyone needed to lighten the fuck up.

If someone wasn't having fun and walked out—it happened with newcomers all the time—Annie and Ira would say, "Well, some people offend themselves when others are having fun. They'd rather be miserable. When that couple left just now, did everyone feel the room transform?" Chorus of "Mmmm's" and nods. "Good. Now we can have fun."

When I waitressed, there were a few customers who complained relentlessly about the food, the music, the lighting, the improperly wiped tables, the portions. "I thought the small would be larger." And yet, they kept coming back. That was me with the Spears. I stuck around hoping while also hating.

"Have you noticed how they keep saying 'a phenomena' instead of 'phenomeNON'?" I asked Ryan. He was the only one willing to shit-talk them with me.

"You seem off," he'd joke, using their language. "I think you're dialing an upset."

"I see that, but actually, I feel well in myself."

"I think you're *doing* being well in yourself instead of *being* well in yourself. I'll bet my brand new boat on it."

Ira used that line at least once a workshop. "I'll bet my brand new boat that you're creating all the negativity around you." "I'll bet my brand new boat that you're not having enough sex."

After hearing about his boat for over a year, I started wondering how new it could be. I'll bet my own brand new boat that he'd bought it in the 1990s.

So why did I keep going back, and "enroll"—their word—in their agenda? Because Gina credited them for her focus, drive, and clarity. *That.* I wanted *that.* I wanted those results. I wanted to be a confident, capable adult who said what was on her mind, took action, created prolifically, made shit happen, and excelled in all areas of life. Steven and I once gave a ride to a talented chef he worked with, who got in the car without his weekend bag. "I can't believe I forgot my bag," he said. "I'm so bad at life." That's how I felt at this juncture: talented but bad at life. I wanted to be great at it, like Gina. So I persisted.

With colleagues and friends, I started listening really hard. With my eyes *and* my ears. "You're quiet tonight," a friend noticed at dinner. "Just listening," I said, feeling the creepy intensity of my own stare. I told people they should come to "this thing I go to" and that it was helping me so much. My close friends told Steven they thought I was in a cult. I doubt he contradicted them.

When I came home that first night and told him about the simple wisdom I'd learned, Steven said, "Sounds like EST." He would often make that comparison to Werner Erhard's notorious 1970s movement, which frustrated me. I wanted him to be impressed with their insights. Steven's older brother had taken him to EST when Steven was a teenager. They were yelled at, broken down, called assholes, and not allowed to go to the bathroom.

Ira actually had trained as a leader in EST. But this wasn't like that, I insisted. For starters, the Spears didn't have a rule against bathroom breaks—although they did point you out if you took one.

"Don't mind Yoga Moe getting up to use the bathroom during the session," they'd say as Moe flipped his hand up—*Yup, that's me*. He was a yogi and a mechanic, but they never called him Mechanic Moe. Just Yoga Moe. As he crouched and tiptoed over a row of feet, they explained, "See, Yoga Moe has an enlarged prostate." I guess he's lucky they didn't call him Enlarged Prostate Moe.

"If it distracts you that he's using the bathroom while we're talking," Annie said, "just notice that you're judging it . . . and include it."

That's what we were supposed to do when something annoyed us: "Include it."

"Gerte has allergies and feels the need to call attention to them by constantly blowing her nose. It's okay, Gerte, it's part of your German culture. So the rest of you, if you're distracted by all the tissues and her noises, just include it."

I struggled to include most of what happened there, but, at the same time, I convinced myself it was working. Over time, I felt closer to saying, "I'm not having kids." I came up with some good ideas at work. I asked for a raise and got it. It wasn't tens of millions, but it was more than I'd ever made before. I went all in, signing up for every weekend workshop—Time and Task Management, Step into Your Brilliance, The Art of Abundant Wealth—even though they were all the same. The Spears would say, "The workshop starts working the moment you sign up." I handed over my credit card for each workshop (especially the wealth one) waiting for it to kick in like an edible. I even signed up for Costa Rica, which was eight months off.

Each week, Steven checked, "Do you have your Monday thing?" My answer: "Yes, always." I felt committed and rigorous in a way that was rare for me outside of working out. And it was entertaining. I'm nosy. I loved hearing people talk about their sordid issues. Sexual hangups, secret credit card debt, HR transgressions at work. I also enjoyed the low-pressure open mic opportunity. Speaking there was like standup, but with zero expectations. I riffed about my dad losing his shit when he saw me throw out a stalk of asparagus, and got some nice laughs—except from the Spears. They said I should cut my dad a break because he grew up in a Depression-era culture . . . and, that I was incomplete with him.

You never knew what would happen when you stood to talk. You could get laughs and approval, or you could get Spear'd.

An architect named Julie got Spear'd big-time when she stood to talk about work stress.

"I don't think you're stressed about work," Annie told her.

"Ahhhh!" Ira said with raised eyebrows, anticipating something interesting.

"I'm not?" Julie asked. "I definitely feel it."

"No," Annie said. "I think you're stressed right now, in front of this room, about your chin."

"Oh. Okay . . . um . . ."

"You hate that your chin wobbles. Your attention is on your chin, so now all *our* attention is on it, too."

What a strange thing to call out, I thought. Yeah, Julie had a fleshy face. But what if it hadn't occurred to her to worry about her chin? Weren't they adding a whole new layer to her stress?

"Okay, I guess I see that," Julie nodded, which made her chin wobble.

"But you see, that's perfect!" Ira said. "It's brilliant that your chin wobbles."

Annie said, "I think it's beautiful—maybe not in the traditional way that we think about beauty, but in that you can simply see it as it is. Just stand there and let that chin wobble."

"Okay," Julie said. She stood there. Her chin wobbled.

"Yeah," Annie whispered, like a gymnastics coach watching a student's perfect dismount.

She and Ira smiled at each other. People coughed into the long, long silence.

Julie finally asked, "Well, is it okay if I sit down?"

"It's okay with us!" Ira said. He and Annie laughed.

She sat, her chin wobbling with the impact.

When this happened, Costa Rica was around the corner. Was I still so sure about spending a week with these people?

When I'd put down my deposit, I'd felt excited. I'd pictured myself on a pool chaise between sessions, marinating on the day's self-discoveries and writing in a notebook with newfound genius. All my creative blocks would dissolve while I observed them without judging and sipped piña coladas. Closer to the date, I started to reconsider. Was I up for seven days of maybe getting validated, but maybe torn down? What body part of mine might I be told to "let wobble"? We got news of an earthquake near the resort, and I wondered, "Is it fair to my husband to go on a self-help retreat where there's just been an earthquake? There could be aftershocks."

I imagined thinking, as I lay dying—crushed by a fallen palm tree with lemurs on it—"I'm sorry, Steven. I love you. And you were right, this IS a cult like EST. The rhetoric IS solipsistic!"

"That's just fear," Gina said, and persuaded me to "feel the fear and do it anyway."

And so I did.

The Spears had described the resort as "sumptuous luxury."
Water bugs scattered when I rolled my suitcase into the room. It
was a barebones cabin with unsanded edges, so you got splinters
if you leaned against the sink. I had asked to room alone, but
they assigned me a roommate, an older woman named Helga.
She was perfectly sweet, but too concerned when I took a long
time pooping, which is always a whole thing after a flight. From
the moment we arrived, I was homesick in a way I hadn't been
since getting a bad bunk at sleepaway camp.

That's how I ended up feeling all week as I pretended to love
things I hated. I was, as the Spears would say, not having fun but
"*doing* having fun."

While at this retreat, I would fake loving the pasta while gagging on the pasta. I would pretend to get incredible value out of
an exercise where Annie put James Taylor on the boom box and
told us to gyrate our hips to "You've Got a Friend." She looked at
my pelvis and mouthed, "too much." Bitch, I was a salsa queen.
I'll tell *you* what's "too much."

I would fake agree, nodding and mmm-ing, when Ryan raised
his hand after an icky group breathing thing, where people
rubbed your arms and legs, and declared, "Can I just say, that was
the most powerful experience I've ever had?" Liar. I knew that
later, I'd go to his and Sadie's cabin to make fun of the exercise
with him, and Sadie would tsk-tsk us for being baddies.

I would fake cheer when they announced we were going
ziplining, but then I'd Google ziplining and see that once in a
great while, somebody died. I said, during dinner, "I don't want
to scare anybody else, but I'm kinda worried about doing something where once in a while someone dies."

"So stop creating commercials about how dangerous it is," An-
nie said. She used my job writing promos against me, often ac-
cusing me of "creating commercials" for what I didn't want.
I got an allergy attack during the mandatory horseback ride
to the disappointing swimming hole and made a big deal of it.
Yeah, maybe I made a commercial. "Good thing I brought my
Allegra!" I said more than once. Afterward, though, I would say,
"That was awesome! So powerful."

And, a pinnacle moment, on a riverboat through thick, muddy
water, along with everyone else, I would fake-yell, "PURA VIDA!"
Few things stink on me like faked enthusiasm. Not even fear
or garlic or Eternity by Calvin Klein, which I wore for a week in
1989. It haunts me. I felt gross the whole retreat, like I needed a
Silkwood shower.

I did perversely enjoy the feedback sessions, the way I enjoy
Real Housewives. I love watching people turn on each other—at
least until they turn on me. The main meat of the retreat, these
made the weekend workshops, which could get vicious, look like
a baby shower. Here, people stood up and said, "So-and-so, I
have feedback for you." It was a sanctioned way of saying, "Here's
how you suck."

Amanda had feedback for Meghan. "Meghan, you're using
your sexuality as a wedge. Last night at the hot tub, you literally
inserted yourself between me and Lorenzo."

It was open season on Meghan and her sexiness. "Who else here
has found Meghan to be using her sexuality in unwanted ways?"

Hands shot up.

Ursula, from Germany, had feedback for her husband, Franz.
"Franz, you've been bossy this whole time. You talk over me, you

tell me what to do, like how to ride the horse even though I was doing fine."

Ira told Franz to stand up.

"Look at you, all tall and blond and stern," Ira said. His elbows out, his hands in fists like a toy soldier marching, Ira aped a German accent: "'*Ja*, I am Franz.' You're like a big, hulking Nazi."

Everyone laughed and clapped. Not because you could still say things like that in 2009, but because Ira could—especially to Germans. A famous ice skater from Hamburg had mentioned the Spears and their work in a local magazine, so they were like David Hasselhoff there.

Next, Ira said to me and Dafna, who was Israeli, "I saw you two sitting on the porch, taking yourselves away from us all afternoon. I told Annie, look at them, it's like the Jewish Conspiracy over there."

Maybe I was Jewish-conspiring with Dafna because Gina seemed to be dodging me. I gave *her* feedback. "Gina, I feel like you invited me into all this and convinced me to come to Costa Rica and then abandoned me."

All week, I'd been arriving at dinner and finding Gina and her fiancé, Dave, already at a full table with Ryan and Sadie.

"Oh no! We love you," Gina said, standing with me. "Let's plan to sit together tonight. But some feedback for *you*: Why didn't you tell me how you were feeling before?"

Fair enough. I wasn't great at bringing things up.

Then, more feedback for me. I'd opened the bottle.

Lexi said, "Laura, the other night at dinner, you brought up the past and I felt unsafe." I'd mentioned seeing her in the end credits of a movie as "Swing Dancer Number One," and asked if she still danced professionally. She'd looked at me like I'd just asked to take a shit in her mouth, and reminded me, "We're not talking about work here. This whole week is supposed to be about the present."

Past and future, a construct we'd been taught didn't exist, were off limits. We were supposed to make observations about the current moment, like, "Oh, I hear a monkey!" or "Look how much passion that waiter brings to clearing plates!" I kept slipping.

I'd slipped with Ira, too. At lunch, I wanted to break the silence—or, more accurately, the sound of him hum-chewing. I asked, "Are you excited about ziplining later?"

He hummed a few bars, or mouthfuls, as if he hadn't heard me. Then, a full year later, after swallowing his terrible ziti and a sip of water, he looked up. "Nope. I'm excited about right now. I'm excited about my pasta."

"I see that I did that," I told Lexi. "I'm sorry." We were now discussing the past, but I didn't mention that.

Joseph, a voice teacher, joined in. "Also, Laura. Last night, when you complained about the pool not having music, I wondered why you were complaining instead of going where the music was—or singing!"

"I was just wishing the pool had a DJ," I said. "I wasn't complaining, I was saying, 'How great would that be?'"

"That seems entitled," Tanya, a stylist, joined in. "You often seem that way."

Tanya was a massive sourpuss, and her pubes stuck out through her leggings, which seemed like a strange look for a stylist. Could I say this as feedback?

Ross, head of a website company in New Jersey who talked a lot about Linux systems, backed Tanya up. "Yeah, Laura, you say you want to make 'tens of millions,' but you don't seem to think you should have to work for it. The definition of entitled."

The Spears jumped in to defend me. Looking back, I think it was because they were about to pitch us on signing up for the following year. Applications were under our seats.

"Laura never said she didn't want to work for it," Annie said.

Nope, I hadn't. It's true, I've never been keen on hard work. I like going hard on work that feels easy. That's how I wanted to generate my bazillions. And hey, if I got paid a fortune for doing nothing? Also great. I don't get my self-worth from efforting. If that made or makes me entitled, sue me. People say you "deserve everything you desire," but then get so upset when you express a desire for money, especially easy money.

"She *just said* she wants to 'make' the money," Annie said, turning to me. "And I think you will."

"And then some," Ira added, like a parent promising sundaes.

I was relieved to have the Spears come to my rescue. Feedback, unsurprisingly, was a lot less fun to take than to watch.

The least fun exercise came on the final day. The Spears instructed, "After lunch, come back in your swimsuits." Like we were going to the beach—which, no. What we were doing, for the grand finale, was dividing into two groups—always nerve wracking on its own, reminds me of gym class—and then standing with our group in front of the other group in nothing but our swimwear for thirty painfully awkward, pale, fleshy, silent minutes. They said it was an exercise in "being seen," but it made me think of the Holocaust. An exercise in pretending we were being shot naked over a pit. They polled us afterward, still in our swimwear: "Who here thinks they have a better body than others? Who's ashamed of their body? If you're hiding your tummy with your hand, that hand should probably be up." Then, we were told we could get dressed. Like a visit to the gynecologist.

"That was powerful," I said, putting my pants back on.

On our way home, at the San José airport, our group ran into the arriving Week Two group. They rushed to tell us the news we'd missed while off the grid: a flight with geese caught in the engines had made an emergency landing in the Hudson. Later, seeing footage of the passengers standing on the plane's wings in the icy water, I felt like my week had had a similar vibe.

After Costa Rica, a friend asked, "How was your cult thing?"

I laughed. "It was great! I got so much out of it." Since coming home, I had persuaded myself of that. A reframe, as they call it. The cult comment, I left alone.

True, no one had to give up their worldly possessions or shave their heads. You didn't have to brand your pubis mons, like we've now seen in that NXIVM documentary, or have sex with a charismatic leader—even if you did have to hear the Spears describe their (*vomit*) lovemaking. There'd been no cyanide Kool-Aid in the jungle. Just overcooked ziti. But I had stood outside myself all week knowing I wasn't being me, and when I was being me, I did everything wrong. Not to mention that half hour being stared at half-naked, like in an avant-garde art performance. So no, maybe it wasn't technically a "cult," but there was, undeniably, a culture. And though I was a dissenter, an outlier who mocked it all behind the scenes and refused to parrot the language, and earned Ryan's secret nickname "Bad Metamorphosis Girl," I was—fuck me—a part of that culture.

"Such good content, right?" Gina and Dave would say to me proudly. They'd been going for over six years. "Yeah," I'd agree, "it is!" And sure, the basic concepts were useful. Listening, being in the moment, resist/persist, yadda yadda, all great. Helpful, even. But I took issue with their stand on pursuing wishes, dreams, desires. In one of the workshops, when I talked about what I wanted—a two-bedroom apartment with a terrace, for instance—Annie chided, "Now you've got everyone in this room wanting what they don't have." She added, "One of your famous commercials." I got the idea of loving what *is*, but what was wrong with wanting more?

And still, I kept going, because sticking around where I didn't belong or even want to belong was my signature style. And, because leaving right after Costa Rica would require admitting to myself that I'd had a terrible time, something I'd made too big an emotional investment to do, not to mention financial. Oh yeah— that application under my seat, for the following year? I'd filled it out, Amex number and all.

Today, I'd be a meme:

ME: I hate all this bullshit.
ALSO ME: PURA VIDA!

The self-help world has a way of getting you to do things that don't sit well: it tells you that if you're uncomfortable, you're doing it right. "All the magic happens outside your comfort zone!" At the same time, you're supposed to listen to your gut: "If your instincts tell you something's off, pay attention." I sat right at the intersection of those directives, before, during, and after the retreat.

But then the weather got warm and things changed. Gina and Dave started skipping Mondays because they liked staying at their beach house. When they tapered off, so did I.

The Spears called me about it from their car.

"Laura," Ira said on speakerphone, "I'm here with Annie. We want to know why you haven't been coming to Monday nights."

"Oh! Well, you know. Things have gotten busy. But I definitely miss it!"

"That sounds to me," Annie said, "like someone who's lost their passion."

Ira jumped in. "It's so clear when someone's lost their zest for life. We saw that passion in you for a while. When you came back from Costa Rica, you were such a gift. Even Steven noticed."

I'd brought Steven once, and they'd asked him, "Isn't she a gift since she got back from Costa Rica?" With a big, scared smile, he said, "Oh! Yeah. A gift." What was he gonna say, No?

"You see," they said from the car, finishing each other's sentences, "you didn't just stop showing up."

"You stopped bringing people and sharing Metamorphosis."

"And the more you share it,"

". . . The more it works."

That's how they got referrals. By commending those who brought guests or handed out flyers: "Everyone who shared Metamorphosis this week seems positively transformed! And those of you who keep it to yourselves aren't just being selfish, you're less alive."

There were few friends I felt comfortable bringing. I knew most would ask, "You really like these people? What's *happened* to you?" I brought my sister once. She liked spiritual stuff. I brought a work friend who seemed down for touchy-feely. She said, "Well, that was interesting," and then I was embarrassed to see her at the office.

I brought my friend Len. He showed up with a copy of Eckhart Tolle's *A New Earth*, which the Spears took as a provocation.

"You want to show us our approach is wrong, and Eckhart Tolle's is right. But you know, being right steals your aliveness. You can either live in the Right House, or the Alive House." Len is a contrarian, but I think he had brought the book to show he was into that stuff. They also took a poll: "Show of hands, how many women in the room were made to feel uncomfortable by Len?" That was the last time I "shared Metamorphosis."

But where *was* all the metamorphosis? The thing that had started to bother me most was the stuck people.

After coming for years, Arlene was still struggling to like her job at the bank. Brad was still struggling to get acting gigs. Dossie, a park ranger, was still struggling to get respect or promoted to Sycamores. Tanya was still struggling to not be . . . a miserable bitch.

Bob, the writing professor with the hugs, talked incessantly about his inability to do any writing. Ira would ask, "Bob, how long have you been coming?" and Bob would say, "Twenty-five years."

"Since we were ten people sitting on cushions," Ira recalled. "And now we're . . ." He counted with his eyes, bobbing his head as he scanned the room. "Seventy-three people." There were always seventy-three people. Even their attendance number was stuck.

"Well, Bob, you have trans . . . formed. Would you say that's because you share Metamorphosis?"

"Without a doubt."

He shared it all right. Once I'd left the Spears, I looked Bob up on a professor-rating site. He was panned across the board. More one-star reviews than for Guy Fieri's restaurant in Times Square. One after another, students warned, *This guy will flunk*

*you unless you come with him to his creepy cult thing. AVOID AT
ALL COSTS.*

Not that it was a cult.

My last straw will seem random and trivial, but it was over a
pop culture reference. A longtime member named Diane, talking
about her stuck dating life, mentioned *Sex and the City.* Anytime
you dropped a proper name—a show, celebrity, or place—the
Spears made you explain. If a guest on their radio show said "I'm
calling from Munich," they'd say, with exaggerated innocence,
"And what is Munich? Is it a town? Is it a country? Because some
of our listeners have never heard of Munich." When I said I was
having trouble cutting back on MSNBC after the election, Ira
asked, "And what *is* MSNBC?" The correct answer was "a cable
news network," but I said, "The Place for Politics." I refused to
play obtuse.

When Diane mentioned *Sex and the City*, she added carefully,
"It's a show . . . a weekly series? On HBO? Which is a cable network? On television?"

That, of all things, was my breaking point. If these people
needed *Sex and the City* explained to them, I was out.

We all left together. Me, Gina and Dave, Ryan and Sadie.
Ryan and Sadie were moving to LA anyway. Gina and Dave
were accused by Tanya of "ditching Metamorphosis"—like it was
school. The Spears suggested they'd lost their passion.

Dave and I both asked the Spears to pay us for work we'd
done. I'd written some marketing copy for them, doing my
damnedest to take out the cringe. Dave had provided the
voice-over intro for their radio show. Ira told us he felt "shaken
down." He added, "I believe in a spirit of volunteering, which I
guess comes from my background in EST." Dave asked Annie

and Ira to remove his voice-over from the show, which is now a podcast.

They had it re-voiced by Randy, an aspiring actor who laughed at all their jokes 'til his ears turned red.

I know, because I continued consuming their content.

The Germans have a word for joy in other people's misfortune. *Schadenfreude.* There should be a word for joy in their discomfort. I love watching or hearing people squirm and be disingenuous, as long as it's not me. It's why I still listen to the Spears' podcast when I'm getting my lashes done. I like hearing the guest's story trail off into the silence with, "So . . . yeah. Listening is . . . so amazing. It's really cool." It's not my highest self, but at least it *is* myself, something I never was around them.

Is this about self-help not working? Not at all. Improving yourself, examining your beliefs, "leveling up," or even—insert sparkle emojis—"manifesting" . . . I love all that shit. Whatever the approach, if it makes you feel great and love your life, then it works. And it's worth paying for or charging for, even to fund your brand new boat . . . from the 1990s.

Do I agree with mind-fuck dynamics where people feel pressure to let their chin wobble? That's a no. I have no beef with the idea that we're enough and have nothing to fix. But the truth is, we all want more—and what's wrong with that? Every great story starts with someone wanting something. Maybe where self-help becomes a problem is when you wait for it to "take effect" and make life happen *for* you. "We're not here to change or improve you," the Spears told us repeatedly. Well, I guess I wanted change and improvement, and I stuck around, refusing to acknowledge that somebody else wasn't going to give it to me. Kinda like staying with a married guy who's never going to leave his wife.

Over a decade later, when I use a gas-station bathroom, the smell of disinfectant and urinal cake brings back to me a time when I was so desperate to be a better me, I was willing to stick it out in a scene that wasn't me at all.

Baby Fever

When I was forty, I got in a cab and knew the driver was going to be one of those—the talkative ones.

My first clue was that he asked, "How was your day?" instead of asking where I was going.

"Great, thanks," I answered. "Tenth Avenue and Twenty-Third, please." I'm thankful for the "no conversation" option we now have in Ubers. (For the record, not wanting to engage now makes you an introvert, as opposed to what it used to make you: an incurious bitch.)

As soon as he turned on the meter, the driver asked *that question*:

"Got kids?"

"No," I said. "You?"

"Yes. A seven-year-old. So, you planning to have kids?"

"Nope."

He spent the whole ride insisting I should.

Driver: What if everyone felt that way? We'd all die out.
Me: I don't think that's an issue.

We'd all die out, sure. But not because people stopped pushing out kids (and bringing them to the farmers' market to touch all the samples). We now know why humans will go extinct: natural disasters caused by climate change, pandemics, viral TikTok challenges where you drink Drano.

Driver: Why'd you get married if you don't want kids? You know, the point of marriage was originally to raise children.
Me: And the point of kids was to have extra hands in the field.
Driver: What if your parents had felt the way you do? Aren't you glad you were born?
Me: Yes, and so are they. But they wanted kids.

You're probably wondering why I bothered.

I could have said "None of your biznatch," or "You're right, kids are the meaning of life," and then busied myself with my iPhone. Thing is, I was finally confident about a decision I'd spent many tortured years trying to make. I was ready to spar. Even though it was just me and a stranger, in my mind I was doing battle for all women like me, who needed this to be a public conversation.

I've never understood why kids are such a sensitive, private topic, except that it takes "private parts" to make one. Correction: Kids are not a private topic. "No kids" is. Not having kids either means something's wrong, y'know, *down there* (and no one wants to open that can of sperm), or it means you're a weirdo. Like me.

When I was five I begged for the Baby Alive doll, as seen on TV. *"Baby Alive, soft and sweet, she can drink; sheee can eat . . .* (Batteries not included.)" Its skin felt like real, live skin! You could feed it baby food, which it actually chewed—or gummed—and swallowed! Best of all, Baby Alive peed and pooped! A refreshing change from the Cookie Monster puppet whose throat I'd slit with my mom's pinking shears. (I'd wanted the Chips Ahoys I fed it to pass into the body.)

I got Baby Alive for my birthday. Praise be! How long did my joy and interest last? Probably as long as the battery (not long), but in any case, my desire for the doll was not a predictor of some later drive to be a mom, in case you were thinking that's where this would go. Many "born to parent" stories start with a doll pushed around in a stroller: "I knew from age five I was meant to be a mommy." It's like business owners who say, "I knew I was born to be an entrepreneur because I had a lemonade stand." Yeah, so did Sheila in Accounts Payable. Who *didn't* have a lemonade stand?

The long struggle to choose between kids and not kids fits my whole late-bloomer profile, but it's not the typical late-bloomer arc. Most modern stories about women who feel behind in life crescendo in a struggle to get pregnant—excuse me, a "fertility journey." They don't find the partner 'til late in the day and thus don't start trying 'til their eggs are "old"—as put by some doctor with a shitty bedside manner.

Should I, or shouldn't I? Rather than a fertility journey, I went through a decision journey. No hormone injections, no husband whacking off in a sterile room to sticky porn mags and bottling his man jam, no devastating calls from a physician about unviable embryos. Just years of uncomfortable fence sitting.

I grew up assuming I'd have kids. No one ever said "*If* you have kids." They said, "When." It wasn't framed as a choice, but an ordained "someday." Starting around age eighteen, any sentence that started, "Someday, when you have kids," washed me in secret dread. But, I told myself, at least someday was far off.

By someday, I figured, I'd be ready to get fat on purpose—or, since that seemed unlikely, maybe I'd adopt? By someday, I'd be ready to (maybe) push out, and then rock, shush, feed, burp, change, and play with a baby. As soon as I was old enough to babysit, I avoided any gigs that involved babies. I wasn't big on toddlers, either. I liked the jobs where I could show up once the kids were asleep, when I could eat their Fruit Roll-Ups while watching *The Facts of Life*. I don't think I've ever asked to hold a baby, though I've been asked plenty if I'd like to hold the baby, and then said, "Um, sure," and wondered how soon I could politely hand it back.

The summer after ninth grade, I took a mother's helper (aka nanny) job in the Hamptons, but I wasn't much help. The mother had to nudge me: "Do you want to get out of bed and watch the boys, or at least fold some of these sheets?" I'd applied for the job so I could spend August in the Hamptons and meet boys my age. I didn't meet any, nor did I win over the little ones in my charge. The younger one, four, wailed for hours whenever his parents left the house. As soon as they drove away, he'd break his sobbing for one chilling moment to tell me, "I'll chop your head off." He and his six-year-old brother liked me only when I was teaching them to moonwalk to the *Thriller* album. My one kid-friendly trick. Even though I had no Hamptons friends to hang out with and nothing to do but master biking hands-free, I lived for my day off, when I could get away from the kids. I was already like the mother in the 2021 film *The Lost Daughter*, feeling suffocated and dreaming of abandoning the family to experience life and pleasure again.

"I never loved babies or children, either," my mom reassured me in my adult years. "And then I had you." Someday, she promised, I'd feel the same way about my own little ones. My mother had given birth to me at the age of thirty-two, and that was in the late 1960s, so—adding a few years for modern timeline inflation—I figured I had 'til at least thirty-six. That's how old my mom was when she had my sister. Although as a kid my sister complained about having old parents, your mid-thirties had later become a common age to become a mom, maybe even early in New York years. I felt comfortable with that age marker. It was far off in the way that, during your school years, Sunday feels far off when it's only Friday. "I have plenty of time to start my homework."

And then, poof, I was in my late twenties. The Saturday of baby-making. Sunday and its *oh fuck, shit just got real* blues were creeping up. I was dating Dylan at the time: so devoted, responsible, and kind it grossed me out. He was marriage material, which meant dad material, which meant I'd soon need to start being mom material. Which is probably why I tanked the relationship.

I wasn't yet thinking, "What if I don't want kids?" Instead, I was waiting to want them. During dinner with my friend Amanda, a mom at a nearby table got up to take her screaming infant outside. As the door shut off the sound of wailing, I sighed, "Thank god," and Amanda sighed, "I have baby fever." Really? I had the opposite: an allergy. Or, I wished it was an allergy so I'd have an excuse. A doctor's note: "Oh, I can't have kids. If I'm even near one I go into anaphylactic shock and my tongue swells to the size of an eggplant." People accept you avoiding just about anything if you carry an EpiPen.

Instead of baby fever, at twenty-nine I came down with dance fever, and that's when I spent all my money on private ballroom lessons and got involved with Antonio, who taught me salsa and posed no threat of stability or planning a family. Although, when I had a pregnancy scare and cried in Duane Reade, buying my first-ever pregnancy test, he was offended rather than comforting. "You're acting crazy. I'm the one who should be upset. You're telling me you wouldn't want to have my baby." He shook his head and snorted, "Unbelievable."

Even after I met Steven at age thirty-two and knew he was The One, I was still waiting to want kids. I felt plenty of longing for Steven (probably more than was healthy), but not for babies. I saw a psychiatrist for depression. Steven had commitment issues, my sister was moving to LA, I wasn't having good ideas at work, my surgically reduced boobs were growing back, I was painfully pre-occupied by the kids question, and depression runs in my family. The psychiatrist, hearing about my slow-to-progress relationship, cautioned me, "Getting pregnant in your early thirties is easy. In your mid-thirties, less easy. By forty, hard." Super! I will take that Wellbutrin prescription, thank you. Along with well-being, does it also promote clarity around reproducing?

I desperately hoped Steven would hurry up, get serious, and propose, so that, if baby fever did suddenly spike, we'd be ready to go. If it didn't, I figured, we'd find a way . . . to not have them. What I didn't know was whether you could have a happy life without babies. All the talk was about having them, or the heartbreak of not being able to have them. The deliberate no-kids route had few advocates and got zero airtime.

Points of reference for not having kids were slim pickings. You had witches: instead of raising children, they stirred cauldrons and grew chin hairs. Everyone knew cat ladies: sad spinsters who made do with their eleven tabbies and a nightly Godiva chocolate. And then there was the play *Yerma*, which we'd read in Spanish class, about a woman who can't get pregnant. A tragedy, natch. The problem is actually with her husband's defective baby batter, but when I Google it now, an updated title is *Yerma: Barren*. In the end, it's always "her" bad. In a couple, *no kids* means they tried and she couldn't. It's never by choice. In these tropes, there's no debate around actually wanting babies. Except, maybe, in sci-fi?

The media was no help. Just as I crossed from the "someday" years to the "on the fence"–slash–"oh fuck" years, baby fever struck *Us Weekly* and all other magazines. Or maybe they'd been running a temperature ever since Demi Moore appeared naked on that 1991 *Vanity Fair* cover, hiding her milky jugs with one hand and cradling her seven-month bump with the other. A mother's love was both precious and HAWT! Maybe I simply hadn't noticed until all the publications in the Price Wise checkout line seemed to be nagging me, personally.

They were positively breathless over baby-making. "Celebrity Tots!" headlines cooed. "Celebrities: They're Just Like US! They Take Their Kids to the Potty!" "Kim Kardashian: Already Back to Her Pre-Baby Bikini Body!" Inside, features like "Bump Watch" now treated the pregnant tummy, which women used to hide, as Hollywood's hottest accessory.

Not having kids made you tragic. A Yerma. Poor Jennifer Aniston: "Jennifer Still Wants Brad's Babies!" "Jennifer Trying for Justin's Babies!" "Jennifer—A Mama at Last!" "Baby

Heartbreak for Jennifer!" The press wept because Jenni Ani still hadn't procreated, but never crowed, "Guess Which Joyful Celeb Isn't Pregnant!" or "*Friends* Star Not Having Kids . . . And She's Over the Moon!"

The craze for celebrity babies, tykes, ankle-biters, or—as a friend calls them at the beach, "sand poopers"—has lasted decades. At a wedding in the early 2000s, I sat at the same table as the editor in chief of one of the big celebrity mags. She took credit for coming up with the whole "bump watch" trend. "I was pregnant, so it's what I was into, and I guess it stuck," she shrugged.

More likely, it stuck because the mommy market is lit (as the kids, which I don't have, might say). So many things to sell: bottles, diapers, toys, strollers, eardrops, chewable vitamins, summer camps, SAT prep tutors, and surface cleaners so your rug rats can sit naked on, and lick, the Caesarstone counter after it's been occupied by a sloppy, raw chicken. Disney vacations, family cruises from hell, and videos on swaddling, sleep training, and tummy time. Books on parenting without yelling or parenting with yelling, on work-life balance, and on coping with mom guilt and practicing self-care, so you can go from "surviving to thriving," and put on your own oxygen mask first, modeling self-love to your kids.

Maybe if there were something to sell to people with no kids. Oh wait, there is: two-door cars, adults-only luxury resorts, priceless ceramics, infinity pools. Head-on, peel 'n' eat shrimp. WHITE SOFAS.

You're not supposed to want *that* life out of the gate, though. You're supposed to earn it by powering through the kid years and then becoming an empty nester. Living large, without peanut butter and jelly on everything you own, is a luxury meant for people with salt-and-pepper hair who relax in side-by-side tubs. You may enjoy the kid-free life only when you've paid your dues and hit the age of needing help with your boner.

Until then, you're to focus on the pursuit of "Having It All." No woman's Having It All kit is complete without:

A happy marriage;

A successful, meaningful career;

Plenty of playtime with her kids.

If you're a man, you can be "the man who has everything" just by owning all the cool, tasteful shit—Rolex, suede Birkenstocks, and a pizza oven—and being hard to shop for. But the woman who has everything, or "it all," qualifies only if she's a mom. Was I willing to have only some of it all?

The question was a constant pebble in my clogs. From the time we started dating 'til a year or two into our marriage, Steven and I had the same kids conversation over and over. "I'm fine either way," he'd say. "I just wish you had a strong opinion on it. I wish you really wanted kids, or definitely didn't."

"Yeah," I'd tell him. "I wish that, too."

If we didn't have kids, would I wake up one day and feel a void? Would Steven? Would we be somebody's sad, childless neighbors, the ones they'd feel obligated to grocery-shop for, or "keep meaning to invite over"? Would we give people our mushy, spoiled fruit because we didn't want it to go to waste? My great aunt, who had no children, used to bring over brown bananas.

I looked around for any sign I'd be okay later in life without kids. Any model. I Googled "older celebrities without kids." There was Oprah—but she had her multibillion-dollar empire, which seemed to be the one legit substitute for offspring. (And still, the world points out, Oprah has a great life, but she doesn't have it all!) Actress Helen Mirren said she loved her child-free life, and that it was the reason she was happy and still looked good. She was unapologetic—for a while. Googling her now, I see endless versions of "Dame Helen Mirren Defends Her Decision Not to Have Kids." No one has to defend their decision to have kids, only not to.

No one in my life, or even strangers, gave me the green light I was looking for to say "I don't want them."

When you're in your childbearing years (or look it), everyone wants you to have kids. Your parents, so they can be grandparents. Your siblings, so their kids will have cousins. People who love you as a couple want you to see what your DNA would look like mixed together. "A combo of you two would be so cute!" You have a pang of agreement with that idea, making the decision harder. Your miserable parent friends want company in their hell. Your happy parent friends want you to experience the joy, just as I do when I plead with people to finally watch *The Wire*. And, admittedly, I'm a bit of a marriage pusher. I love my husband and our life together so much, I want everyone I care about to experience that magic. So I get it.

"You guys should think about having a baby. It's so delightful," a friend told me and Steven at an art museum as she lifted her inconsolable, howling newborn from the pram and smelled her butt. "Oof! That's tangy. I've gotta find somewhere to change her." While happy for her delight in the experience, eye-watering diaper fumes and all, I thought, *Yeah. Hard no.*

Well, I say "hard no," but that was wishful thinking. Two years into our marriage, as I was heading for forty, my response to "Got any kids?" was still a wishy-washy, wistful-sounding, trailing-off "No . . . ," or a fumbling "No, but."

Nope, no kids, but . . . hey, you never know. I'm on the fence, so . . .

Or:

No, but . . . my sister's planning to!

I tried thought experiments. If I accidentally got pregnant, would I want to keep it? Couldn't decide. I made up a mind game called "If it were illegal," where I asked myself, "If having kids were suddenly against the law, a jailable offense, would I (a) be relieved, or (b) march in the streets for justice?" The answer was clear: I wouldn't be out there protesting. I'd even slip a secret note to the Supreme Court asking them not to change a thing.

I arrived at my *hard no* partly by running out the clock and partly thanks to a conversation I had with Steven at the dining table in our one-bedroom. (My mother had taken to asking, gingerly, "Are you still looking for a two- or three-bedroom?" Dodging the subtext, I'd tell her, "Yes—I could really use a dedicated space for my office.")

It was a summer night, two years into our marriage. "If we don't have kids," I asked, playing with my wedding ring, "will you absolutely, definitely be okay with that?" Decisively, and with no trailing off, Steven answered yes. We'd talked about it over and over, but this time it made me feel alive instead of agonized. I felt the same excitement as I would when we'd later put in a real estate bid (on a larger one-bedroom, perfect for a couple with no kids). It was the thought, "Okay, we're going for it!" And we were. We were going for *not going for it.*

And would you believe, ever since I confidently took the non-leap, I've felt active joy at not having kids? It's true. Parents would argue, but as far as I'm concerned, it's as palpable as the joy of having them.

My friends who chose not to have kids agree. I've sought them out not just because they're more available for dinner but also because we can bond over our freedom. A friend of mine and I turn to each other when we hear a screaming kid and say, "So glad."

I wish I'd had that company when I was on the fence. I wish people hadn't responded to my trailing off with a counterpoint like "You can always change your mind!"—implying I *should* change my mind.

What if you said, "I'm going to wear this dress I just bought to the party," and I responded, "I like it! Plus, you can always change your mind"? Not exactly a hearty thumbs up.

Some said I wouldn't know TRUE love until I'd had a baby. Hold my earrings—the ones I can wear because I don't have a baby. (Babies grab earrings and will rip them right out of your lobes like a mugger on a 1970s New York subway.)

Alas, I guess I'll have to settle for off-brand, faux love—the only kind I'll ever know. Sigh.

Then there was the booby prize: "You get to be the cool aunt!"

I know who they were thinking of: the freewheeling, eccentric sitcom aunt who travels far and wide, brings the kids exotic souvenirs (like shrunken heads and hand-carved walking sticks), and regales them with inappropriate tales of her spicy international love affairs. "Oh, that sounds like something Omar Sharif said to me when I turned down his third marriage proposal." (But beneath all the mystery and adventure, there is sadness.)

The subtext is still that I need some sort of caregiving relationship to children to make me whole. Or, at least, a maternal connection to *something*. "You're a mama to words and ideas!" I've heard more than once. "You birth great copywriting!" It's okay, I'm all good.

Mostly, I think people were afraid I was going to regret not being a parent, and that's exactly what worried me, too. But I was way more worried I'd regret having them. Almost everyone said, "I wasn't sure about kids either, but I'd never go back!" One bravely honest friend said, "I regret having kids. If I had it to do over, I wouldn't have them." What I really wanted was to hear from older couples, "We didn't have kids and we never regretted it." As I mentioned, I had only Oprah and Helen Mirren.

If anyone out there is trying to decide about kids and looking for that kind of status update, here you go: So far, so good! No regrets to report.

What do I wish people had said to me? Nothing. I wish they'd nodded noncommittally and moved on, same thing you do if someone says they don't eat scallops.

I'll admit, the public conversation has shifted, but I wouldn't call it a "sea change." One ad for a digital pregnancy test seems to think it covers all the lady bases. In voice-over, we hear the thoughts of three women, each waiting nervously for results from the stick she just peed on. A student in her college dorm: "I. Can't. Even." A wife with a king-sized bed and wedding band: "Please, let this be the time. We've been trying for so long." In between, a busy career woman on the job: "One day. Maybe. But . . . not right now." Her "maybe" is a tiny hat tip to ambivalence, a modern wink of permission. *Go ahead and waver, girl friend, it's cool! You're in your own office and wearing a blazer, which means you have success to replace children if it comes to that! And maybe you can be a proud aunt!* But you can tell she'll come around. This ad is glaringly missing a Woman Number Four, the one who says, "Not today, Satan. And while we're at it, how about never."

And then, in the extended version, a cab driver insists she should change her mind and have kids. As part of his tip, she hands him her negative Clear Blue Easy stick. With a little pee on it.

Company Woman

In fifth grade, our current events teacher gave us the assignment of summarizing an article in any periodical. I took "any" to heart and summarized a letter from *Penthouse Forum*. I understood the assignment, as they say, and did a beautiful job of quoting the key phrase—in this case, "raging hard-on." *The man in the story, upon seeing the beautiful woman, gets a "raging hard-on." . . . In total, the man in this story has four "raging hard-ons."*

I got a check-plus on the piece, along with the comment, "Maybe next time, try *The New Yorker?*" It was a progressive school.

Inappropriate? You bet. Inappropriate is my birth sign, my blood type, my most open chakra, my middle name. I was that kid who led rounds of "Yankee Doodle" where you changed "stuck a feather" to "fuck a feather."

I bring that same "fuck a feather" energy to my business, wherever I can. And it pays off. Sometimes, in outraged email subscribers demanding, "You call this a professional newsletter?

Remove me from your list!" But mostly, in joy. Mine, anyway.
Feeling fully expressed is what keeps me going.

It may shock you that I *have* a business. How does a person
who couldn't even complete a one-week streak of getting to work
on time, who's been quoted in print as saying "I like stasis," and
who had to be *ordered* to take initiative—literally a contradiction
of the term—come to have her own enterprise?

I know I'm supposed to start with an epic origin story. How I
set out to build a business with nothing but a laptop and a dream.
How I quit my soul-sucking nine-to-five and never looked back.
How I started off tens of thousands in debt and sleeping on a
relative's couch (a detail I've heard one entrepreneur swap out for
"homeless," no comment). Anyway, I don't have that story.

More than just a laptop, when I started I had steady clients, a
Greenwich Village apartment with pretty low monthlies, and a
gainfully employed life partner. The boss who later fired me said
we were lucky to be DINKs—Double Income, No Kids. So, not
exactly rock-bottom, desperate times.

As opposed to a nine-to-five, I worked a noon-to-five (at
most) at my long-term TV job, and I was perfectly complacent,
if no longer jazzed by the work. By the end of my tenure there,
I was promoting reality shows for mid-lifers, including a "cou-
gar" take on *The Bachelorette*. It featured a single woman in her
"mature years"—probably forty. Side note, same age as me then.
Middle aged? HOW DARE THEY. Instead of a rose, the suit-
ors who weren't sent home received a long, wet kiss on the lips.
I won't name the show, but my coworkers and I nicknamed it
The Herpes. I knew I was capable of more. Still, I wouldn't say
the job *sucked* my soul so much as tickled it, in the way a stray
hair does when it's stuck in your bra and you can't locate it. But

I had fun at that job, and never would have left if I hadn't been kicked to the curb.

As for a big dream, I had none, unless you count a winning Powerball ticket. And unlike those plucky, big-dream types, I never set out to build a business. I had no desire to be an "entrepreneur." Who knew that before long, an entrepreneur would be anyone with a PayPal account? You've got solopreneurs, mompreneurs, doggypreneurs, flowerpreneurs, tacopreneurs, breastfeedingpreneurs. You can slap "preneur" on anything, like a Lego attachment, and boom—you're in business.

In my mind, entrepreneurs were Visionary Leaders who Disrupted the Industry, with an app or line of slimming shapewear. People who dreamed of ringing the opening bell on the trading floor. People who wanted to be bosses. In other words, not me. I've never once thought, "I'd like to manage a team of people." I don't even like telling friends where to sit at a dinner party.

Nor do I get out of bed thinking, "How can I change the world today?" That's what you're supposed to want, especially as a woman. You're supposed to wake up with the pressing urge to help as many souls as possible. I wake up with the pressing urge to pee. (Several times a night, thank you.) When I get to my work, I'm thinking about what story to tell today. How I can make someone laugh, think differently, get inspired to take action, write better, or write, period, and feel less alone. Even better than getting an LOL or "I snorted my coffee" (which I doubt, but love) is hearing, "You give me permission to be more me." I've realized this is—yes—a form of helping people. I do enjoy that. It makes me feel purposeful and, I don't know, like a good, helpful person? I don't think of myself as a natural helper, maybe because I'm the worst at pitching in with cleanup when we have dinner at someone's house.

I make a gesture of rising from the chair, which probably looks like I'm lifting my butt to fart, and the host says, "No, no, no, no, no, sit." "No! You sure? Okay." I give in way too easily.

So now that I've revealed the ways my business journey falls short of heroic . . . What was that journey?

It started in 2009, when Steven and I incorporated because our CPA said we should. He told us to pick a name, preferably one with an available URL. We wanted a name that could apply to either of us—Steven, a restaurant guy, and me, a writer—and could mean anything or nothing. Voilà: Talking Shrimp. And would you believe? No one had snapped up the URL! Talking Shrimp.com was ours. It was little more than a tax strategy and a web domain, but a company was born. One with a name that, while giving absolutely no hint what I do, has never failed to start a conversation. Whether I'm at the bank, at conferences, in stirrups at the gynecologist, everyone asks, "Why 'Talking Shrimp'?" They also ask, "Is that a seafood business?" and make jokes about tartar sauce.

I decided to use TalkingShrimp.com to showcase my TV promo reel. I ran the site design past Marie Forleo, a friend I'd met in hip-hop class at Crunch. Today, Marie is one of the biggest names in the online marketing and women's empowerment space and #1 *New York Times* best-selling author, and Oprah, no big whoop, has called her "a thought leader for the next generation." She has also helped me make my name, with a course we run together called The Copy Cure. Back then, while juggling two bartending gigs, she had already built a thriving life-coaching practice online. She was dynamite at making money on the Internet and understood this website stuff. (She also had a newsletter called *Magical Moments*, which tells you we all start somewhere.)

Sitting with me at her kitchen table, she said, "You're gonna have a blog, right?"

Well, it was 2009. Wasn't it too late? I figured I'd missed the moment, as always.

"Oh my god," she said. "No! You've got to have a blog. You, of all people. You love to write." She also said I needed a thing called an opt-in, to build an email list. "Your list is gold," she said, looking into my eyes like a dying person giving their most timeless advice. "The money is in the list." On a legal pad, she diagrammed how to set it up, tore it off, and handed it to me. I took home my instructions and, for once in my life, actually followed them.

I started blogging and building a list. Subscribers signed up for my free PDF, called "5 Secrets to Non-Sucky Copy," and then received emails that had zero to do with that. My emails drove to the blog, where I wrote about Menudo videos from the '80s; the horrors of sixth grade; dirty, 1970s New York; video games, porn, the episode of *Little House on the Prairie* where Mary goes blind; and my dad calling his rain boots "rubbers." As I started going down the online business rabbit hole, I wrote about that, too: namely, its self-help-y faux spirituality, and how everyone seemed to whack off to wine-and-media mogul Gary Vaynerchuk.

To attract new business, I should have been blogging about TV or copywriting. Instead of being a top Google result for "promo writer," my blog ranked for searches like "Can you eat toenail clippings?" (Don't ask.)

Oblivious that I was doing it wrong, I loved blogging. Most writing happens in a vacuum. But writing on the Internet? That's practically a live audience. I can see why so many actors live for the stage. Who doesn't want immediate laughs and applause? I loved hitting "Publish" and getting rewarded with shares and comments, including my dad's: "Laura has the best blog in America." He also left notes like, "Tracy Finkel, who commented above, you may be our cousin!" He was forever obsessed with finding relatives, but that's another story.

One day, I got so much engagement, I told Marie, "Holy shit, my blog post today is going viral!" She asked how many shares. I couldn't believe it, but . . . seventy! To me, that was viral. And with my email list of nearly two hundred subscribers? In my mind, I was Lady Gaga. Had I known how small potatoes I was, I probably would have felt behind, said "What's the point," and given up. I wish this cluelessness for anyone starting out. Ignorance isn't just bliss, it's confidence.

My blog was what they now call a "side hustle," except it didn't make money, so I guess . . . a hobby? My career was still in promos. I had a few small TV clients, but my bread and butter was the one main network I worked for. So much so, I considered the VP "my boss." In 2010, after a writer's meeting, she told me she wanted to meet. I figured it was about the new Betty White project, until I entered her office. "Hi," she said, without looking up from her typing. "Whyn't you close the door."

My fat, six-figure contract was up for renewal. And she wasn't renewing it. The network was entering a new phase, of original scripted comedies, and my abiding love for garbage reality shows didn't apply. Wait, what? I felt a defensive lump form in my throat. Sitcoms were, like, where I'd made my name.

I gathered my things, tearfully told one art director on my way out that she might not be seeing me much anymore, and rushed out of the building. For weeks, I cried to Steven, "I'm just so sad." The place had been my work home for a decade and a half.

A home that, if I'm honest, had booted me a few times over the years, usually under the premise of shoddy paperwork, and then brought me back. This time felt like a true goodbye—especially when my ID stopped working. I had to attend writers' meetings through the end of my contract and was now required to line up at security for a humiliating sticker that said "Visitor." It may as well have said "Outsider" or "Has-been." Or how about, "I got sacked."

More than just embarrassed and mopey, I was panicked. How was I going to make up that income? I had a choice: I could dust off my résumé, which still had "ice-cream scooper" on it, and look for a real, J.O.B. job—which appealed as much as eating a bag of hair.

Or I could seek out new clients and expand my offerings.

And so, Talking Shrimp went from a work-adjacent side hobby to an actual business, and we grew up together, my company and I. Okay, semi-grew-up. Cut to me at fifty-something, sleeping teenage hours and working in sweatpants with a lightning bolt on the side—like I'm a Gen Z influencer who gets sent free athleisurewear. Again, I'm not one. Too old. Though I have been offered free whitening strips!

When I was shit-canned from my contract, I had already been hired by a few clients from the online business world. A nutritionist, a life coach, a real estate agent, that kind of thing. I knew there were more of those out there. I put a services page on my website and sent an email announcement to my tiny list, and people started booking me. Before long, I was on track to make up that lost income. So this was what Marie had meant by "The money is in the list."

The copy I wrote for private clients was different from what I did in promos, and, by most definitions, way less cool. In my TV work, I might be asked to write a top-secret *SpongeBob Square-Pants* script to air at Malia Obama's birthday. (Which, *brag*, I was.) Or a Fandango spot for Kevin Hart. (Ditto.) Here, I was helping a massage therapist or an insurance broker with a sales page. But I enjoyed the work. It had tangible, feel-good results: "My new website copy is getting me more bookings," a client might say. Or, "Yay, my copy finally sounds like me!" That's a big deal—sounding like yourself and not like an infomercial for ShamWow. Helping these clients required a skill that came easily to me: writing the way I talked, instead of the way we were taught to write in school—and helping them write the way they talked, too. Most people have a problem breaking rules; it happens to be where I soar.

Less so being a boss, especially my own.

On the one hand, I was a dream to work for.

"Take it easy," I'd tell myself. "You've already worked fifteen minutes, don't you want a Bravo break? It's called 'self-care'!"

On the other hand, I was a nightmare boss:

"Wow, another snack. Is that kettle corn part of the 'creative process'?"

"I know you're in the middle of something, but did you make that doctor's appointment? No, wait, check your email. But what about that blog post, are you gonna finish it? Was it supposed to have a point, or not really? Anything doing on Facebook? Oh my god, why do you keep starting things and not finishing them?"

"I feel a sneeze coming. A–aaa–ch *YOU SUCK!*"

This is why I didn't want to be a boss. Or work for one.

My biggest problem in the early days of my company was a raging case of shiny object syndrome. Even if I hadn't started out with a dream, I saw people all around me in the online space living theirs. They ran group programs, spoke on stages, raked in big bucks. Marie and a partner, Laura Roeder, launched a course called B-School, which taught people how to run and market a profitable online business. The night the cart closed, I joined them for dinner on West Fourth Street. Over skirt steaks with arugula, they tallied their sales, while I ran numbers in my head. Laura R. laughed. "Are you doing the math?" she asked. She must have seen my eyeballs pop out of their sockets like a cartoon wolf's on Looney Toons.

Most of the time, I was proud and surprised at myself for having an actual business, making things happen. The catch was, no matter how booked I got, I still didn't feel like I'd "found my thing," work that didn't feel like work. A path to riches, like what Marie and Laura had built.

As most people do when they enter the online business world, I started snapping up strange domain names on GoDaddy at three a.m. (I thought Beerbellypreneur.com was the score of the century) and collecting courses that taught how to make money on the Internet. How to teach what you know, how to teach others to teach what they know, how to control minds, how to sell anything to anyone, even if you hate selling. Dead Simple Money Maps, Six-Figure Blueprints, etc. (The dark secret about these is, they don't work if you don't open them.) One course taught how to create niche sites, where you'd pick a topic, write blog posts stuffed with key words, and link out to products for a commission. These sites were described as "Set it and forget it." Create something and abandon it? I was born for this! Sold. To the hundred-plus domains I was already sitting on, I added another winner, Makepanini.com. Never mind that I'd never made Uno. Single. Panino. But I loved *consuming* pressed sandwiches, and

figured I could blog passionately for a month about focaccia and
melted cheese, then step back and wait for the riches to roll in.
"Come on in," I'd say to guests of my future waterfront estate.
"Welcome to the house panini built." I never wrote one post
about panini. Never set it and forget it. I did, however, sell Eat
drinktv.com for a cool five hundred bucks. I'd asked for a thousand, but that was something.

So, it wasn't a straight path from going out on my own to
going big. I did, however, grow an impressive client base. I've
written copy for Airbnb hosts, bar soap, cannabis, wine, a sober
companion to the stars, a raw-milk farm, a surprising number
of psychics and mediums, a chocolatier who only made chocolate angels, and an outrageously disorganized personal organizer
I had to invoice many, many times. And, of course, life coaches.
Life coaches had multiplied like Gremlins, and by the 2010s you
couldn't swing a sack of affirmations without hitting one. I tried
to limit them. How many different ways can you say, "I empower
women to be their authentic selves, create abundance, and live
the life of their dreams"?

Over time, although it was my first love, I started phasing out
TV work. My favorite TV clients would ask for "a day of my genius," which, flattering as it was, psyched me out every time. What
if I was fresh out of genius? Plus, promo departments balked at
my prices. "Wow," they'd say. "Even I don't make that much and
I'm the one hiring you." When I quoted my rate to one production
coordinator, she congratulated me: "You are quite the business-
woman." Code for, "Damn, that's some chutzpah." Meanwhile, my
private clients were less taxing, more gratifying, and gladly paid
what I charged. They saw it as an investment in themselves.

Along with my pricing audacity, I can claim a few other natural strengths in areas where go-getters and rule-followers seem to struggle. I don't know if you'd call these superpowers, because they're also weaknesses and not always super. Maybe they're so-so-powers. Or loserpowers. You can develop these, too. Or, if you're like me, you've already got them.

One: Boundaries.

The online-biz world goes on endlessly about boundaries and using them to "protect your energy." Since I started this business, boundaries *are* my energy.

I'm not a morning person. I need to wake when I wake, no alarm, and then I need hours to myself. So no, we're not meeting for breakfast. We're not jumping on Zoom. We're not meeting in any work capacity before one p.m. Noon is a stretch—by my clock, that's still morning. And then, I need my afternoon walk time. My dance class time. I need a breather between meetings, twenty minutes minimum. Preferably, a day. So, my calendar shows more times than not when appointments are out of the question.

In around 2018, I started cutting back on client hours. I loved my clients—most of them—and enjoyed the work we did, once we were in a session. But I dreaded seeing appointments on my calendar. I wanted to look at my day and see blank space, a whole lotta nothing except maybe "dinner." I wanted to sit on the couch, blissfully unaware of the time, and write my emails, which had replaced blogging as my main form of content. They were the most *me* thing I wrote. If I could get paid just to write those, I fantasized, I'd be getting paid to be me. Happily, I found a way to do just that. Once I finally created my own courses and group programs, which, bonus, could help many people at once, I used my emails to sell those. And that, to oversimplify things, is how I got to my first million. Write fun things and then the money comes in, minimal appointments on the calendar. My dream! Sponsored by . . . boundaries.

Two: Laziness.

Some of my laziness is just fear in pajamas, meaning resistance to tackling something I might suck at. That's not good lazy, that's bad lazy. There are two types, like with cholesterol, and I run high in both. The good kind, which I have no need to fix, is the part of me that's perfectly okay with loafing, lying down, doing nothing, or doing less than everyone else. Unlike most ambitious people, I don't measure my worth by how hard I work. If I work too long and too hard, I'm ashamed. Since I've branded myself as an unapologetic lazy person, too much effort feels out of integrity.

Three: Obsession.

When I saw a psychiatrist in my early thirties, he asked, "Your obsession, where is it alighting now?"

I didn't get it. "What do you mean?"

"Obsession is a continuum for you. Over the years, you've been obsessed with . . ." He looked at his notes. ". . . rock collecting, *Donkey Kong* and *Tempest* [the video game, not the Shakespeare play], drug addicts and drug literature, like *Go Ask Alice*, boys who didn't like you back, vintage furniture, salsa dancing, Tasti D-Lite, whether or not to have children, and your current boyfriend. And, always, working out and food and weight. So, obsession lives within you. Like a butterfly."

He made his hand a butterfly—or, more like, a frog—bouncing from one spot to another. As if jumping a checker across the board. "So where has it decided to *alight* right now?"

Still the kid thing, I said. And my boyfriend, and weight, but also, recently, bras? I'd found a kind that worked with spaghetti straps—my holy grail, I added—and couldn't stop buying them. He wrote a refill for my meds.

During the bra spree and all the rest (including my domain-name-junkie phase), I've wondered what I could achieve if only I got that obsessed with my writing.

As business-geeky as this sounds, once I found the right outlet, blog posts and emails, I did become obsessed. Especially since I could write about whatever was obsessing me. I grew self-assured, which kept me in a groove. As my friend Susie says, "Confidence is the best productivity hack." For me, it's confidence *plus* obsession.

Four: Stubborn Refusal.

At one of my magazine jobs, a hilarious Brit I worked with kept turning down an editorial assistant who asked him out every day. Because of his accent, his answer sounded polite: "Oh, shoot, I cahn't. Because I don't want to." That's both my anthem and my handicap, which is why I was a lousy employee and why I often won't try things that work: for instance, Facebook ads back when they were cheap. A colleague described them as putting a dollar in a machine and having a ten-dollar bill pop out. I would have tried it, but I couldn't. Because I didn't want to. Womp womp!

Still, I'm glad I've stuck to my judgy guns and refused to jump on the countless bandwagons rolling by. These bandwagons include: hiring a huge team; giving up TV—*as if*; having a mission statement; niching down to one type of client; shouting about your top company value being "integrity," as if not conning people merits a prize. Most of all, ice baths, jumping off cliffs, and any daring, wet activity that literally forces you to "get comfortable being uncomfortable." Marketing bros love to talk about their daily plunge into cold water, part of their "miracle morning." For me, a miracle morning is when I get up before nine.

Five: Being Me.

While most of the people in my industry were telling you how they'd manifested the life of their dreams, I was broadcasting my procrastination, emotional funks, struggles with writer's block, and pathological greed for free food samples. A buffet of all my loser traits. Some might call my style "vulnerable." I prefer to think of it as "flawsome"—stirred together with good ol' saying things you're not supposed to say. Like when I slipped the word "ballsack" into my father's eulogy. Very *fuck a feather*. He would've loved it. He's where I get it from, this inability to be anyone but myself.

Being different and unapologetically "you" has a ripple effect. It gives others permission to be more "them," and so on. It's like showing up to a fancy party in jeans and feeling obscenely underdressed, until you see that other guest, or, even better, the host, also wearing jeans. Phew. Now you can move on to worrying about whether you're spitting a lot, as people keep rubbing their eyes while you're talking to them, and it seems to happen more when you drink? Just me? Where was I . . .

Six: Being a Slow-Ass, Foot-Dragging, Late-Blooming Motherfucker.

Recently, I had someone read my Human Design, which is like astrology combined with chakras, combined with a bunch of other "woo-woo" systems I don't fully believe in but am open to. I identify as "woo adjacent," which means I'm a hardened New Yorker who thinks most psychics are fake, and I'll wait for you *outside* the crystal shop, but I do think some magic is possible. Plus, I like information that tells me who I am, even if I know. So I forked over good cash to learn I'm a "Generator." I already knew what I wasn't: a "Manifester." One of those people who take fast action. On Monday, Manifesters say, "Let's put on a show." On Tuesday, they're selling tickets. I, on the other hand—a Generator—will wait, stew, and marinate. I'll sit on my idea like an egg, and then will be too comfortable to get up off the egg, which has conformed to my body like a Tempur-Pedic mattress. And, if you believe these kinds of things, that trait was encoded in my being, right when I exited the birth canal. Or, perhaps, light-years ago.

I'd love to be a Manifester. I'd love to go fast, move up and up and up. But my sloth-like pace has its advantages. For one thing, I don't have to look back at my twenties, thirties, or early forties and think, "That was the best I'll ever be." The plumpest my collagen will ever be, you bet. But my writing and career and life? Still improving. I get to enjoy moving toward my peak. I hope I never hit it.

Imagine if I'd struck pay dirt with my set-it-and-forget-it sandwich site. I never would have pushed myself to create anything new. I wouldn't have discovered the work I'm happily obsessed with, that taps my talent, pays me to be me—and, yeah—helps a lot of people. I wouldn't be writing this book, which, I hope you'll agree, would be tragic. Instead, I'd be collecting fancy cars I couldn't drive, and hosting low-life, hanger-on types aboard my super-yacht, *The Flying Panini.*

Make no mistake, though. I'm still me. These days, I'm pretty pleased with myself and the success I've created . . . until I open Instagram. "When I started my business," a caption says, "I felt lost and hopeless and invisible. Today, six months later, I made three million dollars in an hour! Never give up on your dreams."

I know: "If you're jealous of someone, it's an indicator of your own desires!" Yep. And, no matter how far I've come, I feel behind in achieving those desires all . . . the . . . time. That doesn't go away, much as I'd love this book to arc climactically to a moment where it does. "And then, on the morning of my fifty-first birthday, I journaled, showered, ate a fiber-rich breakfast, and finally stopped comparing myself . . . to anyone." Or, "Today, the only person I measure myself against is who I was yesterday. And I always win. The End!" But I haven't lied to you yet, so why start now? Truth is, probably once a day, I make a mean face at people clinking champagne flutes on a private jet. "Sold my company, treating ten besties to a little adventure!" And then I mute or unfollow. Because as long as I don't see people in front of me, I'm not behind.

Then again—and this goes for you, too—maybe there's no such thing.

Acknowledgments

I'll start by acknowledging how hard this book—my first—kicked my hiney. It made me cry for Mama, beg for mercy, question my talents and existence, chow fistfuls of CVS kettle corn, and pluck hairs that weren't there. I finally understood why people do drugs, voiced that thought aloud, then promised I didn't mean it, though I did order a shroom chocolate bar over the Internet because a friend said it gave her lasting clarity. Tried it, and . . . meh.

But I've had plenty of joyful writing moments, too. For those, I thank my dear friend and writing mentor Suzanne Kingsbury, who was essential at every step, a *sine qua non* if we're getting fancy. Endless thanks to Terri Trespicio for connecting us, as well as for the generous feedback, the idea for my subtitle, and all those calming Voxer replies. How lucky to have you right ahead of me in the process, above me on Book Mountain to scope out the next footholds and throw me the rope. (You can tell I've never gone mountain climbing, nor do I want to.)

To my agents, Sarah Passick and Anna Petkovich at Park & Fine, for believing in *Tough Titties* and getting it into the hands of my editor, Lauren Marino, who also believed in it and didn't try to make it an instructional book, the kind with bullets at the end of each chapter or a sidebar outlining "your next steps." In my industry, that's the sort of book I'm "supposed to" write, and we know how I do with "supposed to." Thank you, Lauren, for getting it, and for pushing me to make it better.

A big thanks to the team at Hachette: publisher Mary Ann Naples; head of marketing Michael Barrs; editorial assistant Niyati Patel; art director Mandy Kain—who killed it with the *Tough Titties* jacket design; marketing associate Ashley Kiedrowski; senior publicist Lauren Rosenthal; designer Amy Quinn; senior production editor Sean Moreau; copy editor Katherine Streckfus; proofreaders Annie Chatham and Erica Lawrence; and senior counsel Andrew Goldberg.

Massive gratitude to Sandra Booker, for patiently and masterfully keeping Talking Shrimp running while I was off in book land.

Victoria Cook, from the day we met (see chapter: "Sorry I'm Late"), you've been the friend I wanted and needed, the "Peach Pit" feeling I was looking for, and then a BFF to this book. Also, the rare instant best friend who didn't turn out to be a psycho.

Mark Merriman, thank you for tag-teaming with Victoria on the legal front, and, even more, for championing this project ever since I sent you a few rough stories years ago. You said, "We can sell this." My favorite words.

Rob Lowe, what can I say? I mean, to someone who's never heard of me? You were nowhere to be found my one night at Studio, nor in the bars where I was hoping to work alongside, or go home with, some facsimile of you—even Saxophone you. Still, you've been there for me, if only as an impossible ideal of manly beauty. This is where you say, "I was right here in front of you, loving you all along." But I'm happily married now. Thank you nonetheless.

Susie Moore, thanks for reminding me over and over to "let it be easy." Even if I didn't, the idea made me happy.

Marie Forleo, much love for your unflagging support, especially that day you invited me over before you'd even showered to help me make headway on this beast and to type for me while I bawled and snotted all over my MacBook Pro.

Thanks to my friends, teachers, and mentors who variously lent encouragement, early feedback, industry wisdom, inspiration, connections and referrals, a future shout-out, a long-ago leg up, reassurance, guidance, tough love, regular love, validation, voice notes, tissues: Dani Shapiro, Rebecca Makkai, Kim McCreight, Laura McKowen, Farnoosh Torabi, Rena Ronson, Daisy Florin, Becky Karush, Kara Cutruzzula, Samantha Irby, Michelle Martello, Liz Prueitt, Selena Soo, Stephanie Pastor, Bruce Bernstein, Linda Sivertsen, Marian Schembari, Cathy Heller, Ash Ambirge, Jen Gottlieb, Licia Morelli, Vernon Silver, Abby Miller Pecoriello, Tim Long, Tom Hill, Adam Dolgins, Jana Hollingshead, Lisa Birnbach, David Matthews, Jen Ames, the fearless writers in my Gateless Academy pods, and Ariel Leve—the last of whom advised me to keep these acknowledgments lean. Oops.

Thanks to those who've been part of this, even if by way of a kind "How's the book?" over DM or spaghetti: Jason Lloyd Miller, Levi August Miller, Josh Pais, Avo Samuelian, Hector Manuel Gonzalez, Carla Chammas, Judi Roaman, Jasmine Carey, Anna Chapman, Cricket Lengyel, Monica Lengyel Karlson, Leslie Cohan, all the Patyks, and Kevin Stuessi. Other key friends, you know who you are.

To all the Talking Shrimp subscribers, aka Shrimpers, who've encouraged me for years and promised "I can't wait for your book," I'm so grateful. You'd better mean it!

Thanks to my wonderful, loving sis, Marian Belgray, and bro-in-law, Rob Blatt. Samson and Elena—yes, you're now allowed to say "Tough Titties," if not to read all its chapters yet. Who am I kidding, what's in here that you haven't already seen on someone's iPad at a sleepover?

Mom and Dad, thanks for your unconditional love, and the rent-free lodging (long) after college, including meals, utilities, Diet Sunkist. What a deal! Mom, thanks for passing down the writing skills, even if Dad took credit, calling his own prose "Hemingway-esque." Dad, I miss you and wish you were here to read this. According to some, you're looking down from above, in which case you're asking me to PLEASE ENLARGE THE FONT.

The biggest thank-you of all to my husband, Steven Eckler. You make life great, and you do it with aplomb. Hee hee. *Droppin' a plum*. Jinx!

About the Author

Laura Belgray is the founder of Talking Shrimp and cocreator of *The Copy Cure* with Marie Forleo. She has been featured in *Elle*, *Fast Company*, *Money Magazine*, *Forbes*, *Vox*, *Insider*, *Metro UK*, and *New York Magazine*, and she has written for Bravo, Fandango, FX, NBC, HBO, USA, Nick at Nite, Nickelodeon, TV Land, VH1, and more. Belgray lives with her husband in New York and, except for college, has never lived anywhere else. Not coincidentally, she doesn't drive.

talkingshrimp.com
🔲 in ♪ @laurabelgray
𝕏 @lbelgray